MULTINATIONAL BUSINESS OPERATIONS

II

Long-Range Planning, Organization, and Management

With Introductory Text, Advanced Readings,
and Selected Annotated Bibliography

S. PRAKASH SETHI
School of Business Administration
University of California, Berkeley

JAGDISH N. SHETH
College of Commerce and Business Administration
University of Illinois, Urbana

GOODYEAR PUBLISHING COMPANY, INC.
Pacific Palisades, California

Current printing (last digit):
10 9 8 7 6 5 4 3 2 1

ISBN: 0-87620-594-5

Library of Congress Catalog Card Number: 72-83216

Y-5945-4

Printed in the United States of America

Designed by Art Ritter

MULTINATIONAL BUSINESS OPERATIONS

Long-Range Planning, Organization, and Management

The global profitability of the international corporation is assisted by every influence which eliminates cultural resistance to the consumption patterns of the metropolis. The corporation thus has a vested interest in the destruction of cultural differences and in a homogenized way of life the world over.

Kari Levitt
Silent Surrender,
The Multinational Corporation in Canada

Contents

Editors' Note

The overseas operations of multinational corporations are so multifaceted that research and writings affecting these operations are scattered all over the field and embrace a multitude of disciplines. For example, important papers affecting various aspects of international business operations have appeared in journals in cultural anthropology, communication, business and economics, political science, social psychology, comparative sociology, law, international affairs, and a host of other fields. While most of this material is available to scholars in their respective fields, the students as well as the managers are neither generally aware of these resources nor do they find them easily accessible. We have attempted to fill this gap by bringing together material, directly pertinent to multinational operations, from all possible sources regardless of their origin.

We found it difficult to include, in one book, articles representing current important thinking in what we consider to be all the major areas affecting the operations of multinational corporations. Our primary emphasis has been on the operations of multinational corporations which we define as investing and manufacturing in more than one country. As such, we have excluded topics dealing with international trade theory and problems of imports and exports of manufactured goods for consumption abroad.

This book is the second of four volumes and covers the planning, organizational, and management aspects of multinational business operations: Long-Range Planning; Conceptual Models and Methodological Approaches to Cross-cultural Comparisons; Strategies of Organizational Structure; Cultural and Individual Differences in Managerial Values; Executive Selection, Training, and Development; Compensation and Job Satisfaction; and Public Relations. Volume I deals with the environmental aspects—economic, social, legal, and political—of multinational enterprises. Volumes III and IV deal with various aspects of marketing and financial management respectively of multinational operations.

To a large extent, the selection of articles must be arbitrary as it reflects the biases of the editors. However, in selecting various articles for inclusion in this volume, we have made every attempt to ensure that they represent the best and most lucid explanation of the topics covered. Understandably, some of our colleagues and students may differ with our judgments. The readings in the book are preceded by a lengthy Introduction which sets forth our ideas and also provides a framework to be used as a guide for understanding various readings. For the readers who wish to pursue further study in the field, an extensive Annotated Bibliography of articles selected from a wide range of professional and academic journals and covering various subject areas included in this volume is also provided.

We are grateful to Professor Karlene Roberts of the School of Business Administration, University of California, Berkeley, for her constructive comments on the introductory part of this volume. The assistance in searching for various references was provided by John Hogle and Elliot Stevenson of the School of Business Administration, University of California, Berkeley, and Stephen Harsch, Neil Sutton and Richard Shell of the College of Commerce and Business Administration, University of Illinois, Urbana, and is gratefully acknowledged.

The editors and the publisher also acknowledge, with thanks, the permission granted by authors and publishers—copyright holders—to reprint papers included in this volume.

S. Prakash Sethi
Jagdish N. Sheth

Introduction

The phenomenal increase in the investment overseas by large American and other European multinational corporations (MNCs) has brought forth the complexity of the problems faced by these enterprises in the areas of long-range planning, organization and management. This is one area of international business where extension of domestic practices has been limited. Indeed, it would seem that the organizational structure of the MNC may provide insights for the organization and management of domestic enterprises.

The problems in developing procedures for effective long-range plans, and decision-making structures, at the headquarters level dealing with home office-subsidiary relationships, have several dimensions which make them quite distinct from those involved in a largely domestic organization where superficially similar relationships may seem to exist between headquarters managements and divisional and regional managements. These may have to do with information flows, perceptual biases, criteria for performance and its evaluations; and conflicts in goals, motives, and time horizons of local managers with those of the parent company.

Decision-Making Styles in MNCs

The economics of the question aside, there is another area of the operation of MNCs which is perhaps equally important. This has to do with how decision-making styles of MNCs' organizations are affected by the socio-political and economic aspects of the life of a country. These problems include questions related to demand creation, affecting social structure by altering the reward system, introducing, without adaptation, organizational forms unsuited to a given cultural environment, and the relationships between MNCs and host governments.

The effect of environmental conditions on the decision-making styles in MNCs is likely to vary with variations in the organizational structures of the MNCs and would depend on the latter's flexibility to adapt to different environmental conditions.

Note that the organization structures delineating the relationship between subsidiaries and their parent company are determined by the parent company in a manner best suited to meet the needs of a particular organization. Their suitability for different environmental conditions is not guaranteed. This condition would hold regardless of whether an MNC has a highly centralized or decentralized organization structure. Thus we have a series of concentric influences on the decision-making processes of MNC executives within a *single* environment (Figure 1).

Figure 1

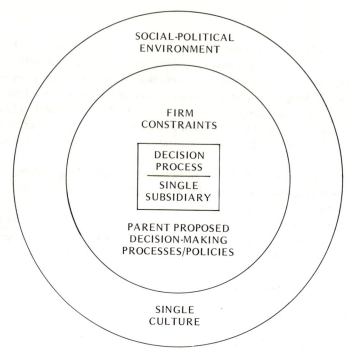

SOCIAL-POLITICAL
ENVIRONMENT

FIRM
CONSTRAINTS

DECISION
PROCESS

SINGLE
SUBSIDIARY

PARENT PROPOSED
DECISION-MAKING
PROCESSES/POLICIES

SINGLE
CULTURE

A Hierarchy of Decisions in MNCs

Large MNC size, the magnitude of decisions in them, and the complexity of their problems (because of involvement in different cultural frameworks and legal structures) make it necessary for the MNC to draw a large number of people into its decision-making process. Those who have ultimate authority and who make final and strategic decisions can be quite remote from the daily operations of their enterprise. The decision making in the MNC may be viewed as a three-stage hierarchy. Level one decisions are those concerned with managing day-to-day operations. Level two decisions have to do with coordinating the production and other functions of the enterprise in a given geographical area, and selecting a course of action from a predetermined finite number of alternatives. Level two decisions are short-term tactical plans. Level three decisions are those concerned with the overall goal determination for the organization and are long-range planning decisions.

In developing effective decision-making structures and processes, MNCs are confronted with a unique set of opposing forces. From the standpoint of the parent firm there is the need to adapt to several or many, often disparate, local environments and operating conditions. This calls for maximum decentralization of authority, which pushes some decision making down closest to the point of impact. Conversely, MNCs' global activities must be coordinated to facilitate the flow of ideas and transfer of resources. This necessitates centralized control and planning at the highest possible level.

As a result of these countervailing forces, MNCs typically make level one decisions at the local level. Level two decisions are made by a cadre of international executives (their nationalities are usually of the parent company's home country or the country of a subsidiary's operation). Level three decisions are invariably made at the parent company's headquarters by executives drawn from the home office nationality. However, even the location of decision making may be modified by the interaction of external environmental and internal organizational variables. The problems posed by such an arrangement are by no means simple and have far-reaching impact on both the organizations and the countries involved. Different decision-making strategies adopted by various subsidiaries obviously influence the efficiency of overall MNC operations. The constraints on decision-making strategies will be discussed later.

Antecedent Conditions of
Decision-Making Strategies and Processes

The factors influencing MNC decision making can be divided into essentially two groups. As indicated in Figure 1 there are influences from the external organizational environment and those from the internal organization.

The external environmental influences can be further subdivided. There are the legal and political constraints imposed by a nation on either the parent firm or subsidiaries of the MNC. These influences must be identified and the nature of their impact on the MNC understood. An example of a constraint a nation may place on an MNC is legislation limiting the amount of authority which can be exercised by a foreign parent firm.

In turn, MNCs may influence the environments in which they exist. An MNC may control a large part of local industry and dominate one or more (generally growth type and high technology) industries. If, under these circumstances, the host nation is relatively small and has been unable to develop strong political and legal administrative functions to deal with MNCs, the influence of the MNC on the host environment can outweigh the impact of the host on the MNC.

The complexity of these multiple influences is illustrated in thinking about executives in subsidiaries of MNCs who may be in a position to play an influential role in the political, social, and cultural life of the country in which they are located because of the country's size in relation to the MNC size. Yet these people may be limited in their firms to what we have labeled level one-type decisions, and unable to develop decision-making talents suitable to level two- and three-type decisions. Thus, the entire nation whose economy is dominated by foreign investment can easily develop a branch plant outlook not only with respect to economic matters but throughout the range of governmental decision making.[1]

Another set of external environmental influences on MNC decision making are those imposed by the culture of the decision maker. Class structure, income distribution, status of business in the culture, other societal values, education, and personal characteristics of the decision maker influence his decisions. Combined, these variables can have deleterious effects on the decision-making process. Traditional cultures may require executives to use only predetermined, considered "sacrosanct," ways of attaining fixed preferences, while the rationality of the situation suggests the development of new procedures to accomplish yet undefined and unattainable objectives.

The necessity to make decisions of a magnitude greater than what is expected of him in his peculiar social milieu is likely to cause an executive to withdraw into indecision and lack of direction. The ultimate result is organizational inefficiency because executives are forced to build defenses against making decisions they are culturally not equipped to make. Conversely, too much centralization of decision making may lead executives in subsidiaries to develop means of subverting home office commands, cause friction between home office and field staff, and clog information channels with inadequate, incomplete, or incorrect information. One effect of such activity is postponement in the execution of home office decisions considered poor by local management.

In addition to external influences there are also internal organizational influences on the decision-making strategy and process. MNC structures, incentive programs, marketing strategies, production organization, expansion plans, limitations on upward mobility, and personnel policies influence the kinds and quality of decisions made at various levels, and the process by which these decisions are made.

MNC compensation programs offer one example of probable internal organizational influence. These programs are generally international in character to encourage mobility of executives. They are often tied to the profitability of the subsidiary and, consequently, the local executive pursues those policies which will increase the profitability of his operating unit though they might decrease the overall profitability of the total organization. Secondly, and sometimes more important, is the fact that monetary compensation means different things in different cultures. People perceive their rewards and inducements to future action differently depending on their cultural milieu. Standardized company compensation packages, then, must be better understood in terms of what they mean and how they are responded to in an individual's cultural framework.

It practically goes without saying that organizational decision making modifies the very internal organizational factors which influence it. These complex relationships must be understood in any study of MNC decision making.

In summary, then, the three-level decision strategy (as defined in the last subsection) must be explicated. Its nature, once defined, is determined by and determines various, external environmental and internal organizational factors. While Figure 1 illustrated the general areas of influence, Figure 2 begins to outline these relationships.

Figure 2

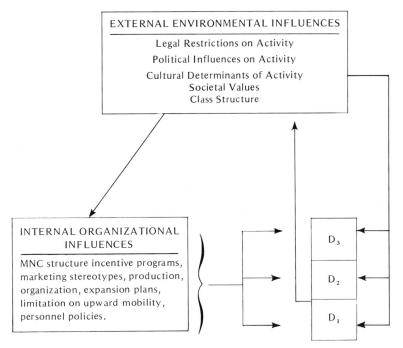

A Consequence of Organizational Decision-Making: Organizational Efficiency

The first concern of an MNC should be the effect of its decision making on the firm's efficiency. Efficiency can best be viewed in terms of economy, but other aspects of efficiency are also important and often not considered. For example, low turnover throughout the layers of a business is preferable to high turnover, if for no other reason than that training new employees is extremely costly. For MNCs some aspects of efficiency are important because of the international character of the firm. These may be less important in single-nation firms.

The selection of various readings in this volume is intended to provide further insights into many points raised above.

Long-Range Planning

Multinational planning is the process by which environmental factors impinging upon an international company are consciously brought to bear in developing both short- and long-term strategic courses of action that best satisfy the basic objective of corporate survival usually indicated by some measure of profit. Planning, therefore, is fundamental to the existence, survival and continued growth of a multinational company.

Planning refers to making present decisions which have future consequences. As such, it does not include future decisions, and forecasting is at best an element in the total process, although it is often a necessary element. Since planning entails present commitments of financial and managerial resources of a company, it implies risk-taking.

Although domestic planning is by now a well-known practice and standardized art in most large-scale companies, its effective and recent use in multinational operations has been plagued with numerous external and internal problems. The external problems are created by (1) rapid changes in environmental factors, (2) protective policies of developing countries, (3) lack of appropriate information to forecast and, hence, to reduce uncertainty, and (4) greater diversity of international markets. The internal problems, on the other hand, are created by (1) domestic orientation of top management, (2) lack of cooperation among units of multinational operations, and (3) differences in philosophy of local managements from one country to another.

Therefore, like the fat person and his weight-watcher program, multinational planning has been found difficult to implement despite the fact that all the necessary skills seem to be known and available.

The article by William Cain points out at least four major problems that seem inherent in any international planning. The first is the susceptibility of international planning to formative problems because of distance, language, management, climate and diversity. Second is the lack of acceptance by top management. Third, international planning has not as yet attained the same quality of planning as its domestic counterpart. Finally, lack of cooperation among international units has not brought about the synergistic effect that international planning mandates.

Based on a total of twelve different criteria, Cain very succinctly summarizes the basic differences between domestic and international planning. Most of these differences can be traced to the inherent greater complexity of multinational business operations.

Leo Welt, in a concise article, recommends a number of specific steps for instituting or extending an international long-range planning system. These range from formats for systematized and comparable business activities, to analysis and screening of possible new business areas.

Conceptual Models and Methodological Approaches
to Cross-Cultural Comparisons

One of the most important problems facing planners and managers of large multinational corporations is the extreme heterogeneity among
various regions and peoples of the world. In a one-country firm, the parameters—external environment—of a given decision-making situation are well-
defined and are either constant or changing at a very slow rate. The only
variables whose interaction needs to be interpreted, in the light of new
information, are the variables with which management already has the most
familiarity and experience. However, the assumption of unchanging external
environment is crucial to the validity of management's evaluation of the
problem, because a changing external environment also will alter the nature
of the problem, thereby rendering inapplicable those solutions which might
have been tried previously and found effective.

MNC managers know only too well that the assumption of the constancy
of external environment is not applicable in overseas markets. The consistency of interpretation of a set of data and its analysis in terms of certain
hypotheses are possible only when exogenous variables remain unchanged.
Failing this, past experience in the understanding of similar facts in somewhat
similar situations, even in different countries of the world, is no longer valid.

The complexity of the situation notwithstanding, it is indispensible that
corporate managements of MNCs must develop some conceptual frameworks
and tools by which they can assess the desirability and usefulness of transferring their experiences from one country to another. How should a country be
evaluated in terms of its market potential and investment risks in the absence
of any data? What are the crucial variables which are likely to determine the
sales potential of a company's products in Country A? Are these variables
similar for Countries B and C? Would the management training programs,
executive compensation, performance evaluation, or the sales and promotion
strategies used in Country A be applicable in Country B? How should the
management go about answering these questions? The remedy lies in the
application of cross-cultural research techniques to the problems of multinational corporations. The articles included in this section demonstrate
that a significant step has been taken in this direction. They also indicate the
urgent need for further research and show the possible direction such research
might take.

The article by Sethi and Curry is an attempt to develop significant and
objective typologies of world markets. The analysis of the data is done
through the BC TRY System of Cluster Analysis.[2] The system provides for
objectively grouping variables or objects, and is a set of about thirty different
programs which may be used to execute some aspect of cluster analysis or
factor analysis on a particular set of data.

The article starts with a general description of cluster analysis in the context of numerical taxonomy and proceeds to a specific discussion of the logic of the BC TRY System. Fifty-six variables are first prefactored by a standard BC TRY V-analysis to reduce their spatial dimensionality and provide independent components on which to scale ninety-three countries. The variable row correlation matrix yields a set of six dimensions that account for over 96 percent of the variance. Next, country clusters are developed by assigning each country a standardized simple sum score on each of the six variable domains. Countries are clustered sequentially in spaces of two, three, four, five and six variable domains in order to isolate the contribution of each variable domain to changes in the country clusters.

The main conclusions are: (1) There is no unidimensional scale or uniform hierarchy on which to rank various countries. (2) The country clusters must be based on one or more composite-unidimensional scales, each scale incorporating one or more variables. Therefore, the composition of country clusters would change on the basis of inclusion or exclusion of (i) variables from a variable domain, or (ii) the number of domains on which the country clusters are based. (3) Specific country clusters should be developed in response to each particular problem.

Charles Ramond's article provides another approach to the problem of analyzing world markets in order to find similarities and dissimilarities between various countries. The World Data Bank is a shared-time computer system for retrieving and analyzing international information. The Data Bank has on-line capacity for analyzing previously stored data on over 100 variables for 154 countries. The data has been collected from over 80 public sources and is constantly updated.

A time-sharing system provides a user instant access to this data. Through a teletypewriter console in his office, he is connected with the central computer via telephone. Through this system, he can use all or any part of this data to perform factor analysis, stepwise regression analysis, cluster analysis, or time series analysis. The user may also include his own internally generated data, with any of the variables from the Data Bank, to generate custom-tailored data matrices for further analysis and develop planning goals or marketing strategies which meet the peculiar needs of his own company. The Data Bank thus offers a potentially, highly useful device for the managers of MNCs, and researchers and students of international business.

The last two articles are closely interrelated and, specifically, they examine the varying degrees of financial and managerial commitments as a consequence of long-range planning. Litvak and Banting found these commitments to vary from simple licensing arrangements to a wholly owned manufacturing subsidiary in a foreign country. The authors examine seven factors—political stability, market opportunity, economic development, cultural unity, legal barriers, physiographic barriers and geo-cultural distance—of a country to classify it as a hot, moderate or cold country in terms of financial and managerial commitments. Litvak and Banting use simple ratings to obtain the temperature gradient of a few select countries.

A better method and analytically more rigorous approach is suggested by Sheth and Lutz. They operationalize the seven factors in terms of a total of 15 variables on which profiles of 82 countries can be drawn. The data were pooled from three independent studies conducted in 1961-1962. Using specialized aspects of factor analysis, the authors obtained a temperature gradient from the viewpoint of U.S. business firms and rank-ordered all the 82 countries from this viewpoint. It was found that the United Kingdom, West Germany, France, the Netherlands, Canada and Belgium were relatively hot countries and North Vietnam, Nepal, Afghanistan, Laos, and Yemen were relatively cold countries. All other countries fell between these two extremes of the hot-cold continuum.

In the area of multinational planning and business arrangements, very little systematic research or thinking has been available in the published literature. The interested reader, however, should find the Annotated Bibliography useful.

Strategies of Organizational Structure

With the substantial increase in world trade and foreign private investment in the last two decades, the area of multinational organization and management has gained considerable significance. This is one area of international business in which extension of domestic business practices has been limited. Indeed, it would seem that the organizational structure of multinational business may provide insights into domestic organizational psychology and management.

Based on their observations of a number of large-scale U.S. companies committed to investment abroad, Clee and Sachtjen find that there are three types of organizational structure relevant to multinational business. The first is the traditional international division structure. It is most frequently used by companies still involved in exporting, rather than manufacturing abroad, where a number of personal and political reasons have impeded a major reorganization required by large-scale international involvement. The second is the geographic structure in which operational responsibility for certain geographic areas is delegated to the line managers, but the worldwide strategic planning and control are retained by the headquarters. Whenever the product is highly standardized, but techniques for penetrating local markets differ, this type of structure is very successful. The oil industry is an outstanding example. The third and more recent organizational structure is the product structure where worldwide responsibility is assigned to managers in charge of one or more related products. In cases where a company has a widely diversified product line and products go to a variety of end-use markets, the product structure seems most desirable. In general, it is probably the most advanced and advantageous strategic structure of all the three structures.

Organizations that have a single or a few related product lines, and organizations with a high degree of vertical integration, tend to be capital-intensive, centrally organized and functionally structured. On the other hand, organizations that have a diversified product line tend to be decentralized and structured in terms of divisions. Fouraker and Stopford, following the theory and research of A. D. Chandler, examined a total of 170 U.S. companies in eighteen different industries that had international operations. They found that, but for a very small number, most companies had the decentralized, division structure. The authors then justify, on a number of criteria, that the multinational strategy of organizational structure is decentralization and diversification rather than centralization and departmentalization.

Stephen Allen discusses the finding and implications of a recent study of concepts aimed at helping managers of multi-unit corporations in formulating organizational designs. He begins by isolating the issues which face the manager in this area. They are: (i) how to constitute organizational sub-units, and (ii) how to achieve coordination within the corporate structure. The multi-unit organization is viewed as a "behaviorally-based system" and is given the following definition: "A complex adaptive system that seeks to survive and grow by coping with changing external conditions and by dealing with its own recurring internal conflicts and performance deviations." Departing from the premise that the firm is sensitive to its environment, the author seeks to study the "interrelatedness" of its sub-units and to trace dynamic interrelationships. He develops a conceptual model in which the factors affecting inter-unit relationships are: strategic decisions and mental set, environmental requirements, and organizational choices of management. Next, an attempt is made to establish the basic pattern of corporate-division relationships and to relate environmental diversity to integrative effort and performance. The author's model of corporate-division relationship patterns (and their operations) traces the impact of organizational design and intervention tactics, and considers the pitfalls of low-performance situations.

The environmental requirements and organizational options are perceived as differences between the conglomerate and vertically integrated firms. The conglomerate is seen to diverge from vertically integrated firms in the following respects: a) its units are more highly differentiated, b) less integrative effort is needed, c) it responds to divisional requests more rapidly, d) its "influence peaks" are at lower levels of the management hierarchy, and e) it has more formal evaluation schemes with more explicit performance criteria. Finally, the author stresses that organizational schemes must be congruent with environmental influences.

In an excellent article, Rutenberg presents a typology of four archetypes of multinational business operations based on the concepts of organizational psychology, behavioral patterns of the headquarters executives and their convictions about the working relationships with foreign subsidiaries. The four archetypes vary primarily in terms of extent of direct and indirect interventions by headquarters in the subsidiary's decision making. Finally, Rutenberg examines differences among the four archetypes in their planning guidelines related to cost of capital, pricing policies, product design, planned managerial rotation, and liquid asset management.

The section on Strategies of Organizational Structure provides a number of viewpoints on the strategies of organizational structures for multinational business. Whatever the organizational structure, it has to be managed and operated upon by individuals brought up in different cultures and climates.

Cultural and Individual Differences in Managerial Values

Given the prevalence of individual differences among international managers, this section attempts to present some fundamental behavioral differences among managers in different parts of the world.

George W. England's article on personal value systems of American managers sets the standard against which other articles can be compared because it is one of the few large-sample studies of U.S. managers' personal values. A total of 66 concepts were developed in these five categories to create a Personal Value Questionnaire: goals of business organizations, personal goals of individuals, groups of people, ideas associated with people, and ideas about general topics. England found that the American managers' primary orientations were pragmatic in that those concepts considered important were also considered relevant for success. However, there were wide variations among American managers in their personal values. England also found that these personal values operate at the corporate level as well as at the level of day-to-day decisions; that organization both influences and is influenced by the personal values of managers; and that differences in personal values may well explain the nature of conflict between individuals in an organization.

In another article, "The European Business Elite," the authors present a study of the characteristics of the men who run the biggest companies in Europe. Based on a sample of 576 chief executives, the study attempts to analyze the career paths, experiences, birthplace, age, social class, educational background, compensations and travels of European business management. In general, European chiefs were found to be not too different from their counterpart American chiefs on the above-mentioned characteristics. However, there were very wide variations among the European managers themselves, which leads one to speculate on the difficulties involved in economic integration of Europe.

Finally, Lauter presents an interesting comparative study of Turkish managers related to the extent of decentralization of authority. His argument is that the concept of decentralization, although proven to be beneficial in the United States by several researchers including Drucker, McGregor and Argyris, is at best difficult to adopt in developing countries such as Turkey. Data collected on 73 Turkish managers clearly indicated that decision making was highly centralized in all organizational activities including most day-to-day operational problems. Even minor matters frequently demand involvement and attention of high-level executives. More interestingly, there were virtually no differences between Turkish and American managers operating in Turkey in their extent of centralized decision making, although one would presume that American managers would manifest their bias toward decentralized policies. Lauter argues that very strong environmental constraints of a socio-logical-cultural and legal nature tend to impede decentralization of authority in Turkey and other developing nations.

The process of selection and development of managers in multinational business is complex because of variety of managerial talents on the one hand and appropriate managerial practices on the other. The following section consists of three articles on this subject and attempts to expose the reader to this area.

Executive Selection, Training, and Development

Hodgson discusses the need for higher quality in American man-agers that are sent overseas in light of the increasing importance of U.S. business involvement abroad and of the political significance it bears. He notices that there are difficulties in selecting men who understand foreign cultures and ways, who are properly motivated for overseas assignments, and who are willing to forego the comforts of home life for the challenge of a foreign post. He feels that companies can reduce the risk of making wrong choices of personnel for their overseas operations by presenting the assign-ments in their true light (i.e., with the pros and cons), integrating foreign assignments with home operations through a job-rotation system, changing the criteria for selection, and offering adequate pre-departure training.

Lee brings out the specific problem of developing domestic managers in developing nations. He identifies five fundamental differences between man-agement selection and development conditions in developing countries and in the United States. These are: (1) limited sources of managerial leadership potential in terms of educated elites, ex-military officers, and college gradu-ates; (2) educational and technical deprivation commonly prevalent in less developed countries; (3) greater hostile attitude toward objectives common to private enterprise such as profits; (4) divergent concepts of the ideal manager; and (5) resistance to typical American development approaches such as face-to-face criticism. Lee then proposes several courses of action in each of the five problem areas. His article is probably one of the most cogent discussions on the problem of developing managers in less developed coun-tries.

According to McKenzie, in "Incompetent Foreign Managers," the sub-optimal performance of a company's foreign general manager may be brought on by headquarters as much as by the individual in question. The article studies the controls and performance criteria to which the local manager is subjected and remarks that they may not be conducive to efficiency and rationality on his part. As a de facto president who is judged on details, the local manager is seen to be filling a dual role. With the view toward giving companies a true means of judging the competence of their foreign managers, the author suggests that:

—the degree of responsibility of the local manager be established explicitly and the control system tailored according to the division of responsibility between him and headquarters.

—the selection procedure be sharpened so that headquarters will be induced to rely more heavily on the capabilities of the manager.

—a set of performance criteria be established at the outset so that it be known to both them and the manager, and thereafter act as the sole yardstick for competence.

Compensation and Job Satisfaction

This section deals with the compensation and job satisfaction aspects of management. In the first article Lesher and Griffith address themselves to the problem of disparate compensations paid to the three common types of business executives in multinational companies, namely expatriate, domestic and foreign national managers. They find that this disparity is due to basic errors of both commission and omission on the part of top management. The former include designing and implementing complicated and, at times, unnecessary hardship allowances. The latter include not making essential adjustments for tax, equalization and cost of living allowances in all cases. The authors suggest that an integrated compensation program should be implemented in view of the fact that there is much greater executive mobility today.

The main thrust of Terry, Michelson, and Vivian's arguments in the article is that multinational corporations operating in Latin America need to be sensitive to changes in their environment when formulating their remuneration plans. The author explains that blind adoption of either an excessively progressive (imported) program or of a paternalistic (low-wage, local) plan will prove inadequate. The suggestion seems to be that the workable wage/benefit structure will derive from the corporation's ability to discern employee backgrounds, be aware of competitive wages, be conscious of taxation considerations, of gaps in statutory benefit programs, and of salary substitutes, and be mindful of the fact that motivation (the major problem) may not be a function of pecuniary benefits alone.

Public Relations

The sole article in this section is that by Lassalle. He narrates numerous examples of how to offend the host country and its government mostly without really trying, but sometimes with lots of trying. He feels that a professional public realtions manager should (1) interpret the culture and social organization of the host country to the company's management, (2) aid management in its contacts outside company personnel such as in government, (3) help management interpret the company to its host country. In addition, Lassalle provides several basic observations that may prove useful to any one in the company in its interaction with the host country.

Finally, an extensive Annotated Bibliography is provided on long-range planning, multinational organization and management for interested readers who may want to pursue some aspects of it for further research.

REFERENCES

1. Stephen Heymar, "The Efficiency (Contradictions) of Multinational Corporations," *Allied Social Sciences: Associations Papers and Abstract of Papers*, New York, December 28-30, 1966, pp. 217-218.
2. Robert C. Tryon and Daniel E. Bailey, *Cluster Analysis* (New York: McGraw-Hill, 1970.)

MULTINATIONAL BUSINESS OPERATIONS

Long-Range Planning, Organization, and Management

1

LONG-RANGE PLANNING

INTERNATIONAL PLANNING: MISSION IMPOSSIBLE?

WILLIAM W. CAIN

International long-range planning works—but not always very well. This seemed to be the consensus of opinion at a seminar earlier this year attended by planners from 30 U.S. companies, among them some of the largest and most successful operating abroad. Most of these companies have conducted long-range planning on an international scale for five years or more. Planners at the meeting agreed that while planning generally has proven to be an indispensable management tool in the United States, neither they nor their top management were altogether happy with the results of planning in their international operations.

International planning today perhaps is at the same stage of development that international marketing was 15 or 20 years ago. The concept of long-range planning and its value have been accepted. Planning procedures and practices are also realtively well known and even, to an extent, standardized. But like the fat girl and her Weight Watchers program, the difficulty has been to make it work. Problems which arose earlier in the sphere of domestic planning have come into even sharper focus in the international field. From the experience of the past five years, it is now possible to identify common problems, to specify their causes and to suggest possible remedies. Shared experience over the next decade should lead to significant improvement.

INTERNATIONAL PLANNING—WHAT IS IT?

Planning has suffered from problems of semantics and definition, much as marketing did in earlier years. Some planners in fact object to use of the term "international planning," claiming that it has no meaningful identification and that it is really no different in concept and practice from what might be termed "domestic" planning. Both are part of the same cloth, they say. At the same time all planners will agree that planning on an international scale has special and unique problems associated with it, primarily with respect to implementation.

Definitions are also not always helpful when it comes to describing and

Reprinted with permission from the July-August 1970 issue of the *Columbia Journal of World Business*. Copyright © 1970 by the Trustees of Columbia University.

3

distinguishing between the different types of planning. Part of the problem is akin to the old tale of four blind men trying to describe an elephant, each feeling a different part of its anatomy. It is perhaps more meaningful to look at what companies are actually doing in terms of their planning practices. One U.S. company, a large multi-division automotive equipment producer, has developed this approach to international planning:

Operational Planning. Shorter range (one- and three-year) planning is the responsibility of each overseas operating unit. Format in general follows that of U.S. divisions and is supplied by the headquarters planning staff. Plans include sales, profit and cash-flow projections by product line, market share, capital requirements, etc. Although plans are integrated at regional levels, individual unit plans are forwarded intact to New York headquarters.

Strategic Planning. Operating units—most of which are national in scope—are asked to plan ahead on a longer-term basis for new products, which might be developed from within or acquired. Headquarters has deliberately provided only very general guidelines as to how far afield a local operation might explore, wanting the local managers to stretch their outlook. However, the scope normally is confined to the unit's country of operation, and plans are subject to review at headquarters.

Corporate Planning. Worldwide plans are developed at international head-quarters, tied closely to overall corporate objectives and plans. This planning takes two forms: 1) "protective planning" and 2) "opportunity planning." The first of these is strategic and long-range in character, anticipating world-wide changes in markets and business conditions relating to the present scope of operation. On the other hand, "opportunity planning" is directed toward seeking new business directions for growth and diversification.

Among the problems which face the nation's most active companies in the international arena, four in particular stand out.

Failure to Take Off. Well known to the planning fraternity are the early failures among companies attempting to launch planning overseas. While getting started has been a common problem in domestic planning, it has been particularly acute on the international scene. International planning is espe-cially susceptible to formative problems because of distance, language, man-agement climate, diversity and other factors unique to individual companies.

Lack of Acceptance by Management. It has been difficult for U.S. companies to get overseas managers—whether nationals or Americans—to accept or use planning. This is often experienced when plans have originated solely at home base and do not reflect the "real world" of the manager. As with planning anywhere, "textbook" plans are doomed to failure.

Quality of Planning. In many companies, foreign operating units have not yet attained the same quality of planning as their domestic counterparts. One reason for this is that planning data are neither as accurate nor as reliable as companies would wish. Perhaps because of this even the most foresighted managements do not seem to plan ahead in the international field with the same confidence, scope and imagination that they display domestically. However, there are notable exceptions to this, including Bendix and Merck, whose international planning units have, in fact, led their corporations into the strategic planning process or pioneered in certain aspects of planning.

Lack of Cooperation Among International Units. Many companies, while recognizing the importance of intra-country cooperation—and of planning as a means of realizing it, have not yet been able to achieve results. This is perhaps the major problem in international planning today. One of the accepted objectives of planning on an international scale is to realize "synergistic" benefits among various independent operations. But there is a basic conflict here. A national manager typically is committed to profit objectives for his own operation and is called upon to develop detailed plans in accordance with those objectives. He knows his own performance is going to be measured by how well he meets the goals set. If he spends his time fitting or adapting his plan into a wider international framework, on an intercountry basis, he is apt to compromise his own short-term profits. He is unlikely to jeopardize his own operation's performance so that a sibling operation in another country will benefit.

While international planners must—and do—think synergistically, management abroad is inclined to think parochially. This of course can be the case with U.S. management as well, even at top corporate levels. Loyalties tend to be national. Achieving international cooperation represents a dilemma which has yet to be resolved, and companies that can solve this will be making a major contribution to planning.

Failure on the Launching Pad

Many planning programs have started off badly, thereby discrediting planning as well as the planning staff and setting back the whole planning process. A sad illustration is the case of a large European company operating on an international basis, which recently disbanded its planning staff, including its vice-presidential head, after two years of operation. When asked why planning has been discontinued, the ex-planning chief said it had not been discontinued; it had never gotten underway.

The basic reason for this failure has since become apparent: top management had neither supported the activity nor had confidence in it. They had in effect attempted to delegate the job to the planning group. It will be a long time before formal planning is undertaken again by this company—which suggests that the ostrich, unlike the dodo, is still alive and well, at least for the time being. Speaking about management support, Irwin Goldman, Director of Planning at Merck International, says: "With us, planning is not just a technique or a system—it is a management philosophy and fundamental to our entire operation."

The same may be said of ITT, where Chief Executive Harold Geneen relies on a comprehensive planning system to run his multifaceted operation. In fact, ITT, of all large U.S. companies, has developed one of the most successful planning systems. This system is a good illustration of how well planning works when it is an intrinsic element in the management of a company. While group and division-level managers are responsible for developing plans embracing some 400 operating units in 60 countries, basic quantitative objectives are first set by Geneen with his top-level product-line managers. While acting in a staff capacity, the product-line managers are on a par organizationally with their corresponding group operating managers. Operating management makes its plans in accordance with these objectives, subject to review by the product-line managers. The central planning group, reporting elsewhere in the corporate staff structure, in actuality does not make plans: it coordinates the planning, essentially an administrative function.

In essence, planning seldom fails because of the competence of the planner or the quality of the planning; it fails because management does not support it. A corollary to this is the principle that planning must remain a prime responsibility of management: it cannot be delegated.

Expectations and Disappointments

Another source of trouble is the expectation on the part of management that the development of a formal planning activity will achieve results "automatically." This is often coupled with a lack of understanding, throughout the organization, of what planning is actually expected to accomplish. When the purpose and goals of planning itself are not well defined and communicated, disappointment will result. Overseas, where communications are more difficult and local management may be less sophisticated in terms of professional management techniques, confusion and misunderstanding often occur.

For the same reason, trying to accomplish too much, too quickly, can lead to trouble. Impatience with planning on the part of top management has often occurred when a new program seems to take too long to get rolling. The experience of many international companies has proven that it requires at least two to three years for planning to function and demonstrate real results.

Another flaw in international planning can stem from a factor which might best be summed up in terms of the old biblical dogma that "God made man in His own image." To initiate overseas planning on the basis of "how it is at home," is a dangerous practice, one planner says, because it inevitably is based on "unspoken" assumptions that sooner or later will come back to haunt.

Perhaps the most common error is to take for granted that foreign management operates by the same fundamental goals and precepts as does U.S. management. Such assumptions as profit growth, financial incentives, free competition and consistency of government policy often do not apply in other countries. This fact, of course, goes without saying among those with experience overseas—some of whom have learned this the hard way—yet it continues to plague good planning.

Corporate planning in France, for example, is tied to government planning to an extent not experienced in the United States. Objectives and programs which are not keyed to government policy and goals can be meaningless. This can present a particular problem to U.S. companies when corporate objectives conflict with the objectives of foreign subsidiaries which must follow government guidelines.

Such a basic philosophical conflict came to light a number of years ago during a planning seminar held in Paris for the management of a number of leading French companies. The purpose of the seminar was to review the long-range planning practices of U.S. companies. Among the subjects included was the setting of profit objectives. As the seminar concluded, the managing director of a well-known company took issue with what he characterized as "the American love affair with growth." He contrasted that with what he considered the prime objectives of his own company—stability of earnings and security of its stockholders. It is difficult to see a common meeting ground between these two philosophies.

Edward G. Ewing of Sylvania International makes an interesting comment about the effectiveness of planning, and what can be expected of managers. The really top-notch manager, he says, will be little helped by formal planning—he already operates according to a plan even though there is no written plan as such, and he often plans intuitively. Also, the really poor manager will seldom benefit very much from a formal plan. It is the managers who fall between these two extremes—and who in fact may represent the preponderance of managers in some companies—whose management skills will be improved the most. This is an important planning consideration abroad, where there tends to be a much greater diversity of management experience and competence than in the United States.

It is surprising to learn how many well-managed companies have proceeded to initiate planning without orienting and educating overseas management in planning concepts and objectives. Thus, planning arrives on their doorsteps virtually unannounced, and headquarters management is dismayed when it is not accepted and used.

A planning executive in a large company based in New York blames the early failure of their planning on this factor. His organization spent months preparing a sophisticated, well-thought-out format and planning system. The planning staff personally delivered the material to individual managers and returned home to await results. In the words of the planning executive, the launching was a disaster. New York management finally did what should have been done in the first place. Seminars were held with their overseas managers to orient them on the concept of planning, its purpose and its expectations.

This gave the managers the opportunity to ask questions and, equally important, to make suggestions concerning format and procedure. This company's planning is now on solid ground, although considerable time was lost through the faulty initial approach.

Clearly, the understanding and acceptance of overseas management is essential to any successful long-range planning program. However, management of overseas organizations may be less accustomed to the workings of planning and unfamiliar with the elements which go into it. Acceptance will often vary according to the sophistication of local management. Problems stemming from this condition have ranged from a complete lack of response, through frustration, to the "boiler plating" of a plan.

Many foreign managers are unaccustomed to sharing their management prerogatives with those reporting to them—much less with staff people. Under this condition, planning activity devolves on the top manager himself. Problems of time and even of disinclination often prevent the job from being done effectively—or even done at all. One international planner sums it up this way: "There is no such thing as planning problems, only people problems."

The practices generally employed for planning in the United States assume the availability of adequate and accurate information and data. Subjects such as the size of markets, growth records, industry projections, competitive standings and profitability of competition are generally not too difficult to determine. In many foreign countries, however, such information is not readily available and may be impossible to develop to the degree of reliability generally achieved in the United States. The planning director of a well-known electronics company admits that the early phase of planning overseas was a "complete fiasco" because the demands of the system forced managers literally to "make up" figures—otherwise unavailable—to satisfy U.S. management. As a matter of fact, a certain degree of this is probably experienced by most companies. In discussing this point, Eric Shane, manager of financial forecasting for Avon Products' international operations, says that he accepts the fact that figures submitted by some overseas units may be "padded." Based on past experience, however, he believes that he can now spot these in most cases, and generally he will ask the manager to revise them, offering guidelines to assure greater accuracy. The lack of business information commonly encountered will probably continue to hinder planning for many years to come.

Planning for Planning

It is perhaps unnecessary to say that the establishment of planning in a company should itself be planned for. Also, this planning should be undertaken with the direct participation of top management. As one executive expressed it, "planning is too important to leave to the planners." In saying this, he was not taking a crack at staff planners, but rather criticizing

DOMESTIC VS. INTERNATIONAL PLANNING

A number of external elements affect plans and planning. They may also differ between domestic and international operations:

Domestic Planning	International Planning
1. Single language and nationality	1. Multilingual/multinational/multicultural factors
2. Relatively homogeneous market	2. Fragmented and diverse markets
3. Data available, usually accurate and collection easy	3. Data collection a formidable task, requiring significantly higher budgets and personnel allocation
4. Political factors relatively unimportant	4. Political factors frequently vital
5. Relative freedom from government interference	5. Involvement in national economic plans; government influences business decisions
6. Individual corporation has little effect on environment	6. "Gravitational" distortion by large companies
7. Chauvinism helps	7. Chauvinism hinders
8. Relatively stable business environment	8. Multiple environments, many of which are highly unstable (but may be highly profitable)
9. Uniform financial climate	9. Variety of financial climates ranging from over-conservative to wildly inflationary
10. Single currency	10. Currencies differing in stability and real value
11. Business "rules of the game" mature and understood	11. Rules diverse, changeable and unclear

continued

continued from page 9

12. Management generally accustomed to sharing responsibilities and using financial controls	12. Management frequently autonomous and unfamiliar with budgets and controls

the managers who may try to delegate the job. This was another way of saying again that planning should be the concern of management and should not be relegated to staff.

Especially in the international company is the pre-planning phase a critical one, where the different conditions overseas must be taken into account including the character of individual operations and their managers. Subjects typically covered in the "planning for planning" stage include:

Development of the planning format to be used for overseas operations and its adaptation for different local conditions and kinds of organizations.

Staging of the planning—what are the steps to be taken and in what sequence and time period?

Organization and staffing of the planning function—who is responsible and where is he located? In Bendix, for example, this varies from a full-time planner in an overseas affiliate to the local manager doing the job himself.

At what organizational levels will various types of planning be done? For example, will planning for new products and operations be the responsibility of operating units or be done at headquarters? In the case of operational plans, the question often arises as to whether it should be done at the regional or local level. This option will vary from company to company.

Careful thought in the pre-planning stage can help prevent fumbling in the initial implementation period.

John Bryan, Vice President of Planning at Bendix International, took a hard look two years ago at the task ahead of him as the newly appointed Director of Planning. In his words, "the first job was to get things sorted out." This was partially crucial because Bendix has diversified interests and, through the years, had "accumulated" various kinds of international operations ranging from licensing to wholly owned manufacturing. Bryan's point was that until everybody had a clear, accurate picture of what they were corporately engaged in doing, planning for the future was unfeasible.

Now, with the "sorting out" completed he plans to move ahead with a phased integrated program that will extend planning to a period of 5 to 10 years. As part of this process, longer-range environmental factors will be examined, and coordination of planning between the different operations and countries will be stressed. Bryan believes that the time spent in getting things squared away in the beginning was without doubt a good investment.

Disagreement appears to exist among companies as to whether the planning system should be used to measure the performance of management. The use of planning as a means of control—to measure the success of an operation —leads naturally to evaluation of the manager himself. Some comapnies feel strongly that the planning process should be separated from managerial control, to insure that management develops realistic plans and does not build in a defense against possible shortcomings in the meeting of objectives. Edward Ewing at Sylvania, for example, believes that combining planning and management evaluation, particularly in the early stages of a company's planning, will hinder its acceptance.

On the other hand, some companies depend heavily on the planning system as a means of control. In ITT, for example, planning is intrinsic to carrying out this management function. It appears that this issue is being resolved differently by various companies, depending on the character of the organization and stage of planning.

Role of the Planner

It is apparent in looking at the companies which have done a good job in planning overseas that the planner has played a key role in their success. International planners are a special breed. They must be particularly skilled and knowledgeable since planning on an international scale is complex and demanding. At the same time, the planner must be practical and not merely a theoretician. Ideally, he should also have a background in international business and a consuming interest in it. Perhaps the most important personal requirement is a high tolerance for frustration—the job typically is beset by a multitude of variables and potentially conflicting loyalties. It can be a hazardous occupation as well.

Basically, the job of the international planner does not differ from that of his domestic counterpart. Communicating what planning is and winning acceptance for it is a key part of either position. However, the job is quite a bit more difficult overseas than it is at home. It requires time, patience, and understanding—and travel. The specialist may find himself away from home as much as one-third of the time.

Above all, fundamental to the international planner's job is one essential function: education. This entails "teaching" planning—often in a truly "foreign" management environment—and showing how it can be a useful management tool. In some cases, the planner has been called upon to organize a study to develop accurate information for the plan. He also may have to "translate" overall corporate objectives into specific goals for a galaxy of operating units and to dovetail the separate plans into a unified supranational form.

Many international companies today are completing the initial phase of a longer-term program for planning. Now that planning has begun to develop and operate, new factors are being introduced into the overall program. Some companies have anticipated this as part of their longer-range "planning plan," while others are adding new elements out of pressing necessity. Some examples of what is presently happening are:

Plans are being "refined" to pick up items which may have been deferred— such as determination of market share and competitive activities. A study is being undertaken by a leading U.S. metallurgical firm concerning technological development trends in Europe. Another company is launching a marketing survey in Europe to develop precise information for the revision of marketing plans. International Dairy Queen, as an example, is demanding more detail and accuracy in plans now, after several years of getting under way. Willard Eggers, who is in charge of international operations there, says of this: "We deliberately started off with a simple and general plan to get rolling quickly." He is now insisting on expanded and more precise planning information.

Companies are extending the time period covered—from 1 or 2 years to as much as 5 or 10 years—based on several years' experience with the plan.

Environmental trends are being examined which will affect longer-range strategic planning, including demographic conditions, housing, transportation, consumer purchasing power and other factors.

A limited number of large companies—oil companies for example—have organized computer-based information and planning systems. Bendix International includes worldwide data on populations, GNP, automotive data such as road miles and vehicles, competitive market shares, as well as forecasts and trends for the 64 countries and 10 major project categories with which its planners are concerned. Long-range planners are looking forward to using such information systems as a basis for simulation. Apparently, little has been done along those lines as yet, and the companies which are reported to be doing so now are close-mouthed about results.

Quantitative objectives are being revised and sharpened, based on actual experience. In particular, profit objectives are being examined in light of the risks in various countries, with standards being revised upwards where investment may be vulnerable to fast-changing political or economic conditions.

Non-quantitative objectives are being incorporated into plans, including management development goals, product development and diversification. Also, an attempt is being made to develop objectives which will assure a greater degree of cooperation among operating units in various countries.

Contingency plans are being developed, considering what is to be done should major political or economic changes occur.

International planning may be under a cloud at present, with both management and planning staff expressing some concern. However, planning on an international scale for the most part is well established in many companies. Experience, even when not altogether satisfactory, has served to clarify problems which are only now coming into focus, and management is taking an honest and critical look at the record. Planning internationally is not easy and will always present special problems.

What is most important at this point is the confidence expressed by companies—many with scars from bad beginnings—in their planning. Along with this confidence goes the belief that long-range planning represents a vital corporate resource, one which can be an important competitive advantage in world markets. With foresighted companies recognizing today that international operations may represent the major source of profit growth in coming years, management is being called upon to insure that its planning overseas is in good working order.

INTERNATIONAL LONG-RANGE PLANNING: SOME BASIC CONSIDERATIONS

LEO G. B. WELT

International operations are becoming increasingly important to many American companies and the attendant problems increasingly complex; for these companies, international long-range planning (as distinct from short-range planning) is now a necessity.

There are fundamental areas of variance between long-range planning on a domestic scale and comparable international planning—yet certain basic, philosophic elements of long-range planning remain constant from the Midwest to central Europe. A systematic approach to long-range planning, anywhere, recognizes two key elements:

The continual imposition of planning discipline on present operations.

A continual reappraisal and updating of a company's definition of its true nature, and of the direction in which it should be going.

After all, the goal of long-range planning is simply to increase in terms of years the company's attempt to do what it is supposedly doing on a short-range basis—come to grips with the opportunities and problems that have, and will have, a real impact on the organization's immediate and future growth.

Besides determining desired avenues of action for the future, long-range planning should stimulate constructive thinking; improve communication throughout the company; generate alternative plans so the company can react

As condensed in *Management Review*, February 1970, pp. 50-51, published by the American Management Association.

sensitively to changing environmental factors; and create a consciousness in management of those environmental factors that cause the need for change in the organization.

WHO SHOULD PLAN?

The questions, or perhaps dilemma, of who is to get this done is, understandably, less distinctly defined. There are more differences between companies than there are similarities, and the position of the long-range planning division, and the composition of that division (if it is indeed a division), depend greatly upon the individual company's characteristics and ultimate goals.

Some companies believe that long-range planning should not, in fact cannot, be separated from other management activities, since planning is one of any executive's most important tasks. It is felt that if long-range planning is carried on elsewhere the executive may ignore this responsibility, creating an actual schism between planning and execution.

A different point of view holds that if long-range planning is not isolated from the responsibility of the executive who is primarily concerned with a week-to-week profit chart, he will not have time to keep that profit curve on an upward swing. And it is true that if long-range planning is to have any validity at all, it must be the end result of a good deal of concentrated effort, painstaking research, and application of specialized skills—many of which the kind of executive we are referring to here often does not possess.

International planning can only be thought of in the context of long-range efforts. Short-range planning in this area will result in short-changing the corporation's future prospects. The systematic approach is essential in the international arena. A chink in the corporate armor is not too difficult to patch up or even replace when operations are limited to the United States. But if a gear or two slips in the overseas office, and there isn't a systematic, well thought-out, long-range plan to resort to, a real disaster may set in.

The major uncertainties about long-range planning for an international operation stem from the simple fact that most U.S. corporations are domestically oriented; this is true both from a marketing and a cultural viewpoint.

Most companies first come in contact with the international scene through exporting. Then if involvement and the nature of business permit, the company establishes an office, or offices, reporting directly to the domestic office. The next step may be to establish its own manufacturing plant. Activities may then expand to other countries.

As long-range planning is vitally concerned with broad strategy and the subsequent design of appropriate policies and programs, a thorough knowledge of markets, of technology, of consumption patterns, and of trends is clearly required. But such information is not generated in anywhere near the desired scope or depth in overseas markets. This becomes the source of many problems for the global planner.

KEY TO SURVIVAL

Here are seven essentials for instituting or extending an international long-range planning system:

1. Appropriately designed, located, and staffed overseas offices, sending back periodic budgets and profit measurement charts.
2. Agreed-upon standards and yardsticks for the overseas office.
3. Gap-measurement and gap-closing programs, preferably originating on both sides of the Atlantic or Pacific.
4. Formats for systematized and comparable business activities.
5. Business plan preparation, coordination, and some form of recycling procedures.
6. Analysis and screening of possible new business areas.
7. A continuous input of new data on market conditions, customer needs, technological opportunities, competition, and a validity check of the overall planning yardstick.

CONSTANT PROBLEMS

Even as a company becomes more deeply involved in international long-range planning, it will find that certain problems continue to crop up. These might be termed the eternal verities of international long-range planning, found even in the most effective and sophisticated company planning systems. Plaguing long-range planning teams will be such problems as:

1. Inducing the overseas management and staff to think in terms of possible alternatives. That is, getting that Brussels office to think flexibly, to assert itself in line with what it uniquely knows about local conditions, instead of simply following, dog-like, whatever might be the current plan.
2. Ensuring overseas line management's commitment to plans. This is not a contradiction of what has just been noted above. There is a crucial difference between altering certain long-range plans in detail and altering them in scope.
3. Securing adequate investment of time in planning by overseas top management. Too many men, whether top executives or not, are satisfied—indeed, are only too happy—to have a nice, fat set of plans sitting on their desks, covering any contingency. As for future planning—they can only hope that this will eventually come from New York by airmail.
4. Obtaining budgets for the trial of new tools and new techniques. This is of

great importance. Technical innovations are the life-blood of profit break-throughs, and overseas competitors are fully aware of this.

5. Recruiting suitable personnel for the staffing of overseas offices, plants, distribution points, and so forth. The availability of good, skilled labor is a major problem everywhere.

6. Validating international comparisons—that is, in investment performance appraisals, market potentials, and so on. This is an area of great specialization, and many corporations either fly their own men or man into the overseas office, or simply transfer such personnel permanently overseas.

7. Allocating the time of overseas personnel equitably between that which is needed for their own duties and that which is necessary for supervision. The executive hierarchy in Europe is distinct. Bosses are bosses and workers are workers, and seemingly, never the twain shall meet. This is a peculiarly European concept that many U.S. executives term their number one problem.

POSSIBLE PROBLEMS

The above list suggests some of the more general problem areas. Other possibilities are:

Your company will find its overseas organization subject to U.S. antitrust regulations, even though its overseas competitors probably will not face any such restrictions.

You may find your company faced with operating in a rapid or even run-away inflation situation.

You must deal with local management, whose appreciation of U.S. business practice may be rudimentary, or even nonexistent.

You may find, in addition, that your business is being discriminated against in favor of local competitors.

Political, economic, social, legislative, competitive, and technological trends should all be studied to highlight problems and opportunities. Given effectively communicated objectives and policies, overseas management can intelligently assess local marketing conditions.

Undoubtedly, long-range planning on the international scene is more involved, and involuted, than it is on the domestic scene. But if it is only recognized that this very complexity requires a like complexity in a company's long-range planning, the results have an excellent chance of being successful.

2

CONCEPTUAL MODELS AND METHODOLOGICAL APPROACHES TO CROSS-CULTURAL COMPARISONS

VARIABLE AND OBJECT CLUSTERING OF CROSS-CULTURAL DATA: SOME IMPLICATIONS FOR COMPARATIVE RESEARCH AND POLICY FORMULATION

S. PRAKASH SETHI
and DAVID CURRY

Introduction

Countries, like all systems, are characterized by an infinite variety of facets and dimensions. It is important that researchers engaged in multinational studies recognize and understand these differences if they are to operate effectively across geographical, cultural, and political boundaries. While the variety of differences among countries may be infinite, not all differences are equally important—either in themselves or from the viewpoint of a given objective. Many may simply be outer manifestations of some basic underlying phenomenon. Differences among countries or groups of countries, which may be minor in themselves, nevertheless may be quite important for a policy planner or researcher, given his specific purposes and his need for understanding certain aspects of the global environment.

While there is a great need for these studies in areas including developmental economics, political science, cultural anthropology, and international business, progress has been slow for want of relevant data and reliable research methodology. Past research has often overemphasized one type of data—typically microeconomic—at the expense of other useful indices. In many cases the researcher can find very few reasons a priori for not dealing with each region or nation separately. There is, therefore, a need for further investigation at the basic level of describing phenomena, the taxonomic level, to develop a classificatory scheme which would group countries into meaningful clusters or types. At the same time, the scheme must reduce a large number of variables into certain basic domains. Typing can provide parsimonious descriptions of nations and facilitate reliable predictions about them based on their status as group members.

The purpose of this paper is the development of significant and objective typologies of different countries of the world. These typologies are based on nonsubjective clusters of variables which define dimensions of national differences. More important, the paper is intended to demonstrate the need and technique for developing new country typologies when changes in variable input are desirable or necessary.

Cluster analysis is useful in confronting taxonomic problems in the social sciences which are analogous to classificatory problems in the biological sciences. Consider these basic reasons why the analyst might expect to find simple structure (homogeneous subgroups) among a large group of countries.[1] First, countries can be characterized as organisms which exhibit *adaptive success* to their environment because of the special value of certain combinations of attributes. Second, some combinations or patterns repeat modally because they are required by natural law. For example, a natural interdependence may exist between levels of gross national product and levels of energy production for a country. Finally, we might conceive a property of gravitation or the tendency for marginal members of a type to gravitate toward the cluster centroid. Obviously, these properties need not be operative simultaneously or serially, and only one or two of the three might contribute to a pattern for any given set of objects.

Before reporting the methods and results of this study, we will briefly review several earlier studies which deal with similar problems of clustering using different clustering techniques. We emphasize that the review is oriented toward the methodology of past studies.[2]

Review of Selected Literature

An early and ambitious project was *A Cross-Polity Survey* by Arthur Banks and Robert Textor.[3] All of the 115 independent polities of the world in 1963 were compared on 57 "raw characteristics," e.g., gross national product, GNP per capita, international financial status, economic development status, sustained growth, population, literacy rate, and others. Banks and Textor's work was an empirical attempt to discern important recurring patterns in their data. The pattern concept was defined as "a concatenation of co-occurrences among attributes considered important by the observer." They stated, "To be of value to the analyst of comparative politics, a pattern must state, or at least imply, some kind of contrast between classes of polities." The 57 ordinal and nominal raw characteristics were dichotomized in a variety of strategically promising ways, and the resulting 194 "finished characteristics" subjected to an exhaustive series of cross-tabulations using the analytical tool, The Pattern Search and Table Translation Technique. Examples of finished characteristics in dichotomous form are "countries formerly under French rule" versus "countries formerly under British rule," and "countries with literacy rates greater than 10 percent" versus "countries with literacy rates less than 10 percent." The technique for evolving finished characteristics from raw characteristics could be described in four steps.

1. The input to the computer program is punched-card data about each polity in the form of dichotomous variables.
2. The technique cross-tabulates each dichotomous variable with every other such variable.
3. It winnows out those resulting two-by-two contingency tables where the strength of association between the two variables is less than $P = 0.15$,

where *P* is the Fisher exact *P*-value. (*P* can range from *zero* to plus *one*, with *zero* indicating the strongest associations.)

4. The remaining strong associations are "translated" to grammatical English sentences according to rules of translation developed by Banks and Textor and the results printed out.

Although Banks and Textor emphasize the political characteristics of countries, the concept of pattern recognition or class structure was nearly analogous to comparing countries by finding homogeneous clusters. A more rigorous method of assessing similarities between countries was discussed by Banks and Gregg where all political variables from *A Cross-Polity Survey* were subjected to a *Q*-factor analysis.[4] The logic of this technique is explained later in this section in the review of work by Bruce Russett.

The research by Banks and Textor emphasized the recognition of clusters of countries while avoiding questions of the efficacy of the attributes or dimensions on which the countries were originally scaled. Adelman and Morris have demonstrated that the techniques of factor analysis can be used to eliminate interdependencies in the variables in order to provide a salient set of independent dimensions on which countries will be scored.[5] The Adelman and Morris study was designed to determine the amount of variance in gross national product per capita predictable or common with the twenty-two other variables used to scale seventy-four underdeveloped countries. The factor analysis recovered four factors for which the communality of GNP per capita was 66 percent. The importance here is that only four domains were actually tapped rather than the twenty-three unique attributes measured for each country. However, Adelman and Morris did not estimate factor scores for the countries in an attempt to cluster them.

In a study with somewhat similar goals, Michael Haas explicitly attempted to reduce 183 carefully selected variables to a smaller set of empirical dimensions.[6] Haas suggested that most, if not all, previous studies which were aimed at recovering some basic structure among a large number of indices, have been pragmatic and problem-oriented and, therefore, limited in generality. In contrast. Dr. Haas developed a broad theoretical scheme as a framework for selecting the indicators in his research. From a principal axis factor analysis of the data, 96 factors representing dimensions of national character emerged. Only 18 appeared relevant in terms of the authors' theoretical criteria, although 43 of them had eigenvalues greater than one. This study possibly represents the most comprehensive attempt to dimensionalize the space of multinational scales, but, like the Adelman and Morris work, does not locate countries or regions of the world in the space.

One last intriguing methodology is illustrated by Bruce Russett,[7] who clustered 82 countries by using the *Q*-technique (or inverse factor analysis) first discussed in detail by Cattell.[8] Russett began his analysis with 54 socio-cultural variables, which were subjected to a standard factor analysis in order to identify interrelationships. The first five factors—labeled *economic development*, *communist influence*, *intensive agriculture*, *size*, and *Catholic culture*—were retained as the most significant. However, the size factor was subsequently excluded from the data base used for country comparisons. Russett reasoned:

Although size is obviously a characteristic of a country, it is not a cultural attribute. Except perhaps in the interplay of international power politics, Luxembourg would be thought of as similar to Belgium or Germany; it is not less European for being small and weak. Thus in the interest of agreement with most intuitive notions of what cultural and social variables are relevant to the delineation of regions, and with existing evidence on what is relevant to integration, we shall hitherto ignore the size factor (number four).[9]

To compare countries, 29 variables from the original 54 were then selected according to the criteria that "only those sociocultural indices which were fairly highly correlated (0.60 or greater) with one of the four dimensions identified as relevant to our concern with regional delineation and integration" be used. The selectively pruned 82 X 29 data matrix was subjected to a Q-technique factor analysis.

The logic of Q-technique follows directly from the basic factor analytic model. Conventional factor analysis or R-technique begins with a data matrix with objects (countries) as rows and variables as columns. The factors identified are linear combinations of the columns or variables. The Q-technique matrix transposes this, having variables as rows and objects as columns. Accordingly, the Russett procedure was to transpose the 82 X 29 matrix to a 29 X 82 data matrix with the countries as columns.

To insure some comparability of scale across countries, each variable was transformed to a uniform zero-to-one scale by the operator function:

$$\frac{X_{ji} - X_{j\min}}{X_{j\max}}$$

where: X_{ji} = i^{th} score on j^{th} variable,

$X_{j\min}$ = minimum value of jth variable,

$X_{j\max}$ = maximum value of jth variable.

This procedure illustrates that a proper approach to rescaling scores in the data matrix for Q-technique typically differs from the standard scores used in R-technique.

Following rescaling, linear combinations of the countries are isolated and indicate which groups of countries within the complete sample are most similar or dissimilar on *all* 29 indices.

The use of Q-techniuqe factor analysis for clustering countries is an imaginative adaptation of the methodology. However, we would like to point out some of the problems confronting the analyst using Q-technique. Jum Nunnally states:

There are some obvious differences between R and Q techniques. . . . [An] obvious difference between the two approaches concerns the number of persons [or countries] and variables required for meaningful analyses. In *R*-technique, the number of [countries] should be much larger than the number of variables, and vice versa in *Q*-technique.[10]

The problem mentioned here is that the order of the resulting square matrix of intercorrelations in *Q*-technique is (number of countries) by (number of countries), or in Russett's research, 82 × 82. Each country is intercorrelated with every other country. The column vectors used for this purpose are 29 × 1. In this case, the problem may not be severe, but the reliability of correlation coefficients based on very short columns of data is normally low. For example, the 82 × 82 intercorrelation matrix generated from a 2 × 82 *Q*-matrix is misleading indeed.

Second, the problem of rotational indeterminacy plagues the factor analyst regardless of the original data arrangement. This problem may or may not affect the actual grouping of countries on a particular dimension, depending upon the clarity versus arbitrary nature of partitioning the factor-loading matrix (matrices).

These problems did not seem to be severe in Bruce Russett's research as he also employed a hierarchial clustering routine, a multidimensional scaling procedure and other grouping routines. He reports that "other methods would produce similar results."

The Methodology of Cluster Analysis

Two interrelated but basic problems confront scientists in virtually every discipline—the measurement and comparison of objects in order to assign the objects to homogeneous groups. Each problem deals with the elements of two different sets—the set of attributes and the set of objects—and this dichotomy emanates directly from the formal definition of scientific measurement. Torgerson states:

Measurement of a property then involves the assignment of numbers to systems [objects] to represent that property.

The essence of the procedure is the assignment of numbers in such a way as to reflect [a] one-to-one correspondence between [the] characteristics of the numbers and the corresponding relations between the quantities [of the attribute possessed by each object].[11]

The second problem, comparing and grouping the objects, presupposes that the comparative analysis will utilize at least one attribute common to the objects. With a single dimension, the analysis is straightforward. Each object is assigned a single scale value; the objects are ordered on the continuum, and high versus low areas of density are sought for clustering purposes. Thus, with one attribute, a complete pre-ordering of objects results. However, the problem is severely complicated if we try to compare the objects simultaneously on a large number of attributes. The objects may permutate order on each dimension, thus providing only a partial pre-ordering and, therefore, no overall basis for comparison.

A Spatial Model

A formal model which satisfies the criteria for multidimensional comparisons is Euclidean space. The objects are represented as points in the space; the coordinate axes are the attributes on which the objects are scored; and a measure of object similarity is the Euclidean distance between points. Suppose the objects of interest are countries and the attributes—assumed to be independent—are descriptions of economic characteristics. To illustrate we will use the raw scores of five countries on two dimensions from this study: population density and income per capita.

To compare the similarity of these countries, we plot each as a point in the two-dimensional space where the attributes are used as coordinate axes and placed at right angles to each other. For each pair of points (i,j), the distance, d_{ij}, is found.[12] The pair with the smallest distance form the "core" of the first cluster and a centroid for the pair is computed. Additional points are added to the cluster until some critical value is reached, either for the number of objects in the cluster or for the distance between the centroid and an object. Figure 1 illustrates the results of such a procedure for our hypothetical example.

The closest pair of points not clustered will then be operated upon to form a second cluster using analogous methods.

The concept of Euclidean distance is easily generalized to spaces of dimensionality greater than two. Let a point i be the row vector $(x_{i1}, x_{i2}, x_{i3}, \ldots, x_{iN})$. Then,

$$d_{ij} = \left[\sum_{k=1}^{N} (x_{ik} - x_{jk})^2 \right]^{1/2}.$$

This generalization allows objects to be represented in a multidimensional space and clustered on the basis of interpoint distances.[13]

Refining Dimensions and Describing Clusters

Several critical problems with the methods described are apparent. These include:

(1) Noncomparability of raw scores for objects on different attributes.
(2) The possibility that the attributes are intercorrelated, requiring that, as coordinate axes, they *not* be set at right angles in space.
(3) The analyst must question whether "real" or significant differences exist between objects in different clusters and provide descriptive statistics for summarizing the "within-group" versus "between-group" distinctions.

Figure 1   FIVE COUNTRIES IN 2-SPACE

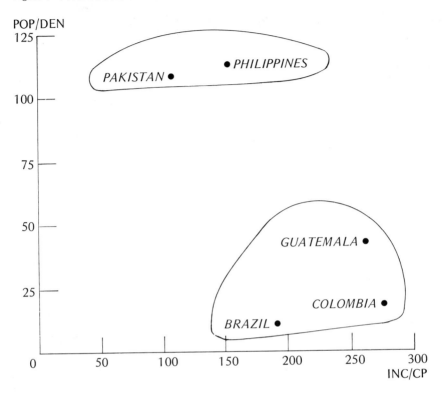

The BC TRY System[14]

We have addressed each of these three problems explicitly by using the analytical techniques and the set of computer programs developed by Tryon and Bailey.[15] The BC TRY System represents a package of about thirty different programs, some combination of which may be used to execute an aspect of cluster analysis or factor analysis on a particular set of data.

The first problem is accommodated in the usual manner by placing all variables in standard form with a mean of 50 and standard deviation of 10.

The second problem is aptly illustrated in Green and Tull. They state:

The Euclidean distance measure technically assumes that the space of (standardized) variables is orthogonal—i.e., that the variables are uncorrelated. While the Euclidean distance measure can still be used, it is useful to point out the (implicit) weighting of the components underlying the associated variables that occur with the use of the Euclidean measure in the original variable space.[16]

If the dimensions are intercorrelated, the effect is to weight each by its standard deviation, thus distorting the Euclidean metric.

V-Analysis

The intercorrelation problem was significantly reduced by following the prescribed procedure for using the BC TRY System. The variables were prefactored to find clusters among them which were maximally independent and yet accounted for a sufficient proportion of the variance between the original raw scores. V-clusters were described by "mutually collinear" variables. Collinearity means that the variables which defined a given cluster (called definers) fell on the same line as defined by the graph of their correlation coefficients over all other variables in a study. The procedure called Key Cluster Factoring—which seeks V-clusters—is similar to orthodox factor analysis in that the definers of separate dimensions are nearly independent. Each object is then given a simple sums score on each dimension defined as the sum of an object's scores on the definers of each V-cluster. These scores are put in standard form with mean of 50 and sigma of 10.

O-Type—Object Clustering

BC TRY O-Type proceeds essentially as described in the cluster-methodology discussion above. However, rather than locating cluster cores by choosing the closest objects of the entire set, all "core O-Types" are located simultaneously as the program searches for sectors in the object space with "high frequency" patterns. The space is normally sectored by cutting each V-dimension at plus and minus one standard deviation from its mean. For one dimension, three sectors are thus formed and, more generally, 3^k sectors are formed for k dimensions. A region must contain at least 2 percent of the total of N objects to qualify as high density.

Next, a centroid is computed for each core O-Type and the distance of all points from all centroids is computed. Points are assigned to their closest centroid. New centroids are computed for all points with common assignments and the process is iterated until the O-Types from two successive iterations are the same.

The final problem of describing and summarizing the differences between object clusters is handled by the OSTAT program. For each O-Type, OSTAT computes the means, standard deviations, and homogeneities of scores on each dimension, and the overall homogeneities of each O-Type across all dimensions.

The variance of the cluster scores initially is σ_i^2 for $i = 1, \ldots, k$ dimensions. The *squared* homogeneity for the gth O-cluster on the ith dimension is:

$$H_{ig}^2 = 1 - \frac{\sigma_{ig}^2}{\sigma_i^2}.$$

The squared homogeneity obviously approaches 1 as the "within O-cluster" variance becomes small relative to the total "between O-cluster" variance. The *overall squared homogeneity* of an O-cluster across all k dimensions is:

$$\overline{H}_g^2 = \frac{\sum\limits_{i=1}^{k} (\sigma_i^2 H_{ig}^2)}{\sum\limits_{i=1}^{k} \sigma_i^2}$$

This statistic represents a weighted average of the homogeneities for the O-cluster across all k dimensions where the weight is the variance of all scores on any particular dimension.

Data Description and Research Procedure

The data included 93 countries and 56 variables and were the latest available, usually 1966. The specific variables were chosen for two reasons: to include measures which might be manifested in the three general reasons for clustering given above; and to make efficient use of currently available data while covering a wide variety of domains. An intuitive breakdown of the indices revealed micro and macroeconomic data, as well as socio-economic, political, biological, transportation, communication, health, education, and trade-oriented statistics. The inclusion of any specific variable was also based on its properties as a scale. All indices were either interval- or ratio-scaled.

Although more than 92 percent of the raw correlation among the 56 variables was accounted for by the first two dimensions, we hypothesized that countries would be significantly differentiated by the other score domains. To verify this, a stepwise procedure was used where countries were clustered successively in spaces of two, three, four, five, and six dimensions. This meant that all 93 countries were clustered under five separate conditions: first, in a two-dimensional space defined by the variables in dimensions one and two; next, in a three-dimensional space where each country now has three standard scores—its scores on the definers of the first three variable dimensions, and so on through six dimensions. The results from all five procedures are reported.

RESULTS

Fifty-six variables were factored to identify latent properties of the variable set. The analysis yielded six highly reliable variable cluster domains (Table 1). Each variable has been plotted, using its augmented factor coefficients, and swarms of points with loadings on this Cartesian basis have

Table 1   CORRELATIONS OF VARIABLES WITH OBLIQUE CLUSTER DOMAINS

(Rotated Oblique Factor Coefficients)

Variables	Clusters					
	1	2	3	4	5	6
1 Airpas	.9970	.5076	−.0497	−.3134	.0444	.0953
2 Aircar	.9942	.5089	−.0498	−.2965	.0712	.0598
3 Gnp	.9909	.5312	−.0551	−.2756	.1053	.1189
4 Rrcarg	.9907	.4861	−.0463	−.2690	−.0134	.0433
5 Elecpr	.9895	.5602	−.0614	−.2450	.1060	.1252
6 Nonsp	.9193	.4243	.0294	−.3620	.0579	.0545
7 For-cf	.8373	.4111	−.0642	−.3616	.0988	.0606
8 Radio	.8193	.7965	−.1258	−.1015	.1748	.3540
9 Urb2	.8033	.3591	.0992	−.4037	.1994	−.0377
10 Area	.5304	.3528	.3189	−.3490	−.2751	.0130
11 Inc/cp	.5551	.9950	−.2026	.0873	.3897	.5196
12 Gnp/cp	.5486	.9888	−.2003	.0858	.4219	.4911
13 Energy	.6142	.9521	−.1858	−.0374	.3627	.4246
14 Cars	.5406	.9364	−.1856	.0176	.3222	.4837
15 Tvrcs	.5146	.9141	−.1571	.0407	.4147	.3738
16 Hspbds	.1885	.8794	−.1940	.0900	.4087	.5679
17 Agricu	−.2710	−.8315	.1348	−.2993	−.4821	−.5340
18 Skool 2	.4740	.8009	−.2361	.2942	.5316	.4560
19 Phones	.4008	.7995	−.1665	.2195	.5224	.4060
20 Nscirc	.1997	.7966	−.1818	.3292	.4583	.6836
21 Elepr/c	.3238	.7899	−.1574	.0640	.1259	.3448
22 Illit	−.2162	−.7800	.2007	−.1050	−.4329	−.5259
23 Gnpagr	−.2691	−.7664	.2842	−.2516	−.3510	−.5286
24 Lifex	.1642	.7381	−.4006	.2586	.4735	.5439
25 Dd-s	.2285	.7281	−.0164	−.1088	.1874	.4411
26 Md-s	.2188	.7226	−.1799	−.0740	.4190	.5655
27 Urbl	.4342	.7116	−.0316	−.0501	.0895	.5185
28 Press	−.2064	−.6489	.1479	−.0762	−.3331	−.3535
29 Teach	.2532	.6361	−.1576	.1674	.0722	.4312
30 Suicid	.0837	.6314	−.0291	.1172	.3953	.3946
31 Infmor	−.1649	−.6301	.1845	−.4267	−.3833	−.3783
32 Workrs	.0769	.6263	−.0777	.1421	.5077	.5726
33 Bks/sc	−.0483	.6001	−.2052	.3967	.2948	.3088
34 Bks/tl	−.0135	.5707	−.1661	.4100	.1753	.3635
35 Skool 1	.2832	.5262	−.1201	.1733	.0817	.4869
36 Bks/al	−.0452	.5131	−.1435	.4006	.1674	.3204
37 Ulcers	.0809	.4179	−.1369	−.1265	.4074	.3519
38 Costlv	−.0463	−.1576	.8546	−.3416	−.2098	−.0555
39 Cnpri	−.0441	−.1819	.8545	−.2465	−.1111	−.1284
40 Imprts	−.2636	.0501	−.3394	.9309	.2754	.1528
41 Xports	−.2327	.0381	−.2661	.8287	.2365	.1481
42 Pop	.3556	−.0205	.1257	−.3832	.0897	−.2281
43 Rrpas	.1527	.0887	−.0246	−.3500	.2859	−.1154
44 Gnpgen	.1474	.1943	−.0418	.3367	−.0247	.1988
45 Dom-cf	.2252	.1041	−.0965	−.3130	.0812	−.0878

Table 1   Continued

(Rotated Oblique Factor Coefficients)

Variables	1	2	3	4	5	6
46 Roads	.1140	.5140	−.1687	.2483	.8645	.2862
47 Popden	−.0076	.1753	−.1473	.2414	.8188	.0028
48 Colleg	.2030	.4176	−.1072	.0958	.5233	.2673
49 Poltic	−.1366	.2454	−.1379	.2707	.2967	.1294
50 Cal/cp	.1762	.6811	.0876	.0756	.2293	.9119
51 Pro/cp	.1963	.6801	−.0765	.0421	.2674	.8779
52 Gnpmnf	.1859	.7157	−.0461	−.0222	.4953	.7824
53 Movie	−.0585	.1000	−.0897	.2221	−.0022	.6671
54 Homicd	−.0250	−.5007	.0146	−.1468	−.3347	−.6199
55 Heart	.2325	.5801	.1247	−.1735	.3731	.5828
56 Cinatt	.0143	.1419	−.0691	.5173	.0809	.5446

Clusters

been identified. The expanded structure for each of the cluster domains, together with associated statistics, is presented in Table 2. The high reliability coefficients of each variable cluster (Table 2) indicated that the clusters represented specific traits or underlying characteristics of the objects—or, in this case, countries. In theory, the property defined by each of these clusters is much more basic than could be measured by any one variable. Figure 2, a SPAN diagram, offers a geometrical interpretation of the intervariable and intercluster relationships in six-space. Since a six-dimensional space cannot be displayed on a two-dimensional page, the SPAN diagram is presented in three parts for better visual effect.

The cumulative proportion of the mean square of raw correlations exhausted by each successive variable domain was C_1 (.3550), C_2 (.9244), C_3 (.9330), C_4 (.9434), C_5 (.9524), and C_6 (.9622). Although the added variance explained by Clusters C_3 through C_6 was minimal (.0378), it would be erroneous to assume that their importance in developing country clusters is proportional to the extent to which they explain variance. As we shall see later, the first three cluster domains, which together explained 93.3 percent of the variance, are relatively ineffectual in discriminating among various countries. Thus, it is the marginal differences which seem to be critical in segmenting countries and therefore deserve our attention.

The cluster titles and interpretations that follow are subjective and have been selected for facilitating the discussion of results.

C_1—Aggregate Production and Transportation

The defining variables of this cluster are: gross national product (GNP), total air cargo/km and passengers/km (AIRCAR and AIRPAS), total railroad cargo (RRCAR), and total production of electricity (ELECPR). The

Table 2 EXPANDED CLUSTER STRUCTURE

(Oblique Unifactor Structure)

	Variables	Oblique Factor Coefficients	Communality	Average[a] R with Definers	B-Reliability	C-Reliability
		Cluster 1—Aggregate Production and Transportation				
1	(D) Airpas	.9970	.9958	.9894		
2	(D) Aircar	.9942	.9899	.9867		
3	(D) Gnp	.9909	.9848	.9834		
4	(D) Rrcar	.9907	.9905	.9832		
5	(D) Elecpr	.9895	.9829	.9821		
6	Nonsp	.9193	.8645	.9123	.9945	.9945(1)
7	For-cf	.8373	.7385	.8310	.9907	.9883(4)
8	Radio	.8193	.8686	.8131	.9945	.9929(2)
9	Urb2	.8033	.7576	.7973	.9911	.9901(3)
10	Area	.5304	.6323	.5264	.9863	.9852(5)

Lbfc = .9877

A—Reliability (definers only) = .9977

	Variables	Oblique Factor Coefficients	Communality	Average[a] R with Definers	B-Reliability	C-Reliability
		Cluster 2—Affluence and Life Styles				
11	(D) Inc/cp	.9950	.9962	.9396		
12	(D) Gnp/cp	.9888	.9825	.9337		
13	(D) Energy	.9521	.9281	.8990		
14	(D) Cars	.9364	.8844	.8842		
15	(D) Tvrcs	.9141	.8501	.8632		
16	(D) Hspbds	.8794	.8876	.8304		
17	Agricu	−.8315	.8047	.7852	.9845	.9845(2)
18	Skool 2	.8009	.7708	.7562	.9836	.9841(3)
19	Phones	.7995	.7115	.7549	.9822	.9832(5)
20	Nscirc	.7966	.8216	.7522	.9848	.9848(1)
21	Elpr/c	.7899	.7105	.7459	.9821	.9830(6)
22	Illit	−.7800	.6840	.7366	.9814	.9830(7)
23	Gnpagr	−.7664	.6635	.7237	.9809	.9831(9)
24	Lifex	.7381	.7385	.6970	.9825	.9836(4)
25	Dd-s	.7281	.6339	.6875	.9800	.9831(10)
26	Md-s	.7226	.6890	.6823	.9813	.9830(8)
27	Urbl	.7116	.6038	.6720	.9792	.9829(11)
28	Press	−.6489	.4483	.6127	.9750	.9819(19)
29	Teach	.6361	.5003	.6006	.9762	.9822(17)
30	Suicid	.6314	.5177	.5962	.9766	.9823(16)
31	Infmor	−.6301	.5674	.5950	.9778	.9825(15)
32	Workrs	.6263	.6092	.5914	.9788	.9827(13)
33	Bks/sc	.6001	.6190	.5667	.9789	.9827(12)
34	Bks/tl	.5707	.5852	.5389	.9779	.9825(14)
35	Skool 1	.5262	.3956	.4969	.9728	.9814(20)
36	Bks/al	.5131	.5161	.4845	.9758	.9821(18)
37	Ulcers	.4179	.4014	.3946	.9721	.9808(21)

Lbfc = .9142

A—Reliability (definers only) = .9855

Table 2 Continued

(Oblique Unifactor Structure)

Variables		Oblique Factor Co-efficients	Commu-nality	Average[a] R with Definers	B-Reliability	C-Reliability

Cluster 3—Purchasing Power of Money

| 38 | (D) | Costlv | .8546 | .4927 | .7303 | | |
| 39 | (D) | Cnpri | .8545 | .4925 | .7302 | | |

Lbfc = .5270
A—Reliability (definers only) = .7422

Cluster 4—International Trade

40	(D)	Imprts	.9309	.8631	.8190		
41	(D)	Xports	.8287	.6832	.7291		
42		Pop	−.3832	.3262	.3372	.8089	.8089(1)
43		Rrpas	−.3500	.3275	.3079	.8052	.8019(2)
44		Gnpgen	.3367	.2526	.2962	.7906	.7855(3)
45		Dom-cf	−.3130	.2082	.2754	.7796	.7961(4)

Lbfc = .7357
A—Reliability (definers only) = .8722

Cluster 5—Economic Advancement, Higher Education and Political Heterogeneity

46	(D)	Roads	.8645	.7788	.7277		
47	(D)	Popden	.8188	.7018	.6891		
48		Colleg	.5233	.3398	.4404	.8071	.8071(1)
49		Poltic	.2967	.2019	.2497	.7538	.7594(2)

Lbfc = .6948
A—Reliability (definers only) = .8451

Cluster 6—Health and Entertainment

50		Cal/cp	.9119	.9885	.7044	.9105	.9105(1)
51	(D)	Pro/cp	.8779	.8641	.6782		
52		Gnpmnf	.7824	.8852	.6044	.8887	.9870(2)
53	(D)	Movie	.6671	.5384	.5154		
54		Homicd	−.6199	.5020	.4789	.8143	.9263(5)
55		Heart	.5828	.6372	.4502	.8340	.9350(3)
56		Cinatt	.5446	.5814	.4207	.8207	.9279(4)

Lbfc = .6370
A—Reliability (definers only) = .7998

[a]Average R with definers is computed with communalities in the diagonals.

Note: (D) denotes a defining variable. Nondefining variables are assigned to a cluster by their highest oblique factor coefficients:

A-Reliability = reliability coefficient of cluster score on full set of defining variables.

B-Reliability = reliability coefficient for expanded cluster scores of definers plus a single nondefiner.

C-Reliability = cumulative reliability coefficient of expanded cluster score for definers plus nondefiners added by the size of their B-reliability (number in ( ) indicates order of addition).

Lbfc = lower bound of factor coefficient that (theoretically) maximizes the C-reliability.

Figure 2 SPAN DIAGRAM FOR VARIABLES

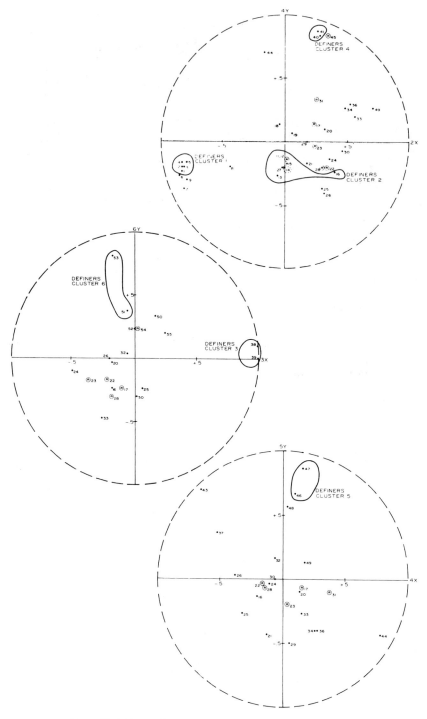

Note: Variable numbers correspond to those given in Table 2.

nondefiners include, among others: the total number of newspapers and the number of cities with populations of 100,000 or more. The factor loadings of all the defining variables in C_1 are greater than 0.989 and, except for one nondefiner—AREA—all other nondefiners have a factor loading of more than 0.80. It is significant that every variable in the cluster, save RADIO, represents aggregate data.

From this we might conclude that the ownership patterns for radio receivers have reached saturation levels in most of the countries under analysis and that these patterns do not significantly differ between various countries.

Not all indices that might be intuitively classed as measures of transportation are included in C_1. Although AIRCAR and AIRPAS are highly correlated and group together, cargo and passengers carried by railroads (RRCAR and RRPAS) appear in two different clusters, C_1 and C_4, respectively. As we shall explain in the ensuing analysis of country clusters (O-Types), the C_4 variable domain is able to develop two O-Types where only one existed for predominantly less developed countries. Similarly, another measure of transportation —namely, road density per 100 sq km of surface area (ROADS)—appears as a defining variable in C_5, which is found to be the most effective cluster in discriminating between various O-Types.

C_2—Affluence and Life Styles

This cluster contains a total of 27 variables, six of which are definers. The factor loadings for the defining variables on C_2 are greater than 0.879 in each case, while in the case of nondefiners—except for deaths from ulcers per 100,000 (ULCER)—factor loadings exceed 0.5. The defining variables are: per capita measures of gross national product (GNP/CP), personal income (INC/CP), energy consumption (ENERGY), passenger vehicles (CARS), television sets (TVRCRS), and hospital beds (HSPBDS). These variables are "micro" oriented, versus the macro or aggregate orientation we discovered in C_1. The nondefining variables can be broadly grouped into three categories—education and information, personal consumption, and health.

It may be interesting to note that although most of the measures of education—SKOOL 1 (enrollment in primary education), SKOOL 2 (enrollment in high school, secondary school, and vocational training), BKS/AL (production of books in art and literature), BKS/SC (production of scientific books), BKS/TL (total production of books), ILLIT (percent of illiterate adults 15 years and over), and TEACH (number of teachers per 10,000 population)—appear in C_2, one of the more important educational variables, COLLEG (university and professional school training) is clustered in C_4. Another important fact worth noting is that while such indicators of health as life expectancy (LIFEX), infant mortality (INFMOR), number of physicians per capita (MD-s), and number of dentists per capita (DD-S) are in C_2, two similar measures of health, per capita calorie and protein intake (CAL/CP) and (PRO/CP), are clustered in C_6.

C_3—Purchasing Power of Money

The two variables which alone form this cluster are the cost of living index (COSTLV) and the consumer price index (CONPRI). We have tentatively interpreted the cluster as indicating the purchasing power of money. Other equally likely alternatives might be the stability of the monetary system or growth in consumer spending. Normally, clusters which are very specific—say defined by a doublet as C_3—exhibit low reliability. This is the case here. Table 2 indicates that C_3 is the least reliable of the six variable domains.

To clarify the idea of reliability we should review briefly the basic model of domain sampling assumed in the BC TRY System. First, the domain of an individual variable is a very large set of theoretically observable variables, but not observed for any particular study, each of which is exactly collinear with the observed variable. For example, a variable, X_j, abstracts certain information about the objects for which it is scored. We can theoretically find variables X_j^k ($k = 1, \infty$) which also measure or abstract this same information for these objects. Second we have a larger domain or a *set* of variables (a cluster) which together relate more general or systematic information about the objects. The domain composite for a cluster domain is defined as the sum of the variable domain composites corresponding to the variables defining the cluster.

Theoretically, then, a cluster domain is defined by an infinitely large number of variables of which the variables defining a cluster in our study are only a small sample. We wish to see if our sample is really representative or general. The index of representativeness (reliability) used in this research is the Spearman-Brown reliability coefficient or simply the correlation between the variables defining our cluster C_1 and some other possible sample of variables from the same domain—i.e., C_i.

The results from the O-analysis which follow somewhat ease our apprehensions concerning the use of the variables defining C_3 when we discover that the dimension has little effect on relationships between countries.

C_4—International Trade

The two defining variables for this cluster are imports and exports measured as a percent of GNP. Their factor loadings on C_4 are 0.93 and 0.83 respectively. Other variables included in this cluster are population (POP), railroad passengers/km (RRPAS), proportion of GNP generated by general government spending (GNPGEN), and a measure of domestic conflict (DOM-CF). It is interesting to note that all the nondefiners have low factor loadings of below 0.38. Population and railroad passengers/km are negatively related to imports and exports. This partially confirms Russett's earlier findings where his analysis revealed that countries with smaller total populations tended to be more foreign-trade oriented.[17] The trade dimension consistently appears to be important in distinguishing countries and has been recovered in each of several previous studies we have conducted.[18]

C_5—Economic Advancement, Higher Education, and Political Heterogeneity

Clusters 5 and 6 are more difficult to interpret. On the surface the relationships between the several variables included in each of the two clusters is not obvious. However, as we shall see, cluster 5 is by far the most important of all variable domains in discriminating between various country clusters.

The defining variables for C_5 are: road density per 100 square/km of surface area (ROADS), and population density per square/km (POPDEN). These two variables have factor loadings of 0.864 and 0.819 respectively. It seems that a combined index of population density and road density is a more discriminating measure of urbanization and economic sophistication than the number of cities with population over 100,000, total population, total GNP, or intensity of railroad or air transport usage all of which load heavily on clusters which contribute little to defining country clusters.

The two nondefining variables included in C_5 are higher education and professional training (COLLEG), and a measure of political heterogeneity as represented by the number of political parties in a country (POLTIC). The factor loading for POLTIC on C_5 at 0.297 is the lowest of the four variables in the cluster. The coefficient of correlation between POLTIC and some other selected variables are POPDEN (0.268), GNP/CP (0.309), LIFEX (0.418), NSCIRC (0.161), TEACH (0.533), SKOOL 2 (0.464), and COLLEG (0.053).

C_6—Nutrition and Movie Entertainment

The two defining variables for this cluster are protein intake per capita (PRO/CP) and cinema seating capacity (MOVIE). The nondefining variables included in this cluster are: proportion of GNP orginating in the manufacturing section (GNPMNF), per capita caloric intake (CAL/CP), cinema attendance (CINATT), deaths by homicide per 100,000 (HOMICD), and deaths caused by hypertension with and without heart disease (HEART).

The reliability of the definers only for C_6 is relatively low. However with the addition of the nondefining variables the overall reliability of the cluster increases to a respectable level of more than 0.90. This "empirical wisdom," however, is little consolation to the analyst attempting to interpret the dimension. Of course the health indices included might have been expected to correlate highly, as would the two entertainment variables. Together these two subsets are quite ambiguous but also quite collinear as indicated by the empirical selection of definers for the set as a whole.

Like C_3, C_6 does not contribute substantially in differentiating countries except in two important cases which are discussed later in the section on O-analysis.

O-Analysis

Each country was given a standardized simple sums score on each of the six dimensions derived from the preceding V-analysis. These scores were used as the coordinates for each country in Euclidean space, and their values were instrumental in determining the similarity for any pair of countries.

The results from the five separate O-analyses are reported in this section in order of ascending dimensionality. First we examine the country clusters derived in two dimensions and comment on the implications of these findings. In three dimensions there is little change from the two-dimensional solution, but the four-dimensional results again require a thorough discussion. The maximum number of O-Types is attained in five dimensions. The breakdown of country clusters, their score profiles, and the general sufficiency of the O-Types in five dimensions will be addressed. The six-dimensional solution provides some small surprises but is essentially the same as the five-dimensional result.

Two Dimensions

The first two dimensions obtained in the V-analysis are by far the most important in terms of explaining variance in the raw score correlation matrix. Cluster 1, *Aggregate Production and Transportation*, and cluster 2, *Affluence and Life Style*, explain more than 92 percent of the mean square of raw correlation. These two indices together summarize a considerable amount of information concerning the aggregate or macro attributes of nations (C_1) and the per capita or micro characteristics of the nations' populations (C_2).

The O-Types obtained from the two-dimensional solution suggest that these "important" scales are not the finely calibrated instrument required by the analyst who would discriminate between countries. Only two large clusters of countries are obtained in two dimensions. A look at Table 3 shows that O-Type 2 is composed of 19 countries typically considered to be the most highly developed in the world. The United States was rejected from O-Type 2 with a distance of 95.20 units from the O-Type centroid compared to the average D-value of 5.54 for the countries included. O-Type 1 contains 73 countries which, relative only to O-Type 2, might be labeled "less developed." Certainly one hesitates at this stage to indict any of the members of the first O-Type as underdeveloped or some similar stereotype, because of the sheer size of the cluster and the inability of the first two dimensions to discriminate finely between countries. The score patterns for the two clusters show the greatest difference on the second dimension. The O-Type means are respectively 48.33 and 51.46 on C_1, and 45.27 and 66.12 on C_2. Members of the second O-Type have slightly higher scores on C_1—Aggregate Production and Transportation—but clearly exceed O—Type 1 members on the second factor, scoring more than 1.5 standard deviations above the mean on C_2.

Affluence and Life Style

Let's attempt to pinpoint the reasons for the large aggregations of countries in two dimensions. First, it is important to examine the sufficiency of the two-cluster solution. Are these large clusters well defined or merely poorly distinguished conglomerates? O-Type 1, even though it is the larger of the two, has homogeneities of 0.9977 and 0.9526 respectively on the two dimensions from V-analysis. The overall homogeneity of O-Type 1 is an impressive 0.9754. This means, for example, that on the first dimension the variance of the scores of the countries in O-Type 1, expressed as a percent of the variance of all countries on the dimension, was nearly zero. Thus the homogeneity for the O-Type on dimension one approaches the maximum of one. O-Type 2 is slightly less dense with homogeneities of 0.9412 on dimension one, 0.8515 on dimension two, and 0.8975 overall.

These statistics indicate that the country clusters themselves are quite sufficient. The indices on which the countries are scored are incapable of creating any additional breakdowns.

This result is important for several reasons. First, many studies in the past, which have relied on a subset of the variables included in variable clusters one and two, may report spurious, forced, or insignificant differences between countries. Second, because the range of the variables defined and included in these two dimensions is so large, it is likely that many previous studies have used highly intercorrelated variables to scale countries and have omitted other important and more discriminating domains.

It should be noted at this point that Table 3 is so arranged that country clusters which develop in spaces of higher dimensionality are tentatively identified by appropriate spacing in the O-Type membership lists. The last partition in most lists is composed of countries which do not remain together as the spatial dimensionality changes.

Three Dimensions

There is little change in the O-Type membership as the variable space dimensionality is increased from two to three. Again two large clusters of countries emerge. O-Type 2 is a repeat of O-Type 2 in *two* dimensions. O-Type 1 has changed slightly but the change is important. In three dimen-

Table 3   COUNTRY CLUSTERS—STEPWISE IN DIMENSIONS TWO TO SIX

Two Dimensions

O-Type 1

Algeria, Argentina, Bolivia, Cambodia, Camaroon, Chad, Chile, Colombia, Congo (Leopold.), Costa Rica, Dominican Rep., Equador, Ghana, Guatemala, Honduras, India, Iraq, Ivory Coast, Mexico, Morocco, Nicaragua, Niger, Nigeria, Pakistan, Panama, Paraguay, Peru, Philippines, Senegal, Syria, Tanzania, Thailand, Tunisia, Turkey, Uganda, United Arab Rep., Uruguay, Venezuela, S. Vietnam

Ceylon, El Salvador, Greece, Israel, Jamaica, S. Korea, Portugal

Congo (Brvlle.), Gabon, Libya, Sierra Leone

Trinidad and Tobago, Hong Kong

Brazil, Indonesia, Afghanistan, Burma, Central African Rep., Dahomey, Ethiopia, Guinea, Iran, Jordan, Lebanon, Liberia, Malaya and Singapore, Mali, Saudi Arabia, Somalia, South Africa, Spain, Sudan, Togo, Upper Volta

---

Three Dimensions

O-Type 1

Algeria, Argentina, Bolivia, Cambodia, Camaroon, Chad, Chile, Colombia, Congo (Leopold.), Costa Rica, Dominican Rep., Equador, Ghana, Guatemala, Honduras, India, Iraq, Ivory Coast, Mexico, Morocco, Nicaragua, Niger, Nigeria, Pakistan, Panama, Paraguay, Peru, Philippines, Senegal, Syria, Tanzania, Thailand, Tunisia, Turkey, Uganda, United Arab Rep., Uruguay, Venezuela, S. Vietnam

Ceylon, El Salvador, Greece, Israel, Jamaica, S. Korea, Portugal

Congo (Brvlle.), Gabon, Libya, Sierra Leone

Trinidad and Tobago, Hong Kong

Afghanistan, Burma, Central African Rep., Dahomey, Ethiopia, Guinea, Iran, Jordan, Lebanon, Liberia, Malaya and Singapore, Mali, Saudi Arabia, Somalia, South Africa, Spain, Sudan, Togo, Upper Volta

---

Four Dimensions

O-Type 1

Algeria, Argentina, Bolivia, Cambodia, Camaroon, Central African Rep., Chad, Chile, Colombia, Congo (Leopold.), Costa Rica, Dominican Rep., Equador, Ivory Coast, Malaya and Singapore, Mexico, Morocco, Nicaragua, Niger, Nigeria, Pakistan, Sudan, Syria, Tanzania, Thailand, Tunisia, Turkey, Uganda, United Arab Rep., Uruguay, Venezuela, S. Vietnam

Ghana, Greece, Guatemala, Honduras, Iran, Iraq, Panama, Paraguay, Peru, Philippines, Senegal, Somalia, South Africa, Spain

Ceylon, Jamaica, S. Korea

El Salvador, India, Israel, Portugal

O-Type 2

Congo (Brvlle.), Gabon, Libya, Sierra Leone, Trinidad and Tobago, Hong Kong

---

Five Dimensions

O-Type 1

Algeria, Argentina, Bolivia, Cambodia, Camaroon, Chad, Chile, Colombia, Congo (Leopold.), Costa Rica, Dominican Rep., Equador, Ghana, Guatemala, Honduras, Iraq, Ivory Coast, Mexico, Morocco, Nicaragua, Niger, Nigeria, Pakistan, Panama, Paraguay, Peru, Philippines, Senegal, Syria, Tanzania, Thailand, Tunisia, Turkey, Uganda, United Arab Rep., Uruguay, Venezuela, S. Vietnam

Greece, Malaya and Singapore, Sudan

O-Type 2

Ceylon, El Salvador, Israel, Jamaica, S. Korea, Portugal, India, Italy

O-Type 3

Congo (Brvlle.), Gabon, Libya, Sierra Leone

O-Type 4

Trinidad and Tobago, Hong Kong

Six Dimensions

O-Type 1

Algeria, Argentina, Bolivia, Cambodia, Camaroon, Chad, Chile, Colombia, Congo (Leopold.), Costa Rica, Dominican Rep., Equador, Ghana, Guatemala, Honduras, India, Iraq, Ivory Coast, Mexico, Morocco, Nicaragua, Niger, Nigeria, Pakistan, Panama, Paraguay, Peru, Philippines, Senegal, Syria, Tanzania, Thailand, Tunisia, Turkey, Uganda, United Arab Rep., Uruguay, Venezuela, S. Vietnam

O-Type 2

Ceylon, El Salvador, Greece, Israel, Jamaica, S. Korea, Portugal

O-Type 3

Congo (Brvlle.), Gabon, Libya, Sierra Leone

O-Type 4

Trinidad and Tobago, Hong Kong

Table 3   Continued

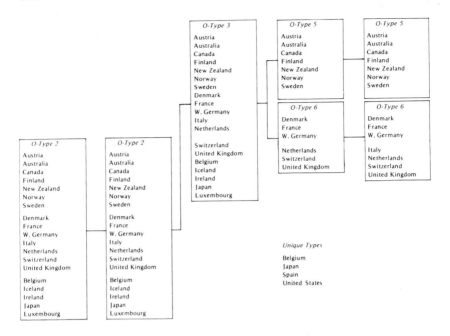

O-Type 2	O-Type 2
Austria	Austria
Australia	Australia
Canada	Canada
Finland	Finland
New Zealand	New Zealand
Norway	Norway
Sweden	Sweden
Denmark	Denmark
France	France
W. Germany	W. Germany
Italy	Italy
Netherlands	Netherlands
Switzerland	Switzerland
United Kingdom	United Kingdom
Belgium	Belgium
Iceland	Iceland
Ireland	Ireland
Japan	Japan
Luxembourg	Luxembourg

sions both Brazil and Indonesia have been rejected from membership in O-Type 1; in fact, they are rejected altogether. The SPAN diagram of country clusters, Figure 3, indicates that Brazil and Indonesia maintain their similarity through the six dimensions and cluster together in space. The original cluster score matrix (not included here) shows these two score patterns across all six dimensions for:

	C_1	C_2	C_3	C_4	C_5	C_6
Brazil	50.50	45.73	91.75	38.74	43.71	47.07
Indonesia	48.45	42.68	126.18	39.23	48.47	45.13

Both countries obviously fit in two dimensions with O-Type 1, but their scores on dimension three are higher than any other two countries in the study. This interesting discovery is contrary to an intuitive estimate of the similarity between these two nations.

That the addition of dimension three does little to affect the initial clustering found in two dimensions is not a surprise. This presumption follows from a cursory examination of their profiles (Figure 4). This figure

Figure 3 SPAN DIAGRAM OF COUNTRY TYPES (6 Dimensions)

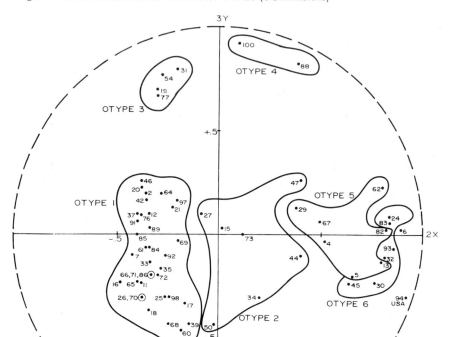

No.	Country	12	Camaroon	21	Costa Rica	39	India	65	Niger	72	Philippines	90	Turkey
		16	Chad	25	Dominican Rep.	42	Iraq	66	Nigeria	76	Senegal	91	Uganda
2	Algeria	17	Chile	26	Equador	46	Ivory Coast	68	Pakistan	84	Syria	92	United Arab Rep.
3	Argentina	18	Colombia	33	Ghana	60	Mexico	69	Panama	85	Tanzania	96	Uruguay
7	Bolivia	20	Congo	35	Guatemala	61	Morocco	70	Paraguay	86	Thailand	97	Venezuela
11	Cambodia		(Leopold.)	37	Honduras	64	Nicaragua	71	Peru	89	Tunisia	98	S. Vietnam

illustrates graphically that all six O-Types eventually described in this research are in sector one on dimension three, and, in addition, indicates that the United States level on C_3 is virtually identical with all other countries. Dimension six also exhibits no variance in sector patterns across O-Types and also results in little change in O-Types. The patterns for dimensions two, four, and five will be shown to be the most important in defining object clusters.

The cluster score matrix by O-Types, Table 4, shows that the standard deviation of the scores for countries on dimension three is very low. With

Figure 3   Continued

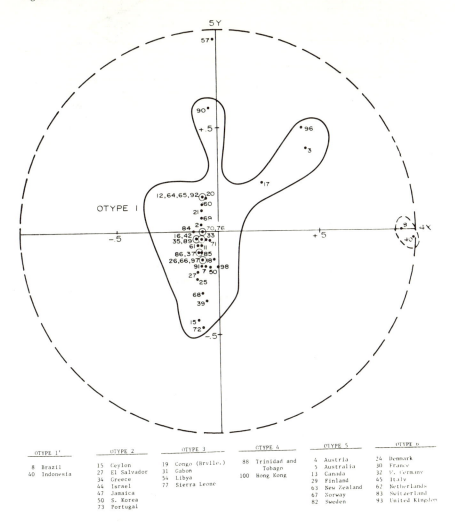

OTYPE 1'	OTYPE 2	OTYPE 3	OTYPE 4	OTYPE 5	OTYPE 6
8 Brazil	15 Ceylon	19 Congo (Brvlle.)	88 Trinidad and	4 Austria	24 Denmark
40 Indonesia	27 El Salvador	31 Gabon	Tobago	5 Australia	30 France
	34 Greece	54 Libya	100 Hong Kong	13 Canada	32 W. Germany
	44 Israel	77 Sierra Leone		29 Finland	45 Italy
	47 Jamaica			63 New Zealand	62 Netherlands
	50 S. Korea			67 Norway	83 Switzerland
	73 Portugal			82 Sweden	93 United Kingdom

Brazil and Indonesia rejected, the scores of all other countries hover around 48. This is another means of prejudging the probable influence a variable cluster will have in determining *O*-Types.

That dimension three has little effect on differentiating countries is perhaps not unfortunate. The discussion of the variable clusters revealed that dimension three is defined by only two variables: the cost of living index and the consumer price index. The cluster has low reliability. In fact the high correlation between the two definers and subsequently their low correlations

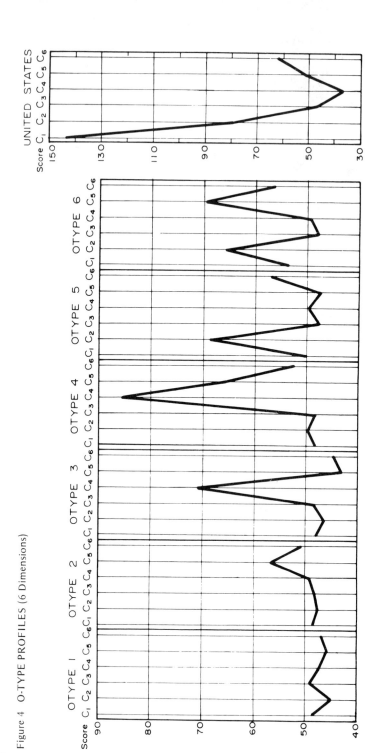

Figure 4 O-TYPE PROFILES (6 Dimensions)

42

Table 4 O-TYPE MEMBERSHIP (COUNTRY CLUSTERS)

O-Type	Countries	C_1	C_2	C_3	C_4	C_5	C_6	D-values Euclidean Distances of Objects from Cluster Centroid
1	Algeria	48.14	45.18	48.06	55.08	43.48	46.46	8.40
	Argentina	49.22	52.50	61.12	39.71	43.74	58.63	20.02
	Bolivia	48.00	45.65	48.56	47.62	43.21	42.03	5.52
	Cambodia	48.02	42.90	48.34	44.20	45.85	44.69	4.18
	Camaroon	48.06	43.76	48.22	52.54	43.36	50.12	6.93
	Chad	47.99	42.53	48.53	44.39	42.20	44.25	5.64
	Chile	48.57	48.11	55.06	42.47	44.52	52.48	10.04
	Colombia	48.87	45.53	49.48	40.69	44.31	43.14	7.54
	Congo (Leopold.)	48.22	43.08	48.49	55.66	42.78	50.12	9.84
	Costa Rica	48.09	47.12	47.72	52.76	45.12	48.94	6.62
	Dominican Rep.	47.84	44.99	47.73	42.50	49.37	42.42	7.49
	Equador	48.08	44.45	47.98	42.39	44.28	43.30	6.10
	Ghana	48.68	43.82	48.50	46.88	46.00	45.80	1.69
	Guatemala	48.43	44.98	47.51	46.59	46.73	46.18	2.01
	Honduras	48.03	43.97	47.71	52.34	44.62	44.13	6.27
	India	51.89	42.58	48.46	39.35	55.72	41.37	14.46
	Iraq	48.11	44.94	47.81	53.77	44.45	45.19	7.14
	Ivory Coast	48.05	44.23	48.19	56.65	43.50	45.36	10.02
	Mexico	49.72	47.31	47.82	38.88	44.83	50.77	9.56
	Morocco	48.18	43.82	47.90	48.68	45.59	45.36	2.73
	Nicaragua	48.02	45.68	47.65	54.60	44.41	50.12	8.44
	Niger	47.99	42.37	48.10	44.16	42.20	50.12	6.18
	Nigeria	48.24	42.44	48.26	45.70	48.19	44.03	4.79
	Pakistan	48.79	42.84	48.03	39.30	52.09	41.37	11.71
	Panama	47.82	48.74	48.07	49.32	44.61	48.50	4.97
	Paraguay	47.92	44.05	48.32	42.72	43.41	46.18	5.06
	Peru	48.35	46.16	49.12	45.47	43.76	45.57	3.05
	Philippines	48.44	43.40	48.13	45.20	52.12	37.06	12.02
	Senegal	48.04	43.56	48.29	52.44	44.37	45.80	5.86
	Syria	48.05	43.85	47.15	48.49	45.62	46.96	2.60
	Tanzania	48.02	43.32	48.12	50.46	45.08	44.03	4.84
	Thailand	48.22	43.21	47.70	45.46	47.47	44.47	4.02
	Tunisia	48.07	44.15	47.73	50.80	45.49	45.80	4.19
	Turkey	48.51	44.72	48.52	37.92	46.54	64.71	20.07
	Uganda	48.03	42.84	48.19	51.73	46.14	42.20	7.00
	United Arab Rep.	48.39	43.86	47.89	48.21	46.11	50.83	4.43
	Uruguay	48.09	49.86	60.60	43.65	44.43	60.88	19.20
	Venezuela	48.81	52.13	47.61	53.28	43.82	43.70	10.32
	S. Vietnam	48.11	43.66	50.29	42.56	50.66	44.69	7.29
2	Ceylon	48.07	44.13	47.67	51.60	60.89	41.26	11.10
	El Salvador	47.82	44.57	47.52	52.89	54.98	45.41	7.52
	Greece	49.99	51.78	47.75	43.19	50.21	57.68	12.10
	Israel	48.60	54.96	48.29	47.52	53.90	59.77	12.16
	Jamaica	47.96	47.72	47.88	57.00	66.08	49.77	12.31

43

Table 4   Continued

O-Type	Countries	C_1	C_2	C_3	C_4	C_5	C_6	D-values Euclidean Distances of Objects from Cluster Centroid
				Variable Cluster Scores				
	S. Korea	48.27	43.04	49.35	40.13	57.97	46.68	10.83
	Portugal	48.36	47.82	47.79	50.05	53.91	53.42	4.26
3	Congo (Brvlle.)	48.03	45.51	48.47	68.41	42.06	46.46	3.24
	Gabon	47.99	47.64	48.19	72.81	42.06	50.12	6.01
	Libya	47.83	49.13	48.15	74.19	41.91	38.16	7.95
	Sierra Leone	47.78	42.98	48.29	67.83	46.08	44.03	5.46
4	Trinidad and Tobago	48.11	52.81	48.21	83.31	69.99	54.62	6.34
	Hong Kong	48.08	47.16	48.06	87.93	60.60	50.21	6.34
5	Austria	48.82	60.68	47.91	48.94	53.39	56.74	10.35
	Australia	51.51	71.89	47.79	44.26	44.26	58.34	7.01
	Canada	56.39	78.36	47.75	45.94	44.08	56.85	12.27
	Finland	48.62	61.69	48.14	52.53	46.06	54.75	8.22
	New Zealand	48.60	67.03	47.85	53.44	48.53	62.70	7.50
	Norway	49.43	65.07	47.93	51.10	45.46	55.86	4.53
	Sweden	50.12	76.16	48.00	50.71	47.87	53.65	8.30
6	Denmark	48.76	68.65	47.97	53.77	66.25	61.95	9.82
	France	56.03	63.48	47.91	42.10	64.51	59.84	10.28
	W. Germany	56.31	67.54	47.81	46.35	71.15	52.43	6.01
	Italy	52.80	58.93	47.99	43.24	62.72	55.86	11.49
	Netherlands	51.05	62.85	47.94	60.09	83.14	51.55	18.16
	Switzerland	49.77	70.33	47.88	52.08	67.38	55.58	6.90
	United Kingdom	58.20	68.12	47.88	47.17	73.18	55.19	6.85
Unique Types								
	Belgium	49.62	65.09	47.82	52.08	99.76	57.73	30.41*
	Japan	56.76	57.39	48.11	N.A.	66.53	51.44	N.A.
	Spain	49.74	50.88	48.41	N.A.	50.18	62.47	N.A.
	United States	143.85	89.08	47.71	36.64	51.08	61.40	96.21†

*(O-Type 6)
†(O-Type 6)

with all other variables may be a function of the type of index—both report movements in price and cost from base year levels—rather than some more fundamental characteristic of the countries themselves.

Four Dimensions

Country scores on the *International Trade* dimension create the first significant division of what has been called O-Type 1 to this point. Four African nations join the island communities of Hong Kong, and Trinidad-Tobago to form a new O-Type, O-Type 2. Some insights are gained into the differences among the three country clusters by examining their profile patterns on the first four dimensions (Figure 4). This group of small countries stands out as being highly trade oriented, so much so that their scores on the fourth dimension are two and one-half standard deviations above the mean.

The O-Types occupy distinct sectors of the space as can be seen from the Euclidean distances between their centroids which are:

	O-*Type 2*	O-*Type 3*
O-*Type 1*	28.08	21.00
O-*Type 2*	0	32.20

These figures can be compared to the *mean* distance from an object to the centroid for each O-Type. For O-Type 1 this distance $(\bar{D})$ is 5.86, for O-Type 2 $\bar{D} = 7.22$, and for O-Type 3 $\bar{D} = 6.84$. The overall homogeneity for each of the three country clusters is 0.9435, 0.9155, and 0.9274 respectively.

Five and Six Dimensions[19]

The most important variable domain in terms of differentiating between countries is defined by the variables in dimension five, labeled *Economic Advancement, Higher Education, and Political Heterogeneity.* "Important" is used to indicate that the five-dimensional solution is the most complex in terms of number of O-Types. The large block of countries in O-Types 1 and 2 from the four-dimensional solution have subdivided to yield four homogeneous country clusters. The overall homogeneity for each of these four is 0.944, 0.908, 0.984, and 0.964. The four African nations have separated from Hong Kong and Trinidad-Tobago. The latter two countries' mean score on C_5 is a high 65.29 where the African nations average below fifty (Table 4).

The block of "developed" nations is also separated by the addition of C_5. The members of O-Type 5 score much lower on the fifth dimension than do those of O-Type 6 indicating the difference between the members of each cluster in population density and road density.

As the spatial dimensionality changes, the behavior of three countries in particular should be mentioned. First, Italy has permuted membership from the most "developed" group in four dimensions to join Ceylon, Israel, Portugal, et al. in O-Type 2 in the five-dimensional solution. This result is contrary to a subjective estimate of Italy's characteristics. A look at Italy's score pattern from Table 4 demonstrates that it is a marginal member of O-Type 2 (five dimensions). A review of the printout from the five-dimensional solution showed Italy to be 13.15 standard units from the centroid of O-Type 2. This distance value is the highest of any of the members of the cluster. The results in six dimensions (Table 4) have Italy's D-value from O-Type 6 to be 11.49, also quite high, indicating that the country is not fitting exceptionally well anywhere.

Second, although Belgium appears in O-Type 3 in four dimensions it has been rejected in spaces of higher dimensionality. Like the United States, Belgium is closest to O-Type 6 but beyond a reasonable limit for inclusion.

Finally, Greece is included in O-Type 1 in five dimensions and is, like Italy, a marginal member. We find that Greece eventually belongs in O-Type 2.

The tabular results for the six-dimensional solutions are offered as the most general examples of the statistics over all solutions and will not be reiterated in the text.

SUMMARY AND CONCLUSIONS

This research has used the formal model—Euclidean Space—to describe the extent and nature of the similarity between countries of the world. The BC TRY System of cluster analysis was used to develop six highly reliable variable cluster domains. Six country clusters (O-Types) were developed based on the scoring of the individual countries on the six variable dimensions. All the variables and country clusters were interpreted and analyzed. A stepwise sequential process was used in developing country clusters in order to identify the contribution of each variable cluster domain in discriminating between countries.

The study has not only demonstrated the feasibility of using empirical methods in classifying variables and objects, but has also pointed out many areas of practical application for economic and political science research dealing with cross-cultural variables.

1. The use of empirical methods in this study has underscored the fact that an intuitive estimate of the relationships among variables may be quite misleading. RRPAS and RRCAR, both apparently manifest measures of transportation, correlate a low 0.128 and exhibit diverging patterns of correlation across other variables as well. Similarly, the intensity of usage of surface transportation (ROADS), defines a totally different cluster (C_5) apart from all other measures of transportation. This argument is further supported by comparing the cluster memberships of health-oriented indices like LIFEX, MD-S, and DD-S (C_2) with other health statistics, HEART, CAL/CP, and PRO/CP (C_6). In this instance, even the high intercorrelations of some of these variables—LIFEX and PRO/CP (0.632) or MD-S and CAL/CP (0.641)— are misleading in that the correlation profiles of the members of the two separate clusters are distinct.

Neither do countries of the world always fit where they "belong." The results reported here often contradict a geographical notion of similarity or other intuitive clustering of countries. Unexpected circumstances such as the pairing of Indonesia and Brazil or the rejection of the United States and Belgium from O-Type 6 have resulted. Greece and Italy change character distinctly as the spatial dimensionality changes. In fact, alterations in the number and types of dimensions used to scale the countries has considerable impact on the entire battery of results.

2. An important problem in the study of cross-cultural phenomena is the lack of available data on different countries which is needed for developing country typologies useful for political and social decisions. The use of the BC TRY System of cluster analysis, as well as other empirical clustering techniques, can be helpful in solving this problem. Since clustering objectively groups these variables and countries which are highly similar to each other, it follows that individual variables and countries can be used as surrogates for certain other variables and countries in developing estimates for defining some parameters. As has been shown in our study, the variation in many of the dimensions is the same—the variables are collinear—and this property can be used to generate clusters of variables. The covariation among the variables in a cluster suggests that, in many cases, one variable may be used as a proxy measure for others in the same domain. For example, the number of passengers carried per year per air kilometer flown (AIRPAS) is nearly a perfect substitute for the air cargo intensity measure, AIRCAR. These two variables correlate 0.998 and, in addition, have the same correlation profiles over the 54 other variables in this study. A much less obvious pair of interchangeable variables would be HSPBDS and NSCIRC which correlates a high 0.817 and are also sufficiently collinear to be members of the same variable cluster.

These examples imply that clustering objects on several highly collinear variables is a redundant process. The effect is to increase the variance of the distance or similarity measure between nations, stretching some distances while shrinking others, or, in other words, implicitly weighting the principal dimensions underlying the variables used.

Similarly, countries which belong to the same O-Type are similar across *all* their basic dimensions and such similarity may lead to interchangeability. This is especially crucial when little or no data are available for one country in a study and estimates for missing data must be based on "similar countries." The simple and most often used method has been to select a country which is similar to the one for which the data are needed on the basis of geographical proximity or administrative convenience. However, our analysis has shown that such intuitive pairing or matching is quite often wrong. Second, these techniques yield "different pairs" according to the needs of the problem—i.e., different variable domains will yield different O-Types.

Future cross-national studies can use the results of this research to sample effectively the range of countries which might be used in comparative research. Preliminary clustering procedures of this type help to insure that the sampling is representative.

3. It may be noted that the criteria used here for including variables are biased due to the constraint of using only interval or ratio scales. Other variables which may be more appropriate for particular problems in discriminating between nations can be used. The promising advances in nonmetric

procedures for describing object similarity suggests that only ordinal scales be required for this purpose in the future. The procedures of cluster analysis are also more general than demonstrated here and can effectively utilize even nominally scaled variables. However, this precludes a prior analysis, say V-analysis, to determine the interrelationships among the variables.

4. The caveat, "You only get from a factor analysis what you put in," applies equally well to the results of a cluster analysis of objects. This is inevitable because the analyst must choose dimensions common to the objects from the infinite number of possible dimensions. However, we have attempted to clarify how a change in the original dimensions affects the analyst's concept of similarity between nations. For example, the large number of variables in V-clusters one and two, and their inability to discriminate between nations, casts doubt on much research which retains only the dimensions accounting for a significant proportion of the raw score variance.

At the same time, the extreme flexibility of the system and the objective nature of the analysis makes it possible to develop "tailor-made" country clusters based on data especially collected to solve specific problems. The BC TRY System program package, for example, provides options for comparing two groups of objects over the same set of variable cluster domains. These options can be used to match problem areas with solution techniques, in different countries—e.g., in international business, job difficulties might be matched with personnel qualifications, or consumer characteristics in several countries with a standardized advertising theme, and so on.

5. The present study was confined to data for one time period only. Further research can be done to study V- and O-Types over different time periods to measure temporal changes. To the extent that changes in O-Type membership can be predicted over time, one might be able to develop and test hypotheses concerning the switching patterns in a country's evolutionary process from economic underdevelopment to economic growth and industrialization. Such a study is also likely to reveal patterns of change for different countries and different variable cluster domains, indicating that "growth"— regardless of how it is defined—is not uniform for all countries over all variables, even when they are starting at the same stage of economic underdevelopment.

FOOTNOTES

This paper is a revised and condensed version of a paper presented by the authors at the Annual Conference of the Western Economic Association at Davis, California, August 27-28, 1970. The authors gratefully acknowledge the assistance and encouragement of Richard H. Holton, Dean of the School of Business Administration, University of California, Berkeley. Financial support for the project was provided by the School of Business Administration, editing and typing services were furnished by the Institute of Business and Economic Research, and the Computer Center supplied the program package and computer time for data analysis. The assistance of all these institutions of the University of California, Berkeley, is greatly appreciated.

1. Adapted from Raymond B. Cattell and Malcolm A. Coulter, "Principles of Behavioural Taxonomy and the Mathematical Basis of the Taxonome Computer Program," *The British Journal of Mathematical and Statistical Psychology*, 19:2 (November 1966), 237-269.

2. For an excellent overview and comparison of the results from much of the literature reviewed here, see Bruce Russett, *International Regions and the International System: A Study in Political Ecology* (Chicago: Rand-McNally, 1967), Chapter Three.

3. Arthur Banks and Robert Textor, *A Cross-Polity Survey* (Cambridge, Mass.: MIT Press, 1963), p. 50.

4. Arthur Banks and Phillip M. Gregg, "Grouping Political Systems: Q-Factor Analysis of 'A Cross-Polity Survey,' " *American Behavioral Scientist*, 9:3 (1965), 3-5.

5. Irma Adelman and Cynthia Taft Morris, "A Factor Analysis of the Interrelationships between Social and Political Variables and Per Capita Gross National Product," *Quarterly Journal of Economics*, 19 (November 1965), 555-578.

6. Michael Haas, "Dimensional Analysis in Cross-National Research," *Comparative Political Studies*, 3:1 (April 1970), 3-35.

7. Russett, op. cit.

8. Raymond B. Cattell, "The Three Basic Factor-Analytic Research Designs—Their Interrelationships and Derivatives," *Psychology Bulletin*, 49 (1952), 499-520.

9. Russett, op. cit., p. 21.

10. Jum C. Nunnally, *Psychometric Theory* (New York: McGraw-Hill, 1967) p. 363.

11. Warren S. Torgerson, *Theory and Methods of Scaling* (New York: Wiley, 1958), pp. 14-15. The three important characteristics of the real numbers referred to are order, distance, and origin.

12. In two dimensions, the distance between points i and j is given by $d_{ij} = (x_{i1} - x_{j1})^2 + (x_{i2} - x_{j2})^2]^{1/2}$, where the ordered pair, $x_i: (x_{i1}, x_{i2})$ represents the point, i.

13. For an excellent illustration and extension of these ideas, see Paul E. Green and Donald S. Tull, "Distance Functions and Cluster Analysis," in *Research for Marketing Decisions* (Englewood Cliffs, N.J.: Prentice-Hall, 1970, pp. 432-463.

14. The influence on this section of Dr. John Myers' work with the BC TRY System is gratefully acknowledged. See, for example, his "Cluster Analysis of Marketing Data," Working Paper No. 51, Institute of Business and Economic Research (Berkeley: University of California, 1970).

15. Robert C. Tryon and Daniel E. Bailey, *Cluster Analysis* (New York: McGraw-Hill, 1970).

16. Green and Tull, op. cit., p. 437.

17. Russett, op. cit., p. 17.

18. S. Prakash Sethi, "Comparative Cluster Analysis for World Markets," *Journal of Marketing Research* (August 1971).

19. The original numbers of countries rejected for O-Type in five and six dimensions are: 14, 23, 28, 36, 38, 41, 43, 48, 49, 52, 53, 55, 58, 75, 78, 80, 87, 95.

THE STRATEGY OF MULTINATIONAL MARKETING ANALYSIS: A CASE HISTORY FROM THE WORLD DATA BANK

CHARLES RAMOND

Major U.S. marketers are finding that an increasing proportion of their sales and earnings come from non-U.S. countries. International marketing management periodically requires swift access to the best information available on sales and profit opportunities around the world. Such information is essential to guide their decisions in advertising and marketing, new product planning, and capital budgeting.

Formerly much needed information about foreign markets was inaccurate, non-comparable, or simply unavailable. The usual solution was to "go and find out." Now the situation has improved dramatically: instead of too few data we have too many. The problem has become one of selectivity, of analysis, of concentrating scarce planning time on just those markets where it is *worth it* to go and find out.

The computer can of course help enormously, but most multinational marketers have yet to realize its benefits. Compilation and analysis of the data is a monumental task, often too burdensome to justify the time of the operating staff. And once the data are stored in the computer, there remains the task of getting them back again, *in usable form*, through a computer staff who may hinder more than help.

In this paper we first describe the World Data Bank, a shared-time computer system for retrieving and analyzing international information. We then present the analytic strategy and tactics used by the World Data Bank, and review a case in which they were applied.

PRESENT SYSTEMS

In many multinational companies the foundation for an information system already exists in the form of fact books, hand tabulations, charts, etc. Periodic reports for management are usually compiled by hand. This method of providing feedback has severe limitations:

1. It cannot be updated as swiftly or frequently as necessary without inordinate demands on internal staff.
2. It does not easily provide the kinds of sophisticated analyses available from the computer, analyses which when done interactively, can cumulate to reveal successively more meaningful or surprising results.

Adapted from an invited address to the American Statistical Association, December 3, 1970. Reprinted with permission of the author.

THE WORLD DATA BANK

The World Data Bank was conceived in May 1970 as an aid to several major manufacturers of consumer products whose sales and earnings came in large part from many non-U.S. countries. Our goal was to relieve them of the manual data-compiling and analytic functions, thereby freeing staff time for interpretation, and focusing their attention on where it was most needed.

Since much of the data was already available, and since several interesting analytic approaches have already been tested by workers in this area (e.g., Marketing Science Institute, 1967), it originally appeared relatively easy to store all necessary information in a form which would permit rapid retrieval, statistical analysis and display.

To do this in comprehensive fashion, however, has been an extremely tedious and time-consuming clerical task, as well as one which required the combined expertise of interactive computer programming and multivariate analysis. As of December 1970 the status of the World Data Bank was as follows:

1. Data

We have compiled and stored the raw data in an IBM 360/65 computer. Currently these consist of over 100 descriptors of 154 countries and non-sovereign areas. A list of all countries and descriptors appears below. A bibliography of the 80 public sources we have examined is available elsewhere (Marketing Control, 1970).

It goes without saying that not every descriptor could be estimated for every country, much less for the same most recent year. Moreover, different users of these data require different matrices for their particular purposes and the same user requires different matrices from time to time. Having assembled a "maximum" data matrix (see Figure 1), we therefore use an interactive program (facetiously called the "data-masher") to draw from it, for a particular user, just that most current complete matrix of desired countries and descriptors.

This custom-tailored public data matrix can then be related to a private matrix furnished by the user. In releasing sales or earnings data for such an analysis, he risks no breach of confidentiality since (a) these data are stored in a computer under a password known only to him; (b) they are named for analysis by his own code; and (c) they may be linearly transformed thus disguising real numerical values without changing the results of multivariate analysis.

2. Hardware

The user of this system faces a teletypewriter console. By dialing the phone he is connected with the central computer and can ask it to display for him, either on the typewriter or a cathode ray display unit, any of the reports listed below. More importantly, he can call on the computer to

Figure 1 THE MAXIMUM DATA MATRIX

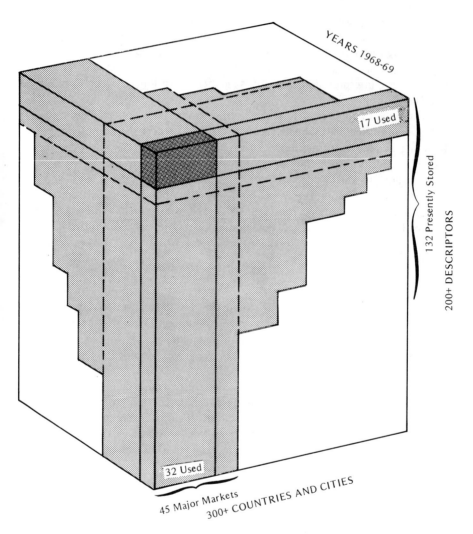

If countries are ranked from most to least developed, descriptors from most available to least available, and years from present to past, then the available data—of all that might be desired, as indicated by the total cube—can be demarcated by the shaded block. The matrix presently stored in the computer consists of only 45 Major Market countries by 132 descriptors. The initial matrix used in this case included those 32 Major Market countries of interest to the client, by the 17 key descriptors identified in the first factor analysis.

perform successive analyses of the same data, varying assumptions or editing files as suggested by the previous analysis. Computer terminals now available are much faster (30 characters per second), quieter (thermal printing) and lighter (25 lbs) than the familiar teletypewriter machine, resulting in a true conversational interface between user and data bank.

3. Software

We have developed proprietary computer programs for generating the five kinds of reports described in the box on page 52. In addition, we have developed programs for connecting the user with standard interactive packages of statistical analysis programs (e.g., the IBM Stat-Pak):

a. Factor analyses for reducing the number of predictive variables to their meaningful minimum.
b. Stepwise regression analyses for predicting sales and earnings from many descriptors.
c. Cluster analyses for identifying meaningful groups of countries, products and country-product combinations.
d. Time series analyses for forecasting sales and earnings years hence.

These latter programs have been used to remotely batch-process data for each World Data Bank subscriber, thereby creating smaller, custom-tailored data banks for ready access through time-sharing terminals.

ANALYTIC STRATEGY AND TACTICS

The search for which marketing forces cause payoff can be completed conclusively only by performing a designed experiment in which a few forces are deliberately manipulated in a random half of a sample and held constant in the other. Any difference in subsequent payoffs between the two halves can then be attributed to the forces.

This is of course impossible in multinational marketing. There the search for causality must be confined to historical data. The best we can do is say that if the amount of or change in a marketing force has in the past been consistently related to the amount of or change in payoff, this will probably continue to happen.

But when we found that certain marketing forces were highly related to *total* payoffs, we were faced with the usual "chicken and egg" problem: did the force cause the payoff, or the payoff cause the force? Or did some group of other forces cause *both* the payoff and the levels at which the marketing budgets were set? Most likely all three processes were at work.

So in trying to predict total payoff we were faced with the common problem of teasing out which way the causality runs. Our way around this obstacle was first to eliminate all variance in payoff associated with those country characteristics we cannot control: its wealth, population size, weather, etc. This done, we then examined the residual payoff for its relationships to the controllable marketing forces.

When this residual payoff is strongly related to those forces, there can be no question of which way the causality runs. It is impossible to imagine how such levels of such residual payoff could lead to management's setting of the marketing budget in correspondence with it; they could not have known what that residual payoff was.

Conceivably there remains the possibility that residual payoffs and budget-settings by management are both determined by the same exogenous variables. Our conversations with international marketing managers, however, have convinced us that most of them allocate the coming year's marketing expenditures on the basis of last year's performance, e.g., as a fixed percent of sales, ignoring those qualitative or unmeasurable variables that cannot be included in our analyses.

Having found a strong relationship between marketing forces and the residual payoff, we are therefore left with only two explanations: either the marketing force caused the residual payoff, or the relationship is due to chance. The probability that the relationship is due to chance can of course be estimated by the usual techniques of statistical inference. Moreover, if the same forces are consistently found to be related to payoffs year after year, we may with even more confidence reject chance as an explanation.

STRATEGY FOR TIME SERIES

The above strategy is indicated mainly when data are available only for one common time period. When *time series* are available for both marketing inputs and payoffs, then a second strategy for inferring causality can be used. It rests in part on the form in which the data are expressed.

Suppose we examine not *levels* of a brand's marketing expenditures but its shares of the total spent by all competitors. Given time series, we can go on to examine *changes* in these shares from period to period. Suppose further that these expenditure share-changes are found to be consistently related to subsequent changes in shares of the total payoff to all competitors. Merely by changing the form of the data, we have eliminated several obvious other explanations of the observed relationship:

Payoff share-changes cannot cause marketing share-changes because the latter come first in time.

Industry-related "other factors," like population growth or a recession, cannot cause changes in shares of both payoff and marketing expenditures; there is no reason why they should affect our brand's payoff or budget-settings any more or less than those of any other brand.

Company-related factors, like temporary fluctuations in our own or our competitors' production or distribution, cannot cause changes in our shares of *both* payoff and marketing expenditures: they may affect changes in *levels of one or the other* for any competitor, but except by coincidence, not changes in *shares of both* for the same competitor.

In short, if we observe that a change in share of one of our marketing forces is consistently followed by a change in our share of payoff, we are again left with only two possible explanations: either that force causes payoff, or we have observed a rare chance occurrence whose probability is known. Again too, the more consistently we see such a relationship in time series for different periods, the less likely it is due only to chance.

In practice such relationships are hard to find. Usually when we try to relate marketing inputs and outputs expressed as share-*changes*, any relationships we may have found between mere levels or shares vanish into the background noise. Management needs the interactive capability of the computer to examine quickly *many* possible relationships in search of those products, markets and product-market combinations where the relationships are strong enough to suggest immediate marketing action.

Because few multinational marketers have recorded comparable data on payoffs and marketing expenditures for long periods of time, and because industry totals of payoffs and marketing expenditures can rarely be found in comparable fashion across many country-markets, this strategy of examining successive share changes must usually be foregone. In one case where such data were available for over 100 brands sold in the domestic U.S. market (Ramond and Sheth, 1970), this approach was applied with considerable success due to the accuracy of the original data: changes in brand shares were successfully predicted for two consecutive years and marketing management was able to act on the implications of the analysis with confidence.

CHOICE OF INDEPENDENT VARIABLES

Having over 100 descriptors of most major countries of the world, we require a way of reducing these to a meaningful few before examining their relationships to payoffs. Here our strategy was twofold: (a) to eliminate redundant variables, and (b) to avoid multi-collinearity among those variables chosen as least redundant. In other words, we needed those few orthogonal descriptors which best represented *all* descriptors of a given set of countries.

Factor analysis seemed uniquely appropriate for this strategy. By choosing those descriptors which loaded most highly on each factor, we had some assurance that each such descriptor:

—represented, to some known degree, all other descriptors which also loaded significantly on the same factor; and

—was by definition orthogonal to every other such descriptor which was most highly loaded on each other factor.

By choosing them in this way we insured that the independent variables in the subsequent multiple regression were truly independent. In the case which follows, this preliminary caution probably explains the remarkably high proportion of variance in payoff accounted for by only a handful of country descriptors. They not only subsumed most of the descriptors available, but also had little overlap with each other.

So our strategy has been to *identify* key publicly available descriptors of countries through factor analysis; then to *remove* from the variability in payoff (during a single time-period, assuming time series analysis must be foregone) that part accounted for by these descriptors, through multiple regression analysis; and finally to relate the residual variance among countries to the client's own private descriptors of those countries, usually his marketing expenditures. Our reasoning is straightforward: these marketing expenditures can be evaluated only in terms of their ability to increase payoff *above that expected from uncontrollable country conditions*. Once we know what these conditions are, we can go on to see whether the residual or controllable payoffs are in fact related—as the client would wish—to his own concurrent marketing efforts.

MULTIPLE REGRESSION TACTICS

But the tactics of multiple regression analysis remain to be chosen. We chose the stepwise procedure, simply because it permitted us to determine, on an objective basis, the *number* of independent variables that were most meaningfully related to a payoff.

As generally executed by standard computer programs, stepwise regression analysis selects first that independent variable which accounts for the most variance in the dependent variable, then that which accounts for the most of the remaining variance, and so on until the user decides to stop. He can make this decision according to any of several defensible criteria—among them the amount of variance he wishes to account for, the size of the standard error of the whole equation, the statistical significance he desires for the whole equation, or the statistical significance he wishes for each new independent variable.

In the case which follows, we simply let the computer add variables until little or no additional variance was accounted for. We then chose that equation after which the next variable either:

1. reduced the significance of the overall equation beyond the 0.95 level (i.e., the probability associated with the F statistic rose above 0.05); or

2. was itself not significant at the 0.95 level, i.e. the probability associated with the F for that variable was greater than 0.05; or
3. did not reduce the standard error of the whole equation.

If neither of the first two conditions was met, and the size of the standard error was much the same from step to step, we simply chose that equation with the lowest probability of F's being due to chance, even though that probability was above 0.05.

CLUSTERING TACTICS

The realities of international marketing demanded one final tactic to guard against being misled by spuriously high or low correlations of a payoff with concurrent or previous marketing expenditures. When the observations come from a large set of countries, say 30 or more, we know in advance that at least two artifactual circumstances can spuriously inflate or deflate the multiple r:

1. One country, e.g., the United States, or a small number of countries that differ radically from all the rest, may, by their extreme values of payoff or marketing expenditures, artificially increase or decrease the apparent relationship between payoff and expenditures.
2. The marketing forces which most closely relate to payoff in one type of country will not necessarily do so in another type. While each country is of course highly individualistic in certain respects, countries do tend to fall into intuitively understandable groups, especially in terms of those uncontrollable country conditions which constrain the payoff. For example, what constrains or enhances automobile sales in rich countries will not necessarily do the same in poor countries.

We therefore decided, in advance, to regress payoffs against marketing expenditures *separately* for each identifiably homogeneous cluster of countries in any total set. Although we factor-analyze all available descriptors for all countries in the set, we also then cluster-analyze, by rotating the data matrix 90 degrees, all countries in terms of all available descriptors. This typically produces three, four or five easily named clusters of homogeneous countries, payoffs in which can then be separately related to the least redundant public descriptors found in the overall factor analysis.

As will be seen below, not every country in a large set necessarily loads highly on only one cluster. A few multi-clustered countries usually are found, and occasionally a single country which either constitutes its own unique cluster or otherwise bears no close relationship to any group. The majority of the countries in the total set, however, do tend to cluster meaningfully. More importantly, the multiple regression equations for payoffs (a) differ from cluster to cluster, (b) are more meaningful than similar equations for the whole set, and (c) have significantly lower standard errors.

Case History

The client, a mlutinational marketer of a well-known, branded product line, selected 32 countries as markets of primary interest to his firm. For each of these countries he provided 1969 data on an unnamed payoff he wished to increase, and ten marketing or other expenditures, coded A through J, for the same year. In addition to having thus disguised all variables, he had also multiplied each by the same constant, which was unknown to our staff. These safeguards permitted no breach of confidentiality, yet left the results of the analysis identical to those which would have been attained from the original untransformed data. In short, we received a private matrix of 11 variables (one payoff and ten inputs) by 32 countries, for the year 1969.

FACTOR ANALYSES OF COUNTRY DESCRIPTORS

Normally, we would have run a single factor analysis of all 1968 public descriptors available for the 32 countries designated, to find those independent descriptors which best represented all the rest. In this case, however, two subsets of country descriptors were a priori so important that factor analyses of each of these sets were done separately:

1. *Weather and related descriptors for the key city in each country.* Four descriptors (sunny days, average monthly temperature, altitude and latitude) represented all seven weather variables studied. Eliminated as redundant were high monthly high temperature, low monthly low and the range between them.
2. *Age distribution.* The populations of five age groups (10-14, 15-24, 25-34, 35-44 and 45+) can represent all seven age breaks studied. Eliminated as redundant were the groups aged 0-4 and 5-9.

Both these findings were somewhat surprising, but for different reasons.

1. We had suspected that the temperature range would be independent of the variables retained; it was not.
2. Then, among age distributions we would have thought the negative correlations between young and old would have made these groups essentially opposite ends of the same factor; this was not so either. Instead, there are at least some countries with every combination: many young, few old; few young, many old; many young, many old; and few young, few old.

We also factor-analyzed a third set of 52 other descriptors of the 32 countries: mainly of economic, transportation, power and media conditions. The variables which loaded highest on the five resulting factors were: total national income per capita, gross national product, passenger cars, telephones and total energy consumption per capita.

Here there were no particular surprises, these results being similar to those of other, not-too-different sets of countries. Note that income per capita and gross national product were independent; previous analyses had shown that GNP per capita and total national income were also independent. We therefore arbitrarily added the latter two variables to those examined in the subsequent multiple regression analysis, partly in view of the above and partly because relatively accurate current data on these variables were generally available for most countries.

From these three factor analyses, then, we chose the following variables for inclusion in the multiple regression analyses and cluster analysis which followed:

A. Weather Variables
   WALT   Altitude Above Sea Level
   WAMA   Average Monthly Average Temperature.
   WLAT   Latitude from Equator
   WSUN   Days Without Rainfall
B. Population Age Groups
   DA14   Population Aged 10-14 in 1969
   DA24   Population Aged 15-24 in 1969
   DA34   Population Aged 25-34 in 1969
   DA44   Population Aged 35-44 in 1969
   DA45   Population Aged 45 and Over in 1969
   DSUM   Total Population, Midyear 1969
C. Economic, Transportation, Power and Media Variables
   EGNP   Gross National Product in 1968
   ETNI   Total National Income in 1968
   EPPC   GNP Per Capita in 1968
   EIPC   TNI Per Capita in 1968
   TCAR   Passenger Cars in Use in 1968
   MTEL   Telephones in Use in 1968
   PCPC   Total Energy Consumption Per Capita in 1968

MULTIPLE REGRESSION ANALYSES OF ALL 32 COUNTRIES

We then stored these variables in the computer in a private file, a matrix of 17 descriptors by 32 countries. We also stored the client's private data—one payoff (dependent) variable and ten marketing expenditures (independent variables)—in a separate private file.

An initial stepwise regression analysis of this latter file showed that variable F, by itself, accounted for 73 percent of the variance in the payoff. Adding variable C accounted for another 19 percent. Expressed in correlational terms, the multiple r between the payoff and variable F was 0.86, and with F and C together, 0.93.

This kind of result is of course ambiguous: it may mean that F and C caused payoffs to the extent indicated, that marketing budgets for F and C were held at some fixed percent of the payoff as a matter of corporate marketing policy, or that some other variable or set of variables caused both the payoff *and* the setting of budgets for F and C. We therefore adopted the analytic strategy described above, in an attempt to get around this common "chicken-egg" problem.

Our next step was thus to relate the payoff first to those 17 public descriptors which best represented all the rest. Another stepwise multiple regression analysis was done for all 32 countries taken together, with the following results:

1. *Per capita income and altitude* were by far the most important "country conditions" affecting payoff, in that order. Together, however, they accounted for only 40 percent variance in payoff ($r = 0.63$).
2. *Gross national product, population aged 45 and over, and passenger cars in use* accounted for the largest proportion of the remaining variance, but inversely. Surprisingly, the richer, older, and more motorized a country
   · the less the payoff.
3. *Population aged 10-14 and 25-34* were next most important, positively and negatively, respectively. The more young people and fewer "middle-aged" people in the country, the greater the payoff.
4. *Sunny days* was positively related to the payoff. This had been expected.

The table below shows, however, that all eight variables accounted for less than two-thirds of the payoff variance.

Ind. Vars.	Mult. r	r^2	b	S.E.
ETNI	.44	.19	8.9	>10,000
WALT	.63	.40	3.8	7,900
EGNP	.70	.49	−5.7	5,000
DA45	.72	.52	.1	4,000
TCAR	.76	.57	−8.3	3,600
DA14	.78	.61	12.2	3,500
DA34	.78	.62	−10.0	3,200
WSUN	.79	.62	90.0	2,350

But this equation was much less meaningful, as will be seen in the next column, than those found for separate country-clusters.

CLUSTER ANALYSIS

In terms of their similarities in the above 17 variables, all but five of the 32 countries clustered neatly into three groups we named:

I. Fifteen Rich European and Far Eastern Countries
II. Nine Poor Asian and Latin American Countries
III. Three Richer Latin American Countries

Of the remaining five countries, four of them were mildly related to two or more of the three clusters above. Israel, the most unusual country, was mildly related to Cluster I as well as to a fourth cluster in which it was the only country.

Countries in each cluster are shown in Table 1. Table 2 shows which countries were most "like" each other.

Table 1   FACTOR-LOADINGS OF THE 32 COUNTRIES ON EACH CLUSTER

(Numbers are loadings of each country on the cluster named)

I. Rich European and Far Eastern		II. Poor Asian and Latin American		III. Richer Latin American	
Sweden	.99	India	.99	Mexico	.95
Switzerland	.98	Thailand	.99	Puerto Rico	.94
Denmark	.97	Pakistan	.98	Argentina	.91
France	.96	Malaysia	.94		
Netherlands	.94	Brazil	.91		
United Kingdom	.94	Turkey	.91		
Finland	.94	Peru	.88		
New Zealand	.92	Philippines	.82		
Belgium	.90	Colombia	.80		
Norway	.88				
Italy	.87				
West Germany	.86				
Australia	.86				
Japan	.81				
Austria	.80				
Israel	.75				
		Chile	.68	Chile	.56
Venezuela	.65	Venezuela	.50	Venezuela	.52
Spain	.62	Spain	.62		
South Africa	.56	South Africa	.60	South Africa	.56

Countries below the line relate closely (0.8 or higher) to no cluster, but rather, relate mildly to two or more clusters. Israel had a factor loading of 0.52 on a fourth cluster, not shown here because no other country was in it—Israel is thus "in a class by itself."

Table 2   SIBLING COUNTRIES FOUND BY SCANNING CORRELATIONS
BETWEEN ALL COUNTRY-PAIRS ON 20 KEY DESCRIPTORS

(Siblings shown are only those for which the
correlation was 0.98 or higher)

COUNTRY	ITS SIBLINGS

Cluster I. Rich European & Far Eastern Countries

1.	Sweden	Switzerland, Denmark, Netherlands
2.	Switzerland	Sweden, Netherlands, Denmark
3.	Denmark	Finland, Sweden, Switzerland
4.	France	U.K., Netherlands
5.	Netherlands	U.K., Switzerland, France, Belgium, Italy, Sweden
6.	U.K.	France, Italy, Netherlands
7.	Finland	Denmark
8.	New Zealand	None (Denmark, Finland 0.96)
9.	Belgium	Austria, Germany, Netherlands, Australia
10.	Norway	Belgium
11.	Italy	U.K., Netherlands, Japan
12.	Germany	Japan, Austria, Belgium
13.	Austria	Belgium, Germany, Australia
14.	Japan	Germany, Italy
15.	Australia	Austria, Belgium

Cluster II. Poor Asian & Latin American Countries

1.	India	Thailand, Pakistan
2.	Thailand	India, Pakistan
3.	Pakistan	India, Thailand, Malaysia
4.	Malaysia	Turkey, Brazil, Pakistan
5.	Brazil	Peru, Malaysia, Turkey
6.	Turkey	Malaysia, Brazil
7.	Peru	Brazil, Philippines
8.	Philippines	Peru
9.	Colombia	None (Turkey, Peru 0.93)

Cluster III. Richer Latin American Countries

1.	Mexico	Argentina
2.	Puerto Rico	None (Mexico, Argentina 0.94)
3.	Argentina	Mexico

IV. Multi-Clustered Countries

1.	Israel	None (not over 0.85)
2.	Chile	South Africa
3.	Venezuela	None (Spain, Colombia, Chile 0.95)
4.	Spain	South Africa
5.	South Africa	Spain, Chile

MULTIPLE REGRESSION EQUATIONS
FOR EACH LARGE CLUSTER

Our suspicion was confirmed: the same variables did not relate to sales in rich and poor countries. Below are the multiple regression equations for the two clusters in which there were enough countries to permit a meaningful equation.

For 15 Rich European & Far Eastern Countries
(Cluster I):

$Payoff = 16(DA34) - 38(DA24) + 2(TCAR) + 44(DA14)$
$+ 3(PCPC) - 7,200 \pm S.E.$ of 3,700

Multiple r $= .993; r^2 = .986$

For 9 Poor Asian & Latin American Countries
(Cluster II):

$Payoff = 16(TCAR) + 5,400 \pm S.E.$ of 5,800;

Multiple r $= .807; r^2 = .651$

As expected, public descriptors predicted the payoff more accurately in each cluster than they did in all 32 countries taken together; the standard errors were less than half as large for these two clusters.

The most surprising difference between these two equations is that age-distribution was more important to payoff in richer countries. Three of the five key public descriptors of Cluster I are populations of age groups. In Cluster II, on the other hand, only passenger cars in use related closely to payoff. In summary, payoff was greater to the extent that:

—In Rich European and Far Eastern Countries, the more people there were aged 25-34 and 10-14, the fewer people there were aged 15-24, the more passenger cars there were in use and the more power they consumed per capita.

—In Poor Asian and Latin American Countries, the more passenger cars there were in use.

Having thus isolated the key public descriptors which conditioned payoffs, we ranked the countries in each cluster in order of their departure from the payoffs expected on the basis of those descriptors.

Ranked by these residuals, one country clearly had the outstanding payoff in 1969. It was 13,000 units above the payoff expected from its passenger cars in use, more than twice the standard error of 5,800. The odds were therefore less than one in twenty that this discrepancy occurred by chance. No other countries departed as significantly from the payoffs expected from their uncontrollable conditions.

It now remained to find whether these deviations from the expected could be explained in terms of the client's marketing expenditures. As before, our reasoning is straightforward: these marketing expenditures can be evaluated only in terms of their ability to increase payoff *above that expected by uncontrollable country conditions.*

MULTIPLE REGRESSION
EQUATIONS FOR THE RESIDUALS

Having accounted for that variance among countries due to their uncontrollable conditions (age groups, wealth, etc.), we then related the remaining variance to those variables under the client's control—his marketing expenditures. These controllable payoffs were related to his private descriptors as follows:

Controllable Payoff = $10A - 15C - 11B - 83 \pm$ *S.E. of* 2,300
(Cluster I)

$$Multiple\ r = .73;\ r^2 = .53;\ p = .05$$

Controllable Payoff = $20C - 19H + 28E - 1,400 \pm$ *S.E. of* 3,700
(Cluster II)

$$Multiple\ r = .84;\ r^2 = .71;\ p = .07$$

Again our suspicions were confirmed: different marketing forces worked better in different kinds of countries. Indeed, marketing force C was inversely related to payoff in Cluster I but positively related to payoff in Cluster II! Since we did not know what C stood for, we could not reasonably guess why this should be so. (The client had no trouble in interpreting this result, we might add.) But it was clear that the relationship of any marketing force to payoff could be understood only in combination with the other forces in its equation: thus C lowered payoff in combination with A and B in rich countries, but raised payoff in combination with H and E in poor countries.

The marketing implications of these equations were quite important; note the high positive weights on at least one marketing force in each equation. All figures the client gave us were expressed in the same units. We could therefore recommend that to increase payoff:

—In Cluster I, *reallocate funds from C and B to A.*
—In Cluster II, *reallocate funds from H to C and E.*

For example, if in a certain country in 1970 the client had increased A 200 units, taking 100 each from variables C and B, substituting these new values in the recipe for controllable payoff in Cluster I we find that the odds are two out of three (± 1 standard error) that the resulting residual payoff in that country would have increased between 3,500 and 7,100 units, always assuming that the relationships remain stable for a year. In 1969, this country's residual payoff was plus 770 units, so this is an increase of between

2,730 and 6,330 units of payoff—without adding a dollar of marketing expenditures.

Similar "what if" games were played with other countries in both clusters. The "Payoff Recipe" program of the World Data Bank permitted rapid examination of many such alternatives, thereby suggesting the best countries in which to increase, decrease or reallocate marketing budgets.

But before we took the step of storing these Payoff Recipes in the computer, we had to confirm or reject our assumption that they do remain stable from year to year. We have therefore gone on to repeat the entire analysis for 1968 and 1970 data. Results are unavailable at present. But if these relationships do remain stable, the client will have at his disposal a powerful tool for improving the efficiency of his marketing expenditures, usable as needed from the console of his own remote terminal.

References

Grafflin, Mary Ellen and Charles Ramond. *Sources of Data Stored in the World Data Bank: Annotated Bibliography*. New York: Marketing Control, 1970.

Marketing Science Institute. *A Comparative Analysis for International Marketing*. Boston: Allyn and Bacon, 1967.

Ramond, Charles and Jagdish Sheth. "Controlling Marketing Performance: Two Case Examples" in *Proceedings of the Workshop on Marketing Information Systems*. New York: Association of National Advertisers, 1970.

APPENDIX

CODES, DEFINITIONS AND SOURCES
(ALL DESCRIPTORS)

Descriptor Codes

Descriptors in parentheses include those they follow; those ending TOT include whole class. For printout definitions, sources and formats of each descriptor, see following pages.

Advertising Expenditures

ACIN	Cinema
AMAG	Magazines (APRI)
ANEW	Newspapers (APRI)
AOUT	Outdoor
APRI	Print Media Total
ARAD	Radio
ATOT	Total
ATRA	Trade Press
ATVS	Television

Consumer Expenditures

CBEV	Beverages
CCAP	Domestic Capital
CCAN	Non-monetary (CCAP)
CCAR	Passenger Cars (CTRC)

CCLO	Clothing
CFOD	Food
CFUR	Furniture, Household
CHEA	Health (CPEH)
CNON	Total Non-monetary
COTH	Non-car Transport (CTRC)
CPEH	Personal Care, Health
CPER	Personal Care (CPEH)
CTOB	Tobacco
CTOT	Total
CTRC	Transportation, Commun.

Demographic

DA04	Population Aged 0-4
DA09	Population Aged 5-9
DA14	Population Aged 10-14

DA24	Population Aged 15-24
DA34	Population Aged 25-34
DA44	Population Aged 35-44
DA45	Pop. Aged 45 and Over
DAGR	Pop. in Agriculture
DBIR	Live Birth Rate
DILL	Percent Illiterate
DINC	Income Inequality Index
DLAN	Land Inequality Index
DLEF	Female Life Expectancy
DLEM	Male Life Expectancy
DMAN	Manufacturing Workers
DMOR	Infant Mortality
DPAG	Annual Growth of Pop.
DPOD	Population Density
DPOP	Total Population
DURB	Pop., Cities Over 100MM

Economic

ECPI	Consumer Price Index
EEXR	Exchange Rate
EGNP	Gross National Product
EIMP	Total Imports
EIPC	Total Income Percap
EMAN	Manufacturing Output
EPAG	Ann. Growth of GDP
EPCG	Ann. Growth of GDP Percap
EPPC	GNP Percap
ETNI	Total National Income
EXPC	Export Concentration
EXPO	Total Exports
EXRC	Receiver Concentration

Foreign Affiliations

FDPL	Diplomatic Posts
FDPR	Diplomats Received
FDPS	Diplomats Sent
FMEM	International Memberships
FMIN	Non-UN Orgs. (FMEM)
FMUN	UN Organizations (FMEM)
FSOV	Soviet Aid
FUSA	Total US Aid
FUSE	US Economic Aid (FUSA)

Government

GAGE	Age of Present Form
GCEN	Centrist Seats
GCOM	Communist Seats
GCON	Conservative Seats
GDEF	Defense Expenditures
GELE	Elections Missed
GISM	Ideological Skewness
GLEF	Leftist Seats
GMIL	Military Manpower
GPFI	Press Freedom Index
GSEC	Internal Security
GSTS	Diversity by Seats
GVOT	Diversity by Votes

Health

HCPC	Daily Calories Percap
HDEN	Dentists
HMID	Midwives
HPHA	Pharmacists
HPHY	Physicians
HPPC	Daily Protein Percap
HPPH	Pop. per Hospital Bed

Media Availability

MACI	Cinema Tickets Sold
MCIR	Newspaper Circulation
MCIS	Cinema Seats
MCPC	Newspap. Circ. Percap
MMAI	Domestic Mail Traffic
MPPC	Newsprint Cons. Percap
MPRI	Newsprint Consumption
MPRO	Newsprint Production
MRAD	Radios in Use
MSCI	Scientific Journals
MTEL	Telephones in Use
MTVS	TV Receivers in Use

Power

PCPC	Energy Cons. Percap
PELE	Electric Power
PSTE	Steel Consumption
PSPC	Steel Cons. Percap
PTOT	Total Energy Consumed

Religion

RCAT	Number Roman Catholics
RCHR	Number Christians
RETH	Number Ethnic Groups
RIND	Number Independents
RLIN	Number Linguistic Groups
RMOS	Number Moslems
RORT	Number Orthodox
RPRO	Number Protestants

Transportation

TAIR	Passenger Kms. Flown
TCAR	Passenger Cars in Use
TCHI	Air Fare to Chicago
TLON	Air Fare to London
TNYC	Air Fare to New York
TPAR	Air Fare to Paris
TTOK	Air Fare to Tokyo
TVEH	Comml. Vehicles in Use

Weather (Selected Cities)

WALT	Altitude
WAMA	Avg. Monthly Avg. Temp.
WAMH	Avg. Monthly High Temp.
WAML	Avg. Monthly Low Temp.
WLAT	Latitude
WRAN	Range of Monthly Temps.
WSUN	Days Without Rainfall

CODE	PRINT-OUT NAME OF DESCRIPTOR	SOURCE/TABLE	REPORT UNITS	FIELD DIGITS	DECIMAL PLACES
Advertising					
ACIN	Cinema Advertising in 1968	IAA-WAE	$ Million	4	1
AMAG	Magazine Advertising in 1968	IAA-WAE	$ Million	5	1
ANEW	Newspaper Advertising in 1968	IAA-WAE	$ Million	5	1
AOUT	Outdoor Advertising in 1968	IAA-WAE	$ Million	4	1
APRI	Print Media Advertising in 1968	IAA-WAE	$ Million	5	1
ARAD	Radio Advertising in 1968	IAA-WAE	$ Million	5	1
ATOT	Total Advertising in 1968	IAA-WAE	$ Million	6	1
ATRA	Trade Press Advertising in 1968	IAA-WAE	$ Million	4	1
ATVS	Television Advertising in 1968	IAA-WAE	$ Million	5	1
Consumer Expenditures					
CBEV	Expenditures for Beverages	UNB17-2	$ Million	6	0
CCAP	Gross Domestic Fixed Cap Formation	UNB11-3	$ Million	6	0
CCAN	Non-Monetary Gross Dom Cap Formation	UNB11-3	$ Million	6	0
CCAR	Expenditures for Passenger Cars	UNB17-10A	$ Million	6	0
CCLO	Clothing & Other Personal Effects	UNB17-4	$ Million	6	0
CFOD	Expenditures for Food	UNB17-1	$ Million	6	0
CFUR	Expenditures for Furniture, Household	UNB17-7	$ Million	6	0
CHEA	Expenditures for Health Expenses	UNB17-9B	$ Million	6	0
CNON	Non-Monetary Consumer Expend	UNB11-1	$ Million	6	0
COTH	Expenditures for Trans Other Than Cars	UNB17-10B	$ Million	6	0
CPEH	Expenditures for Personal Care, Health	UNB17-9	$ Million	6	0
CPER	Expenditures for Personal Care	UNB17-9A	$ Million	6	0
CTOB	Expenditures for Tobacco	UNB17-3	$ Million	6	0
CTOT	Total Consumer Expenditures	UNB11-1	$ Million	7	0
CTRC	Expenditures for Transport, Communicat	UNB17-10	$ Million	6	0

CODE	PRINT-OUT NAME OF DESCRIPTOR	SOURCE/TABLE	REPORT UNITS	FIELD DIGITS	DECIMAL PLACES
Demographic					
DA04	Population Aged 0-4 in 1969	UN-C6	Thousands	6	0
DA09	Population Aged 5-9 in 1969	UN-C6	Thousands	6	0
DA14	Population Aged 10-14 in 1969	UN-C6	Thousands	6	0
DA24	Population Aged 15-24 in 1969	UN-C6	Thousands	6	0
DA34	Population Aged 25-34 in 1969	UN-C6	Thousands	6	0
DA44	Population Aged 35-44 in 1969	UN-C6	Thousands	6	0
DA45	Population Aged 45 and Over	UN-C6	Thousands	6	0
DAGR	Population Dependent on Agriculture	UN-C4	Thousands	2	0
DBIR	Crude Live-Birth Rates	UN-C12	Births/1000	3	1
DILL	Percent of Population Illiterate	UN-D32	Percent	6	3
DINC	Income Inequality, 1960	ICPR-I20	Percent	6	3
DLAN	Land Inequality, 1960	ICPR-I21	Percent	2	0
DLEF	Life Expectancy at Birth-Female	UN-C3	Years	2	0
DLEM	Life Expectancy at Birth-Male	UN-C3	Years	5	1
DMAN	Employment in Manufacturing	UN-A82	Thousands	3	0
DMOR	Infant Mortality Under One Year	UN-C42	Deaths/1000	3	1
DPAG	Annual Rate of Population Increase	UN-C1	Percent	2	0
DPOD	Population Density	UN-C1	Pers Per Sq Km	3	0
DPOP	Population, Mid-Year	UN-C4	Thousands	6	0
DURB	Population in Cities Over 100,000	UN-C5	Thousands	6	0
Economic					
ECPI	Consumer Price Index, 1968 Base 1965	UN-A175	Annual Averages	3	0
EEXR	Exchange Rate in 1968	UN-A184	Curr Units/Per $	7	3
EGNP	Gross National Product in 1968	UN-A178	$ Million	7	0
EIMP	Total Imports in 1968	UN-A142	$ Million	6	0
EIPC	Total National Income Percap in 1968	UN-A177	$ Percap	4	0
EMAN	Manufacturing Output in 1968	UN-B2-3	$ Million	5	0
EPAG	Avg. Annual Growth of GDP in 1968	UN-A180	Percent	3	1
EPCG	Avg. Annual Growth Percap in 1968	UN-A180	Percent	3	0
EPPC	Gross National Product Percap in 1968	UN-A178	$ Percap	4	0

Code	Description	Source	Units		
ETNI	Total National Income in 1968	UN-A177	$ Million	7	0
EXPC	Export Commodity Concentration, 1965	ICPR-I19	Index 0-1	5	3
EXPO	Total Exports in 1968	UN-A142	$ Million	6	0
EXRC	Export Receiver Concentration, 1965	ICPR-I19	Index 0-1	5	3

Foreign Affiliations

Code	Description	Source	Units		
FDPL	Diplomatic Representations, 1963-64	ICPR-126	Countries	3	0
FDPR	Number of Diplomats Received, 1965	ICPR-129	Persons	4	0
FDPS	Number of Diplomats Sent, 1965	ICPR-129	Persons	4	0
FMEM	Total International Memberships, 1965	ICPR-126	Organizations	4	0
FMIN	Memberships in Non-UN IOs, 1965	ICPR-126	Organizations	2	0
FMUN	Memberships in UN Organizations, 1965	ICPR-126	Organizations	2	0
FSOV	Total Soviet Aid, 1954-1965	ICPR-125	$ Thousand	8	0
FUSA	Total US Aid, 1958-1965	ICPR-126	$ Million	6	1
FUSE	Total US Economic Aid, 1958-1965	ICPR-126	$ Million	6	1

Government

Code	Description	Source	Units		
GAGE	Age of Present Institutional Form, 1970	ICPR-129	Years	3	0
GCEN	Centrist Percent of Legislature, 1965	ICPR-126	Percent	5	1
GCOM	Communist Percent of Legislature, 1965	ICPR-126	Percent	5	1
GCON	Conservative Percent of Legislature, 1965	ICPR-127	Percent	5	1
GDEF	Defense Expenditures, 1965	ICPR-124	$ Million	4	0
GELE	Electoral Irregularities, 1965	ICPR-127	Index 1, 2, 3	1	0
GISM	Ideological Skewness Measure, 1965	ICPR-127	Index 0-10	6	4
GLEF	Non-Com Left Percent of Legislature, 1965	ICPR-126	Percent	4	1
GMIL	Military Manpower, 1965	ICPR-124	Thousands	5	1
GPFI	Press Freedom Index, 1965	ICPR-127	Index -4 to $+4$	5	2
GSEC	Total Internal Security Forces, 1965	ICPR-128	Persons	6	0
GSTS	Party Diversity Based on Seats, 1965	ICPR-126	Index 0-1	5	3
GVOT	Party Diversity Based on Votes, 1965	ICPR-126	Index 0-1	5	3

CODE	PRINT-OUT NAME OF DESCRIPTOR	SOURCE/TABLE	REPORT UNITS	FIELD DIGITS	DECIMAL PLACES
Health					
HCPC	Calories Per Capita Per Diem, 1965	ICPR-123	Calories	4	0
HDEN	Number of Dentists in 1968	UN-A198	Individuals	5	0
HMID	Number of Midwives in 1968	UN-A198	Individuals	6	0
HPHA	Number of Pharmacists in 1968	UN-A198	Individuals	6	0
HPHY	Number of Physicians in 1968	UN-A198	Individuals	6	0
HPPC	Proteins Per Capita Per Diem, 1965	ICPR-123	Grams	5	1
HPPH	Population Per Hospital Bed in 1968	UN-A198	Units	4	0
Media Availability					
MACI	Cinema Tickets Sold in 1968	UN-A206	Thousands	4	0
MCIR	Total Daily Paper Circulation in 1968	UN-A204	Thousands	5	0
MCIS	Cinema Seating Capacity in 1968	UN-A206	Thousands	4	0
MCPC	Paper Circ Per Thousand in 1968	UN-A204	Units	3	0
MMAI	Domestic Mail Traffic in 1968	UN-A155	Thousands	6	0
MPPC	Newsprint Consumption Per Cap in 1968	UN-A171	Units	3	0
MPRI	Total Newsprint Consumption in 1968	UN-A171	Thousand Met Ton	4	1
MPRO	Total Newsprint Production in 1968	UN-A104	Thousand Met Ton	4	0
MRAD	Radio Receivers in Use in 1968	UN-A207	Thousands	6	0
MSCI	Number of Scientific Journals, 1961	ICPR-I19	Journals	4	0
MTEL	Number of Telephones in Use in 1968	UN-A157	Units	7	0
MTVS	Television Receivers in Use in 1968	UN-A208	Thousands	5	0
Power					
PCPC	Energy Consump Percap Coal Equiv in 1968	UN-A136	Total	4	0
PELE	Total Electric Power Production in 1968	UN-A138	Kilowatt Hours	7	0
PSTE	Total Steel Consumption in 1968	UN-A166	Thousand Met Ton	6	0
PSPC	Steel Consumption Per Capita in 1968	UN-A166	Kilograms Percap	3	0
PTOT	Total Energy Consump Coal Equiv in 1968	UN-A136	Million Met Ton	4	2

Religion

Code	Description	Source	Unit		
RCAT	Number of Roman Catholics in 1969	ICPR-I14	Thousands	6	0
RCHR	Number of Christians in 1969	ICPR-I14	Thousands	6	0
RETH	Ethno-Linguistic Diversity Index in 1969	ICPR-I14	Index 0-1	5	3
RIND	Number of Independents in 1969	ICPR-I14	Thousands	6	0
RLIN	Linguistic Diversity Index in 1969	ICPR-I14	Index 0-1	4	3
RMOS	Number of Moslems in 1969	ICPR-I14	Thousands	6	0
RORT	Number of Orthodox in 1969	ICPR-I14	Thousands	6	0
RPRO	Number of Protestants in 1969	ICPR-I14	Thousands	6	0

Transportation

Code	Description	Source	Unit		
TAIR	Passenger Kilometers Flown in 1968	UN-A151	Hundred Thousand	6	0
TCAR	Passenger Cars in Use in 1968	UN-A146	Thousands	5	1
TCHI	One-Way Economy Air Fare to Chicago 1970	OAG	Dollars	3	0
TLON	One-Way Economy Air Fare to London 1970	OAG	Dollars	3	0
TNYC	One-Way Economy Air Fare to NY 1970	OAG	Dollars	3	0
TPAR	One-Way Economy Air Fare to Paris 1970	OAG	Dollars	3	0
TTOK	One-Way Economy Air Fare to Tokyo 1970	OAG	Dollars	3	0
TVEH	Commercial Vehicles in Use in 1968	UN-A146	Thousands	5	1

Weather

Code	Description	Source	Unit		
WALT	Altitude Above Sea Level	PAA	Feet	4	0
WAMA	Average Monthly Average Temperature	PAA	Degs. Fahrenheit	4	1
WHMH	Average Highest Monthly High Temperature	PAA	Degs. Fahrenheit	2	0
WLAT	Latitude from Equator	PAA	Degrees	2	0
WLML	Average Lowest Monthly Low Temperature	PAA	Degs. Fahrenheit	2	0
WRAN	Range of HMH to LML Temperature	PAA	Degs. Fahrenheit	2	0
WSUN	Days Without Rainfall Per Year	PAA	Sunny Days	3	0

SOURCES CITED

UNA   United Nations Statistical Office. *Statistical Yearbook*. (New York: U.N., annual)
      The world's statistical abstract with data on population, production, consumption, trade, finance, housing, education and communications. 1969 issue, pub. 1970, contains 1968 data.
UNB   ————. *Yearbook of National Accounts Statistics*. (New York: U.N., annual) 2 vols.
      Vol. I, Individual country tables, Vol. II, International tables. Internationally comparable data on production; national income; finance; capital formation; private consumption; government; household and external transactions. 1968 issue published 1970.
UNC   ————. *Demographic Yearbook*. (New York: U.N., annual)
      Data on population, natality, mortality, nuptiality and divorce and latest available data on life expectancy; features natality statistics. 1969 issue, published 1970, contains 1969 data.
UND   United Nations Economic, Scientific and Cultural Organization. *Statistical Yearbook*. (Paris: UNESCO; N.Y.: UNESCO Publications Center, annual)
      Data on education, books, libraries, newspapers, paper consumption, film, radio, T.V.
IAA   International Advertising Association. *World Advertising Expenditures*. (New York: I.A.A., biennial)
      1968 issue published 1970. Most comprehensive source of advertising data, much of which was obtained for them by International Research Associates.
ICPR Taylor, Charles T., et al. *World Handbook of Political and Social Indicators*. (2nd ed. in preparation)
      A compendium of demographic, economic, social and political data for every country collected around four base dates; 1950, 1955, 1960, and 1965. Much data is easily available through U.N. sources and useful primarily for historical time series. Data not readily available elsewhere refer to military expenditures, inequality indices, trade concentration indices, and political and cultural data. Prepared by the World Data Analysis Program of Yale University, the published volume will contain approximately 2/3 of the data collected. The entire collection will be available on computer tapes from the Inter-University Consortium for Political Research, Ann Arbor, Mich.
PAA   Pan American Airways. *New Horizons World Guide; Pan American's Travel Facts About 138 Countries*. Ed. Gerald W. Whitted. (New York, Pan American World Airways, 1970)
      A truly world-wide travel guide, most useful as a convenient source of basic weather statistics.
OAG   *Official Airline Guide*. (Chicago: American Aviation Publications, monthly)
      The basic American airlines timetable, including information on air distances and rates. Domestic and international editions.

A CONCEPTUAL FRAMEWORK FOR
INTERNATIONAL BUSINESS ARRANGEMENT

ISAIAH A. LITVAK
and PETER M. BANTING

The more unstable a foreign environment is, the more difficult it becomes for the international firm to establish and maintain control over its marketing arrangements in foreign countries. This is particularly the case in developing economies. Therefore, it becomes vital for the international marketer not only to evaluate those environmental elements which impinge upon his pattern of foreign involvement, but also to structure feedback systems which will enable him to minimize external threats to his firm's development in foreign countries. This paper presents a classification system which permits the international marketer to determine the marketing arrangement best suited for the foreign country, and the vulnerability of the firm's international structure to change.

Most comparative studies to date have been descriptive and general rather than analytical and specific. In the words of an eminent marketing authority, Professor Reavis Cox:

Much of the literature of comparative marketing combines observations by perceptive travellers with the results of inquiries among a few informed people and a survey of the easily available published materials. Most of it, however, does not dig very far beneath the surface. Someone takes a quick look in the course of a short trip made for some other purpose and reports back on what he has seen. He makes no systematic or thorough search for data that would be available if he had time to seek them out. He gathers no new materials through extensive field work.[1]

This absence of information, particularly in the case of the marketing middleman, is a serious omission because he has been and will continue to be a key factor in the stimulation of foreign investment, and the formation of international businesss arrangements.

Few companies when going international initiate their activities by establishing manufacturing facilities in the foreign country. They are more likely to take a cautious approach, where the risks associated with heavy investments may be minimized. Rather than having wholly owned distributive arrangements, they tend to employ the services of an established resident agent or merchant middleman. This first distributive arrangement is rarely the ideal. Pressures within the foreign environment, together with the company's desire to optimize its foreign market potential result in continual re-evaluation and reorganization of its international marketing arrangements. Because

From *Marketing and the New Science of Planning*, AMA 1968, no. 28, Fall 1968, pp. 460-467, published by the American Marketing Association, reprinted with permission of authors and publisher.

utilizing the manufacturers' agent is the most simple and least costly method of probing the foreign market for both small and large companies, and because the manufacturers' agent is frequently superseded by other middlemen, this article will focus on the agent as the starting point in the evolution of international business arrangements. A classification system will be formulated for evaluating the marketing middleman's vulnerability to change when he is employed by the foreign principals, and the relations will be shown between country-type and the direction in which the marketing-oriented middleman is most likely to adapt.

Much of the empirical data was obtained from personal interviews conducted by the authors with manufacturers' agents, merchant middlemen, and manufacturers in the United States, Canada, and South Africa, and from a questionnaire sent to manufacturers' agents associations.[2]

THE FINDINGS HIGHLIGHTED

The data collected suggest that there are certain strategic factors that have affected the development of distributive arrangements, particularly during the post-war era. These factors include nature of the product, concentration of customers, intensity of competition, resources of the middleman, market potential, degree of industrialization, cultural, lingual and geographical distance, legislation, and degree of political stability. Alone or in combination, they influence the way the distributive arrangement evolves and the middleman's role in international business arrangements.

The results of the study indicate that in both domestic and foreign markets the marketing middleman is more likely to evolve from being a pure agent:

a) the greater his resources are,
b) the more complex the product is,
c) the greater the market potential and regional concentration of customers are, and
d) the more competitive the market is.

The findings further indicate that the manufacturers' agent will more likely be utilized to both probe the market and participate in international business arrangements:

a) the greater the degree of political instability that exists in his country,
b) the greater the distance between his country and that of his principal in miles, language, and culture, and
c) the greater the proliferation of rules and regulations governing foreign investment in either the agent's or his principal's country.

SIGNIFICANT ENVIRONMENTAL FACTORS

These findings apply equally to the United States, Canada, South Africa, and other countries. Nonetheless, there are certain differences in the way the agent has developed from one country to another. Upon closer scrutiny, it may be seen that the rate at which an agent has developed in any one country, and the direction of his evolution within that country, are the result of the environment within which he operates. These differences are most apparent in agents who represent foreign principals. For example, numerous agents in South Africa and Mexico tend to evolve into manufacturers, while in Canada and the United States they tend to become merchant wholesalers.

The following paragraphs will first develop a classification system indicating the likelihood of an agent being vulnerable to such evolutionary environmental influences, then propose a theoretical framework which shows what institutional character the adaptable agent will be most likely to assume.

THE "HOT-COLD" COUNTRY CLASSIFICATION

Countries may be viewed as lying along a temperature gradient. "Hot" countries are those in which the environmental forces irresistibly push the agent toward new institutional structures. If he does not adapt, he finds he no longer has any principals to represent, or competitors have taken most of his business away. In other words, the environment is "too hot" for his continued existence as a pure agent.

At the other end of the gradient, the manufacturers' agent finds few threats to his continuation as a pure agent. His principal is more inclined to let the agent handle his accounts as he sees fit, and competitive pressures toward institutional change are less dynamic. This is the comfortably "cold" country.

The factors which lead to a country being classified as "hot," "moderate," "cold," or somewhere in between are defined as follows:

1) Political Stability—a system of government which permits representation of the major segments of its society, enjoys the confidence of its people, generates conditions for continuity of business operations, and is sympathetic to private enterprise. A "hot" factor when stability is high.
2) Market Opportunity—a sufficient number of customers with incompletely satisfied needs and the necessary resources with which to satisfy those needs for the product or service in question. A "hot" factor when opportunity is high.
3) Economic Development and Performance—the level of a country's eco-

nomic growth, efficiency, equity and stability, which shape the environment for private enterprise. Applying Rostow's classification[3] within the context of this definition, levels could be grouped as follows:

Low—the traditional society, the pre-conditions for take-off, and the take-off. A "cold" factor.

Medium—the drive to maturity. A "moderate" factor.

High—the age of high mass-consumption. A "hot" factor.

4) Cultural Unity—the values, goals, attitudes, social relationships and interactions between distinct segments within a country's people in terms of shared heritage, unassailed by competing groups. A "hot" factor when unity is high.

5) Legal Barriers—a proliferation of public measures in the form of laws and regulations which either deliberately or unintentionally restrict or discourage existing business activities and the future environment for private enterprise. A "cold" factor when barriers are high.

6) Physiographic Barriers—the obstacles to the development of efficient business operations created by the physical landscape or land forms of the country. A "cold" factor when barriers are high, and infrastructure is weak.

7) Geo-Cultural Distance—barriers created by geographical separation, cultural disparities between countries and problems of communication resulting from differences in social perspectives, attitudes and language. A "cold" factor when distance is high.

The matrix configuration of this temperature gradient classification is shown in Exhibit A.

Exhibit A THE COUNTRY TEMPERATURE GRADIENT—
A CLASSIFICATION SYSTEM OF ENVIRONMENTAL CHARACTERISTICS

Degree of Environmental Characteristics	HOT Country	MODERATE Country	COLD Country
Political Stability H-L	High	Medium	Low
Market Opportunity H-L	High	Medium	Low
Economic Development and Performance H-L	High	Medium	Low
Cultural Unity H-L	High	Medium	Low
Legal Barriers L-H	Low	Medium	High
Physiographic Barriers L-H	Low	Medium	High
Geo-Cultural Distance L-H	Low	Medium	High

Thus, for example, an agent in Canada who represents a United States manufacturer would find his country classified as follows:

Political Stability . . . . high (a hot factor)
Market Opportunity . . . . high (a hot factor)
Economic Development and Performance . . . . high (a hot factor)
Cultural Unity . . . . medium (a moderate factor)
Legal Barriers . . . . low (a hot factor)
Physiographic Barriers . . . . medium (a moderate factor)
Geo-cultural Distance . . . . low (a hot factor)

Since we find five "hot" and two "moderate" factors, we conclude that Canada is a relatively "hot" country under this classification system, and the manufacturers' agent probably will be forced to evolve as a marketing institution.

There are several reasons for likely evolution of the distributive arrangement away from simple agency representation. In a "hot" country, such as Canada, the foreign principal will experience a set of conditions conducive to foreign investment. The market potential for his product-mix is excellent. Few restrictions are imposed on direct injection of foreign capital and managerial skills. The government in power has shown its willingness to permit foreign-owned and controlled companies to repatriate part of their earnings. The government does not discriminate against foreign-owned firms in favor of domestic companies. In short, the U.S. company would perceive opportunities for greater profits through increased control over its distributive system in Canada, while the risks of its greater involvement would be minimal.

On the other hand, an agent in South Africa who represents a United States manufacturer would find his country classified as follows:

Political Stability . . . . low (a cold factor)
Market Opportunity . . . . medium (a moderate factor)
Economic Development and Performance . . . . . medium (a moderate factor)
Cultural Unity . . . . low (a cold factor)
Legal Barriers . . . . medium (a moderate factor)
Physiographic Barriers . . . . high (a cold factor)
Geo-cultural Distance . . . . high (a cold factor)

It can be seen that this classification with four "cold" factors and three "moderate" factors, represents South Africa as quite a "cold" country, and thus the agent is less vulnerable to being forced to evolve.

In this situation, the U.S. firm foresees high risks in committing capital investments to South Africa. While the governmental attitude toward foreign investment is not negative, latent unrest among the populace, uneven distribution of personal income, and the social policies practised by the government act as obstacles because they portend possible social upheaval and commercial uncertainty.

Exhibit B APPLICATION OF THE CLASSIFICATION SYSTEM

Environmental Characteristics	Canada		Gt. Britain		W. Germany		Japan		Greece	
	Hot	Cold	Hot	Cold	Hot	Cold	Hot	Cold	Hot	Cold
Political Stability	H		H		H		H			L
Market Opportunity	H			M	H		H			M
Economic Development and Performance	H			M	H		H			M
Cultural Unity		M	H		H		H			M
Legal Barriers	L		L			M	H		L	
Physiographic Barriers		M		L	L			M	M	
Geo-Cultural Distance	L		L			M		H		H

Environmental Characteristics	Spain		Brazil		S. Africa		India		Egypt	
	Hot	Cold	Hot	Cold	Hot	Cold	Hot	Cold	Hot	Cold
Political Stability		L		L		L	M			L
Market Opportunity		M		M		M	M			L
Economic Development and Performance		M		L		M	L			L
Cultural Unity		M		M		L	M		M	
Legal Barriers		M		H		M		H		H
Physiographic Barriers		H		H		H		H		H
Geo-Cultural Distance		H		H		H		H		H

Charts for several countries illustrate further the application of this classification system (see Exhibit B). These countries could then be ranked, when viewed as agent outlets for a U.S. based manufacturer, on a gradient ranging from "hot" to "cold" as follows:

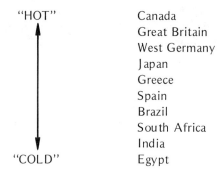

"HOT"

"COLD"

Canada
Great Britain
West Germany
Japan
Greece
Spain
Brazil
South Africa
India
Egypt

ADDING PRECISION TO THE MODEL

It should be noted that such ratings of countries will change over time. The changes may result from factors both internal and external to the country, necessitating continual surveillance and possible revision of the country's classification. For example, within a country a change in government may bring about a dramatic shift in its policy toward foreign business involvement. In the international business sphere, regional economic realignments, new resource developments, economic assistance programs, and international financial movements may force a re-examination of the country's rank. Within the foreign principal's own country, such phenomena as guidelines for foreign investment, restrictive trade practice rulings, and shifts in the political climate may have a similar effect on the country's evaluation. Of no less importance are the results of changes in the objectives and resources of the principal.

It is widely recognized that within a country the environmental elements tend to develop along parallel lines as the country matures. Thus, it is the exception when one environmental element predominates to such an extent that it negates the other environmental factors in placing a country along the temperature gradient. For example, the possibility exists that a country at either end of the distribution channel may institute a policy which completely precludes foreign commercial involvement, *e.g.* application of the U.S. "Trading with the Enemy Act" against Communist China, or severely hampers involvement, *e.g.* other communist countries.

Further, countries ranked according to the temperature gradient classification system are approximately positioned. Although several countries may exhibit an identical classification mix, finer calibration of their relative position is dependent upon additional subjective weights. Rarely will two firms give identical rating to the same country. One manufacturer may be in a far better position to establish a strong buyer franchise, and thus view the foreign country as relatively "warmer," than another manufacturer who does not enjoy a similar advantage. On the other hand, a manufacturer's greater international business sophistication may lead him to evaluate a country as being relatively "cooler" than his less experienced counterpart would evaluate it.

Product characteristics may warrant similar adjustments in the classification of a country. For example, for a highly technical and costly product, the country might be rated much "warmer" in the gradient than for a simple, inexpensive product.

INTERNATIONAL BUSINESS ARRANGEMENTS

The temperature gradient shows how susceptible an agent might be to evolutionary influences. But, it serves a further purpose. When superimposed upon the various types of business enterprise which may be used in a particular environment, it also predicts the type of institutional structure into which the manufacturers' agency is most likely to evolve. (See Exhibit C.)

The degree of control which a principal can exercise in a foreign market is related to the "temperature" classification of the country.

In a "hot" country, by definition, the environmental elements force the agent to evolve. His very survival hinges upon his ability to adapt to changing market conditions, and expectations of his principal. In fact, this is true of all marketing middlemen. Thus, in such an environment, the foreign principal can exercise maximum control over the evolutionary process. He may establish a branch sales office, a branch plant assembly operation, or a wholly owned manufacturing subsidiary. It is then within his discretion whether to retain the agent in a different capacity such as sales manager, salesman, branch manager, or distributive contact with the trade. On the other hand, he may choose to sever all ties with his former agent.

The foregoing situation is in fact the case experienced by Canadian agents representing American principals. Many of the present giants in Canadian industry originally employed agents to probe the Canadian market at the turn of the century. As the country developed, it rapidly moved up the temperature gradient from "cold" to extremely "hot" and, as a consequence, foreign principals bypassed Canadian agents. Thus, today, more than one-half of the manufacturing sector of the Canadian economy is controlled by non-residents, of which more than three-quarters is in the hands of American firms.

Modifying the exclusion of the Canadian agent has been the size of the foreign principal. While large principals have completely by-passed Canadian agents by establishing wholly owned Canadian subsidiaries, smaller principals have established sales branches and assembly plants, and in many instances, have absorbed the agent into their sales organization.

The case is completely reversed in a "cold" country where the agent is least susceptible to evolution. Here the agent shapes his own evolutionary

Exhibit C INSTITUTIONAL STRUCTURE GRADIENT FOR INTERNATIONAL BUSINESS ARRANGEMENTS

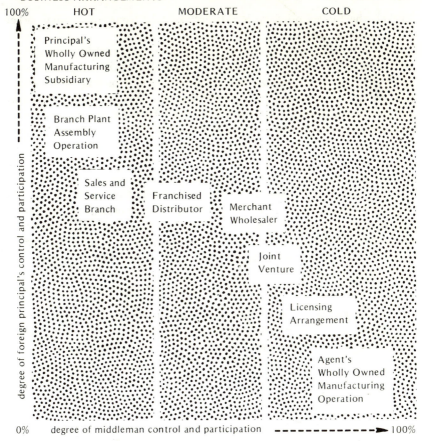

process. If he does not wish to change, he may continue as a pure agent unassailed by the influence of his foreign principal. On the other hand, if internal conditions such as competition, the agent's financial and managerial resources, and market expectations exert pressure upon his functioning as an institution, he is most likely to adapt by establishing his own manufacturing operation, entering into a licensing arrangement, participating in a joint venture arrangement, or becoming a merchant wholesaler. In any case, he retains maximum control over the way in which he evolves and it is extremely difficult for the foreign manufacturer to exercise any significant power in the relationship.

Egypt provides an illustration of this condition:

The machinery used to sell foreign goods has usually followed one of two forms: (1) selling through exclusive agents or representatives, and (2) selling through the manufacturers' own branches. Manufacturers' own branches have dwindled in importance as a result of import restrictions and exchange control. The exclusive agent is now the basic importing institution. He is the authorized representative of the foreign manufacturer and is responsible for selling and distributing the goods throughout Egypt.[4]

In fact, the foreign principal is virtually excluded from probing the market except through agents.

In South Africa, although foreign principals are not restricted from operating in the domestic market by such stringent legal barriers, the economy is still "relatively cold" and the internal market conditions exert evolutionary pressure upon the pure agent as an institution. Thus, when the marketing-oriented agent changes his institutional role, he does this because he so chooses. Consequently, he may actively negotiate joint venture and licensing agreements with his foreign principals or decide to engage in manufacturing on his own.

Foreign principals frequently may wish to enter such relatively "cold" countries as South Africa and Brazil, but are unwilling to experience the risks attendant to the country's "coldness." Thus, a foreign principal may seek out and initiate an arrangement with the agent, but does so in a situation where his control over the foreign operation is severly limited due to the agent's superior bargaining power over the negotiatory process. The following illustrations are examples of actual situations encountered in the South African market:

1) Certain agents in machinery and automobile distribution have recently decided to become assemblers or manufacturers on their own account through licensing agreements with their former principals.

2) In the cosmetics, hosiery, household appliances, and in consumer and industrial chemical fields, various agents have initiated their own manufacturing operations, some to the exclusion of their original principals, and others in partnership with them in the form of joint ventures. This new institutional arrangement has not prevented the South African entrepreneur from continuing in his capacity as an agent for other foreign manufacturers in non-competitive fields.

3) Some foreign manufacturers working through agents with limited resources have agreed to grant franchises to other South African entrepreneurs on the condition that the agent be retained in his capacity as a necessary distributive link. The most recent example has involved an agreement between an American foundation wear manufacturer, a South African clothing manufacturer and the manufacturers' agent.

Those countries lying in the moderate range of the temperature gradient exhibit an environmental setting wherein the pressures between agent and principal provide neither with absolute control. Thus, under pressure from his foreign principal, the agent may be persuaded to assume additional functions, but he retains sufficient flexibility to decide the course of his evolution. At the same time, he is still subject to domestic environmental pressures which in many instances have forced him to evolve into a merchant middleman in the capacity of either a merchant wholesaler, or a franchised distributor.

IMPLICATIONS

The theory proposed here has been developed to explain and predict the way in which distributive arrangements evolve over time within different environmental settings. To do this, it isolated the key environmental elements which make the manufacturers' agent vulnerable to change, and dictate the institutional direction of his evolution.

Today, firms in the United States are becoming increasingly aware that their very survival will depend on their business success in foreign markets. Whether the company is currently using any particular type of marketing middleman, or is planning to establish a new distributive arrangement, the conceptual framework is sufficiently flexible to predict the most favorable intermediary to employ, and what is likely to happen to that distributive arrangement. For example, in establishing a new distributive relationship, the company is better able to select the most effective intermediary and to determine whether it is necessary to build flexibility for change into the relationship.

On the other hand, a firm, already operating in, say, a "hot" country, with heavily commited investments, may be guided by this concept to relinquish control if the environment becomes "cooler." Without .this guidance, the company may find control wrested away at a high cost both financially and in terms of continuing goodwill. This information is critical to any company's attempt to plan its international operations effectively in a highly competitive and volatile world market. Moreover, because of the need to continually audit the firm's commitments in a rapidly changing multinational environment, the necessity of having operational concepts is intensified.

The temperature gradient theory is useful to those marketers who are either intending to explore foreign markets, or are already engaged in international business. It suggests:

a) the favorability of foreign markets, and the ease with which their opportunities may be realized,
b) the degree of control the foreign principal can exercise over his distributive arrangements, and
c) the degree of control the foreign principal can anticipate in the planning and development of his own operations in the foreign country.

REFERENCES

1. Reavis Cox, "The Search for Universals in Comparative Studies of Domestic Marketing Systems," *Proceedings of American Marketing Association Fall Conference, September, 1965*, p. 145.

2. The authors are indebted to the Canadian Department of Labour, under whose commission part of the research was done, and to Dr. Andre van der Merwe, Graduate School of Business, University of Cape Town, for his assistance in South Africa.

3. For a detailed description of Rostow's classification, see W. W. Rostow, *The Stages of Economic Growth* (Cambridge, Mass., Cambridge University Press, 1960).

4. H. W. Boyd, Jr., A. A. E. Sherbini, and A. F. Sherif, "Channels of Distribution for Consumer Goods in Egypt," *Journal of Marketing*. Vol. 25, (October, 1961), p. 32.

A MULTIVARIATE MODEL OF
MULTINATIONAL BUSINESS EXPANSION

JAGDISH N. SHETH
and RICHARD J. LUTZ

Introduction

Recently, Litvak and Banting [2] have developed a useful conceptual framework for international business arrangements based on empirical
data collected from a large number of manufacturers, their agents and other
middlemen in the United States, Canada and South Africa. A major aspect in
their conceptual framework is the threefold classification (hot-moderate-
cold) of countries with the use of the country's following environmental
factors: (1) political stability, (2) market opportunity, (3) economic development and performance, (4) cultural unity, (5) legal barriers, (6) physiographic
barriers, and (7) geo-cultural distance from the U.S. A hot-cold gradient or
index is then suggested in which the first four factors are considered hot
factors and the last three factors are cold factors.

Depending upon the intensity of each of the seven factors (high-medium-
low), Litvak and Banting suggest classification of a country as a hot, moderate, or cold country for foreign investment. If a country is found to be hot, it
is considered most profitable for a U.S. multinational corporation to heavily
invest its financial and managerial resources. On the other hand, if a country
is found to be a cold country, it is advisable to leave the financial and
managerial investment to the company's local agent. Litvak and Banting
describe the suitability of a number of business arrangements ranging from
simply exporting to establishing wholly owned subsidiaries in a foreign
country based on the threefold classification.

This conceptual framework seems to offer several advantages from the
point of view of long-range planning and expansion decisions of a multinational company. First, it presents, though somewhat crudely, a method of
allocating scarce resources selectively to some countries and some parts of the
world. Second, it specifies both the magnitude and the type of foreign
investment involvement depending upon the hotness or coolness of a country.
Accordingly, it gives insights into the relevance of a variety of foreign
investments ranging from joint ventures, through franchised operations, to
manufacturing and marketing the company's products. Third, the conceptual
framework neatly summarizes the evolutionary process of emergence of a
multinational corporation from a simple export house. Finally, and perhaps
equally important, the conceptual framework suggests how a large body of
secondary data on environmental factors can be effectively utilized to undertake long-range planning and business expansion.

Although the Litvak-Banting framework is conceptually useful and exciting, it suffers from a number of methodological and analytical problems. First, no analytical scheme is developed which will transform the values of the environmental factors into the gradient of hotness. Second, although the environmental factors are explicitly described, no attempt is made to suggest their operational indicators from the secondary data banks. Third, the three-fold classification of countries is at best judgmental and arbitrary rather than empirically derived. Fourth, there is no discussion about the relative impor-tances of various environmental factors: Is political stability more important than economic development or performance? Finally, it would seem that the environmental factor called market opportunity is considerably different from the other six factors: it is specific to an industry or product while other factors are invariant to type of foreign investment. Furthermore, it is gener-ally necessary that primary data be collected to estimate market opportunity of a product or industry, whereas one can get by with secondary data for the other six factors. Accordingly it might be best at first to classify countries on the six factors and then to investigate the market potential in those countries which promise to be serious candidates for foreign investment.

The purpose of this paper is to operationalize the Litvak-Banting frame-work with the use of a secondary data bank. In the process, it is hoped that some insights will be presented to remove, or at least minimize, the method-ological problems enumerated above. Finally, a multivariate model is at-tempted which suggests one analytical approach to the development of the hot-cold gradient on which countries can then be graded from the point of view of future investment and business expansion.

SOURCES OF SECONDARY DATA
AND OPERATIONAL DEFINITIONS

The secondary data related to the six environmental factors were obtained from three separate sources: (1) The Yale Political Data Program, (2) The Dimensionality of Nations Study, and (3) The Bank-Dextor Cross-Polity Survey. These data are a part of the data archives stored at Survey Research Laboratory, University of Illinois. All three data sources are related to 1961-1962 and represent profiles of a total of 82 countries. However, the USSR and Communist China were not included in the final analysis due to their large ideological differences with the United States. Accordingly, a total of 80 countries were included in the development of the hot-cold gradient from the point of view of U.S. corporate foreign investment.

From the complete profile on each country, a total of 26 variables were found to be related to the six environmental factors. However, due to missing data on a number of these variables, a final list of 15 variables was prepared. The list is reproduced in Table 1 along with the brief description of each environmental factor as given by Litvak and Banting.

Political stability is indicated by the following three indices: (1) govern-

Table 1 ENVIRONMENTAL FACTORS: THEIR DESCRIPTION
AND OPERATIONAL DEFINITIONS

---

(1) *Political Stability*

  (a) A system of government which permits representation of the major segments of its society, enjoys the confidence of its people, generates conditions for continuity of business operations, and is sympathetic to private enterprise.

  (b) Variables used to represent political stability:

Governmental stability	4-point scale
Freedom from group opposition	4-point scale
Political enculturation	3-point scale

(2) *Economic Development and Performance*

  (a) The level of a country's economic growth, efficiency, equity and stability, which shape the environment for private enterprise.

  (b) Variables used to represent Economic Development:

Economic development scale	4-point scale
Energy consumption	megawatt hours

(3) *Cultural Unity*

  (a) The values, goals, attitudes, social relationships and interactions between distinct segments within a country's people in terms of shared heritage, unassailed by competing groups.

  (b) Variables used to represent Cultural Unity:

Religious homogeneity	3-point scale
Racial homogeneity	3-point scale
Linguistic homogeneity	3-point scale

(4) *Legal Barriers*

  (a) A proliferation of public measures in the form of laws and regulations which either deliberately or unintentionally restrict or discourage existing business activities and the future environment for private enterprise.

  (b) Variables used to represent Legal Barriers:

Import plus exports	millions of U.S. dollars
Tariffs on imports/Total value of imports	percentages

(5) *Physiographic Barriers*

  (a) The obstacles to the development of efficient business operations created by the physical landscape or land forms of the country.

  (b) Variables used to represent Physiographic Barriers:

Air passenger km flown	in 10,000s
Road density	km/100 km^2
Railroad density	km/100 km^2

(6) *Geo-cultural Distance*

  (a) Barriers created by geographical separation, cultural disparities between countries, and problems of communication resulting from differences in social perspectives, attitudes, and language.

  (b) Variables used to represent Geo-cultural distance:

Degree of westernization	6-point scale
Air distance from U.S.	inches on global map

mental stability, (2) freedom from group opposition, and (3) political encul-
turation. The latter reflects the political consciousness of a country.

Cultural unity is represented by three different indices of homogeneity.
They are (1) religious, (2) racial, and (3) linguistic homogeneity, each being a
three-point scale.

Economic development and performance is reflected by two variables: (1)
an economic development scale (a four-point scale), and (2) energy consumption in megawatt hours.

Legal barriers are indicated by two indirect variables. The first is the level
of imports and exports measured in millions of U.S. dollars. It is argued that a
greater degree of international trade will be present in a country characterized
by fewer legal barriers, and vice versa. Similarly, the second variable is the
level of tariff on imports as a percentage of the total value of imports. Again,
the greater the number of legal barriers, the more likely it is to find a higher
levy of tariffs, and vice versa.

Physiographic barriers are also indicated, although indirectly, by the three
modes of transportation. It is assumed that the greater the physiographic
barriers present in a country due to mountains, deserts, and rivers, the less
will be the density of air, road, and railroad transports. By simultaneously
taking into account all the three major surface and aerial methods of transportation, we presume that substitution effects among them, if any, are
included.

Finally, geo-cultural distance is measured in two ways, both of which are
related primarily to the distance of a country from the United States. The
first measure is an index of westernization, a six-point scale. The second is the
air distance from the United States.

The Multivariate Model

Multivariate methods are becoming more common in international business. Perhaps the single most common method has been cluster
analysis to classify countries on a profile of economic and demographic
characteristics. Our objective here is to derive an index or gradient on which
countries can be located. As such, the objective is somewhat different from
strict classification. A specialized multivariate method, therefore, is proposed
in this paper to achieve this objective. We may also note that the procedure
resembles factor analysis, but it differs from it at various stages of calcula-
tions.

Let X_{Nxn} be a data matrix with x_{ij} elements, $(i = 1, 2, 3, \ldots N, j = 1, 2, 3,$
$\ldots n)$ where x_{ij} refers to the ith country's value on variable j. Each row of the
data matrix represents the profile of a country, and each column represents
the distribution of values of a given variable.

If X is a rectangular matrix $(N > n)$ and all the cells have values, it is possible to state X as a product of three other matrices following the basic structure theorem. Thus $X = U\Gamma W$ where U and W are orthonormal matrices $(U^1 = U^{-1}$ and $W^1 = W^{-1})$ containing vectors associated with the data matrix and Γ is a diagonal matrix containing roots associated with the data matrix.

By selecting only some of the vectors and roots from the U, Γ and W matrices (generally equal to the rank of the data matrix X), it is possible to construct an approximate data matrix, $\hat{X}$, which is the best approximation in the least squares sense. Thus

$$X \sim \hat{X}_{Nxn} = U_{Nxr}\Gamma_{rxr}W_{rxn}$$

It is now possible to state that the U_{Nxr} represents projections of the rows (countries) on some r-dimensional space $(r < n < N)$ and W_{rxn} represents simultaneous projections of the columns (variables) on the same r-dimensional space.

Each of the r-dimensions, after proper rotation, can be looked upon as a hot-cold gradient from the viewpoint of that country which is most closely associated with that dimension. The closeness of association of a country with a dimension is represented by the size of the projected value of that country. It is then easy to read off relative values of all other countries in terms of their degree of hotness or coolness on that dimension by examining the elements of the rth vector.

In order to obtain the basic structure of a data matrix, Sheth [4] has suggested the use of Eckart-Young theorem stated below:

$$X = U\Gamma W$$
$$XX^1 = (U\Gamma W)(W^1\Gamma U^1)$$
$$= U\Gamma^2 U^1$$

because $W^1 = W^{-1}$ and therefore $WW^1 = 1$. In other words, by obtaining the *cross-products* matrix of a data matrix, it is possible to derive two of the three matrices on the right hand side of the equation. It is relatively easy then to obtain the W matrix:

$$W = \Gamma^{-1}U^1X$$

Once the three product matrices are derived, it is equally easy to choose the first r roots and associated vectors to form the approximate matrix $\hat{X}$.

The above multivariate method underlies factor analysis because a factor loadings matrix is defined as the $U\Gamma = A$ matrix and a factor scores matrix is defined as the $W = F$ matrix. Thus

$$X = AF$$

However, there are a number of subtle and significant differences between the model and factor analysis:

(a) In factor analysis typically the interest is in the correlational structure among variables (R-type factor analysis), whereas in our model the interest is in the structure among countries (Q-type factor analysis).

(b) Typically, factor analysis is performed on a correlation matrix. In our model, we obtain the rank of the data matrix X through its cross-products matrix.

(c) The emphasis in factor analysis is the overall parsimony of the data matrix. In our model, parsimony is directly related to the specific viewpoints the researcher is interested in. Accordingly, the rotational procedures may vary between the two methods.

Results and Discussion

From the three sources of secondary data, a data matrix $X_{N \times n}$ was constructed consisting of 80 countries ($N = 80$) and 15 variables ($n = 15$). The data matrix was converted from raw scores to standard scores in order to remove the effects of varying types of units of measurement of variables. This is especially necessary in multicountry, multitrait data because the latter typically combine economic, social, and demographic types of information. Consequently, income is measured in U.S. dollars, whereas distance is measured in miles and population is measured in terms of density. In our data also, the units of measurement are disparate in several instances; e.g., energy consumption, import plus exports, etc.

The standard scores matrix was then decomposed through the use of its cross-products matrix. Since this study is an attempt to operationalize the Litvak-Banting framework specifically in terms of U.S. corporate investment, our interest is in only one viewpoint—the viewpoint represented by that dimension on which the United States is most closely associated. Table 2 reproduces that dimension. It represents a hot-cold continuum based on the six environmental factors. The relative positive values of countries reflect the degree of hotness, and the relative negative values of countries reflect the degree of coldness from the viewpoint of U.S. corporate foreign investment in those countries.

A number of observations can be made on the results:

(a) Most other advanced countries have the highest "hotness" values. These include United Kingdom, West Germany, France, Netherlands, Canada and Belgium. Conversely, most developing and small countries have highest coldness values. These include Yemen, Laos, Afghanistan, Nepal, North Vietnam, etc.

(b) Although Canada and Mexico are closer in geographical proximity, numerous other countries are shown as better candidates for foreign investment.

Table 2 THE "HOT-COLD" GRADIENT FROM U.S. VIEWPOINT

Country	Value	Country	Value
U.S.A.	13.22	Venezuela	− .40
U.K.	4.60	Panama	− .41
W. Germany	3.44	Costa Rica	− .47
France	2.64	Turkey	− .47
Netherlands	2.12	Bulgaria	− .47
Canada	2.01	Ecuador	− .52
Belgium	2.00	Libya	− .60
Denmark	1.33	Bolivia	− .61
Italy	1.32	Philippines	− .64
Taiwan	1.16	Egypt	− .72
Japan	1.13	Peru	− .73
Sweden	1.13	Lebanon	− .80
Poland	.93	Haiti	− .88
Switzerland	.86	Guatemala	− .93
Ireland	.83	Liberia	− .94
Argentina	.81	Ceylon	− .97
Australia	.76	Albania	− .99
Norway	.73	Thailand	−1.00
Austria	.73	Mongolia	−1.07
E. Germany	.72	Paraguay	−1.13
Mexico	.58	N. Korea	−1.16
Finland	.47	Iran	−1.23
Brazil	.46	Indonesia	−1.23
New Zealand	.40	S. Korea	−1.24
Czechoslovakia	.33	Ethiopia	−1.25
Spain	.23	Cambodia	−1.28
Colombia	.22	Saudi Arabia	−1.31
Greece	.16	Syria	−1.32
Hungary	.05	S. Africa	−1.33
Portugal	− .00	S. Vietnam	−1.37
Uruguay	− .13	Jordan	−1.42
Yugoslavia	− .16	Iraq	−1.44
Honduras	− .16	Pakistan	−1.52
El Salvador	− .17	Burma	−1.55
Chile	− .18	Israel	−1.57
India	− .19	N. Vietnam	−1.62
Nicaragua	− .23	Nepal	−1.68
Cuba	− .26	Afghanistan	−1.86
Dominican Rep.	− .29	Laos	−1.89
Rumania	− .29	Yemen	−1.99

(c) Portugal acts as the "true" neutral country from an investment view-point. It is neither hot nor cold because of its zero value. It should, however, be remembered that this neutrality is *relative* to other countries and not in any absolute sense.

(d) The East European and the other communist countries in Latin America, Africa, and Asia do not systematically cluster together in the cold spectrum of the continuum. For example, Poland, East Germany, Czechoslovakia, and Hungary have positive values.

(e) It is somewhat surprising to find that even the "hottest" country, the United Kingdom, is considerably separated on the continuum from the United States. This implies that overseas investment in general is more problematic than domestic investment.

Conclusion

In summary, we have attempted in this paper to show how one multivariate method can be effectively utilized to transform the Litvak-Banting conceptual framework into an analytical model of overseas business expansion. It is also demonstrated that the secondary data, which are readily and cheaply accessible, can be meaningfully utilized if one at first derives a conceptual framework.

REFERENCES

1. Liander, Bertil (ed.) *Comparative Analysis for International Marketing* (Allyn & Bacon, 1967).

2. Litvak, I. A. and P. M. Banting, "A Conceptual Framework for International Business Arrangements," in R. L. King (ed.) *Marketing and the New Science of Planning* (American Marketing Association, 1968), pp. 460-467.

3. Nunnally, J. C., *Psychometric Theory* (New York: McGraw-Hill Book Company, 1967).

4. Sheth, J. N., "Using Factor Analysis to Estimate Parameters," *Journal of American Statistical Association*, Vol. 64, September 1969, pp. 808-822.

3

ORGANIZATION AND MANAGEMENT

Strategies of Organizational Structure

ORGANIZING A WORLDWIDE BUSINESS

GILBERT H. CLEE
and WILBUR M. SACHTJEN

Actions and reactions of U.S. firms in evolving different management structures to tackle complex international problems.

In recent years substantial numbers of major U.S. corporations have committed themselves for the first time to full-scale, long-term participation in the intense and sophisticated rivalry of worldwide enterprise. A survey by McKinsey & Company indicates that 100 leading U.S. companies, accounting for more than half of total U.S. corporate investment abroad, have been increasing their overseas investments almost five times as fast as their domestic assets. Moreover, a growing number of American companies plan on deriving a significant share of their sales, profits, and future growth from overseas activities. Already, as another survey of U.S. corporate activity overseas indicates, more than 20 important U.S. corporations are earning more than half their profits abroad.[1]

Both the rise in U.S. financial commitments overseas and the stepped-up foreign competition in our domestic markets reflect a significant change in the nature of international competition. Increasingly, the tempo and character of this competition are being determined by management decisions in a growing group of true world enterprises. Headquartered in London, Brussels, Tokyo, Geneva, or New York, these companies no longer plan their strategy in the manner of domestic companies with interests abroad. Instead, they apply their corporate resources on a global basis to exploit growth and profit opportunities wherever they may be found in the world.

NEW PRESSURES

In undertaking the commitment to world enterprise, however, U.S. businessmen have found themselves confronting a whole new range of problems. If managing a domestic business is complex, managing an interna-

From *Harvard Business Review*, November-December 1964. Copyright © 1964 by the President and Fellows of Harvard College; all rights reserved.

tional enterprise is infinitely more so because of the many new variables bearing on crucial management decisions. Consequently, organizational structures and relationships that may have worked smoothly for an export-oriented domestic company soon show signs of strain when management begins to wrestle with problems like these:

What kind of relationship should we establish between domestic and foreign operations to enable the more experienced domestic companies to give effective technical and functional guidance to the less advanced overseas subsidiaries? What incentive can we give them to do so, particularly if we lack majority control?

What position should we take with respect to local ownership participation? Do we need the tight control that only majority or 100% ownership will provide? Or can we operate successfully as a minority partner where necessary (as in India, Japan, and some of the emerging countries)?

How do we develop a flow of managerial manpower with the background, technical capability, and breadth of perspective to function effectively in different national environments?

How do we develop a system for planning and control that will (1) coordinate objectives, strategies, and action programs for all worldwide activities; and (2) provide an information flow to keep key executives informed on our progress, alert management to important external developments, and provide consistent and accurate cost data?

How do we resolve the complex financial problems faced by all world enterprises? In raising funds for overseas expansion, for example, what capital market should we go to, who should issue the debt or equity, and how should the financing be timed in light of foreign exchange considerations? Again, when cash flow exceeds current internal requirements, where and how can the surplus funds be most profitably put to work?

As overseas commitments increase, these growing problems begin to exert severe pressures on existing organizational alignments. In this article, we shall be concerned with the organizational actions and reactions of those U.S. corporations that are confronted with the problems and pressures of managing a true world enterprise.

Dominant Patterns

At the outset, it should be noted that no two world enterprises pass through the same organizational stages in the same way. No two arrive at precisely the same organizational pattern. Nor should they. Companies and circumstances both differ. Indeed, some companies, either because of the nature of their product or because of the limitations of management capacity, will never have a sufficient volume of international activity to be concerned with these problems at all.

Nonetheless, it is significant that among the major U.S. companies committed to investment abroad, three basic organizational structures have evolved in response to the growing pressures, and enough experience has now been accumulated to permit some meaningful evaluation of them. Each of the structural patterns—which are, of course, subject to many variations and modifications—has its own distinctive rationale. Each offers advantages for companies in particular situations and at particular stages of their transition to world enterprise.

These basic organizational patterns are:

1. Variants of the traditional *international division* structure, all displaying a shift of responsibility for policy and worldwide strategic planning to the corporate level.
2. The *geographic* structure, replacing the international division with line managers at the top-management level who bear full operating responsibility for subsidiaries in assigned geographic areas.
3. The *product* structure, replacing the international division with executives at the top-management level who bear worldwide responsibility for development of individual product groups.

In the balance of this article, we propose to describe these dominant types, give detailed examples of each, and explore the advantages and problems they raise for top management. Such an analysis, we believe, should be useful to any company entering or experiencing the transition to world enterprise.

INTERNATIONAL DIVISION STRUCTURE

In some companies, responsibility for broad policy and strategic planning for overseas operations, once in the hands of an international division or actually carried out by affiliates acting independently, has shifted to executives at the corporate level without significant change in the traditional formal structure (see Exhibit 1). Operational responsibilities, such as running the overseas plants and developing markets in individual foreign countries, are handled by the subsidiaries and affiliates, with corporate or international division assistance given as required. The international division may continue to coordinate export sales from the U.S. operation to foreign affiliates and export markets. But it may also function as a coordinating "middleman" between production facilities anywhere in the world and the corporation's total complex of worldwide markets.

Transition at Alpha

The Alpha Corporation,[2] a giant automobile manufacturer with plants in 20 countries, its own sales operations in 18 others, and more than 100,000 workers overseas, has approached the problems of managing a world

Exhibit 1 INTERNATIONAL DIVISION STRUCTURE

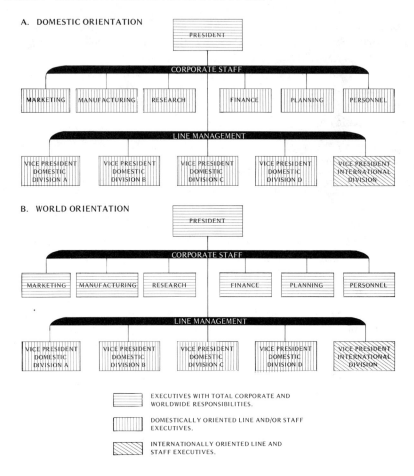

A. DOMESTIC ORIENTATION

B. WORLD ORIENTATION

EXECUTIVES WITH TOTAL CORPORATE AND WORLDWIDE RESPONSIBILITIES.

DOMESTICALLY ORIENTED LINE AND/OR STAFF EXECUTIVES.

INTERNATIONALLY ORIENTED LINE AND STAFF EXECUTIVES.

enterprise without any major departure from the international division struc-ture. Within that framework, however, its managerial setup has undergone important shifts in recent years.

During the lifetime of Alpha's founder, its foreign affiliates had been handled more in the fashion of personal investments than as extensions of the U.S. operation. To be sure, the founder and a few corporate officers main-tained close contact with the foreign affiliates. But in practice—beginning in the late 1920's, when they were given control of foreign sales and assembly—the two big foreign manafuacturing affiliates had been making virtually all the key decisions regarding overseas activities.

Need for Tighter Control. In 1948, three years after taking command of the company, Alpha's new chief executive turned his attention to interna-tional opportunities and problems. Aware that a potentially huge car and truck market was almost certain to emerge in postwar Europe, he realized that this market could never be won with high-cost U.S. and Canadian output. To wage an effective competitive battle, it was clear, would require European production bases. And this, he reasoned, meant tighter operating control over the big foreign manufacturing affiliates, which were hardly prepared to exploit in an effective, coordinated way the massive opportunities that would soon be developing.

For more than 20 years these two subsidiaries had been virtually autonomous companies with strongly entrenched local managements, exercising ownership control over all the other foreign affiliates. But then the new chief executive made it clear that he wanted ownership control of all foreign activities to rest in the United States, with broad policy and strategic planning for the international activities emanating from a single U.S. office.

Therefore, in addition to supplying the foreign affiliates with technical and management skills to help them recover from the havoc of World War II, corporate headquarters began increasingly to assume control of key management decisions for these operations.

Domestically Oriented Managment. Two years before corporate headquarters "reached out" for control of the foreign affiliates, an international division had been set up in New York to channel and coordinate the dealings between the domestic company and its foreign affiliates. From 1948 on, however, decisions on policy and strategic planning for the overseas operations were increasingly made directly by top corporate management. The responsibilities of the international division were, and continue to be, mainly confined to coordinating overseas activities, providing advice and assistance to its foreign companies, developing markets in individual countries, and channeling output from producing affiliates to distributors in areas without assembly facilities.

Practically speaking, however, Alpha continues to be a domestically oriented company. The most urgent pressures and preoccupations of corporate headquarters executives involve meeting competition on the domestic front, not overseas. And Alpha's foreign expansion plans are also heavily influenced by the international strategy of its most powerful domestic competitor. Moreover, there has been a discernible tendency to fill key positions in the international division with seasoned domestic managers.

Meanwhile, the overseas activities are being carried on within an increasingly apparent framework of corporate policy and strategy. Corporate headquarters exercises fairly strong worldwide control over all products and planning, and the individual foreign units are functioning much more like operating entities than like the autonomous companies they were in the past. The international division now has responsibility for running the overseas plants, determining minor product modifications from country to country, and increasing penetration in individual markets. At the same time, though, considerable flexibility remains to the overseas operating units. A manager responsible for sales development in a particular market, for example, is free to explore the opportunities for more economical vehicle sourcing for his operations.

Expansion at Beta

Another example of the continued use of the international division pattern in an important world enterprise is Beta, Inc., a large manufacturer of computers and other business machines. Beta's top management has
always devoted a great deal of attention to worldwide problems and opportunities. For many years, the overseas activities have been grouped together in
a separate corporation, quite apart from Beta's domestic divisions. Historically, this international corporation has operated with considerable autonomy,
though most major product-development activity has emanated from the
United States divisions.

Unlike Beta's domestic operations, which are laid out along product and
functional lines, the operations of the international corporation are organized
on a geographic basis. The range of products sold by any one geographic unit
in the international corporation is limited only by the state of development
of local markets and by local import policies. Some of Beta's foreign units
have manufacturing facilities to produce part of the product line, but they
depend on the domestic manufacturing operations for items which are not in
heavy demand overseas.

As Beta's international operations have expanded—in many cases reaching
a level of development comparable to that of its domestic divisions—management has felt a growing need for worldwide policy determination, for effective global product strategy, and for the development of better ways to meet
the needs of individual users on a worldwide basis. In response, the corporate
staff, which has long had worldwide functional responsibilities, is devoting an
increasing share of its time and effort to overseas activities.

Variety of Reasons

How is a company such as Alpha able to alter long-standing
management decision-making patterns for its foreign operations so completely without making major changes in its basic organizational pattern?
Why does Beta's management continue to favor the international division
form while setting worldwide policy and controlling the approval of worldwide operating plans at the corporate level? And why do other companies as
deeply committed as these two to worldwide activities sometimes prefer to
retain the international division form?

Analysis indicates that they may do so for one or more of five reasons:

(1) Formal organizational changes sometimes threaten to disrupt delicate
working relationships, particularly in the case of long-established overseas
subsidiaries under strong, well-entrenched local managements who are used to
running their operations without interference. In this situation, it may be
desirable to avoid major organizational realignments while seeking closer
coordination between domestic and overseas activities or strengthening corporate control of worldwide policy and strategy. The same considerations are
likely to apply where the parent company lacks majority control.

(2) Top management may believe that the foreign activities will get better direction with an international division than with a different organizational form. Under the international division pattern, overseas operations (particularly individual subsidiaries) can benefit from extra management attention that may be needed at the outset. Later on, some other organizational structure may prove more appropriate.

Where the domestic operations are many times larger than those overseas and where corporate management finds it difficult to get a diverse group of domestic divisions to devote adequate effort to their overseas counterparts, the international division form has a good deal of merit. Multiple-product-line companies have the option of organizing the international division on a product, rather than a geographic, basis, thereby encouraging a closer liaison with domestic divisions.

The international division recommends itself with special force in situations where broad-scale international activities are relatively new to a company and where most members of senior operating management lack experience with worldwide problems. Later, as overseas interests become more important to the company and top management gains assurance in handling global problems, a shift in the organizational pattern may become desirable.

(3) Because management views domestic performance as the primary measure of success, the company's key executives may be domestically oriented even though they participate in policy and strategy formulation for the overseas activities. In such a situation, the big foreign affiliates often bypass the international division on major matters and deal directly with corporate management. As long as it achieves tight and effective financial control, top management generally has little inclination to tamper with the existing organizational framework, despite this shortcut in the chain of command.

(4) The company may have worked out special ways, peculiar to its own situation, of deriving the key benefits of another organizational pattern without relinquishing the international division form. If so, it has no compelling motive to make a purely structural realignment.

(5) Finally, the company may not have enough trained, capable executive personnel to staff a worldwide organization effectively.

Problems & Disadvantages

The international division form can become ineffective when a company's overseas activities shift significantly from "exporting" to self-contained operations at many points on the globe. Under these circumstances, too strong an international division can hamper corporate direction of worldwide activities. Ironically, the more independent an international division becomes, the more it tends to insulate corporate management from overseas problems and opportunities.

For a worldwide company with a reasonably diverse product line, the international division form may impede management's efforts to mobilize the resources of the total company to accomplish a global objective. Even with superb coordination at the corporate level, global planning for individual products or product lines is carried out at best awkwardly by two "semi-autonomous" organizations—the domestic company and the interantional division. To add a series of country (or area) managements makes the problem still more difficult.

GEOGRAPHIC STRUCTURE

The second basic organizational form that has emerged as companies evolve toward functioning world enterprises is the geographic structure (see Exhibit 2), which is characterized by the assignment of operational responsibility for geographic areas of the world to line managers, with

Exhibit 2 GEOGRAPHIC STRUCTURE

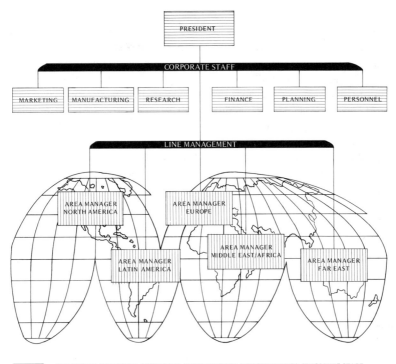

EXECUTIVES WITH TOTAL CORPORATE AND WORLDWIDE RESPONSIBILITIES. CORPORATE STAFF ACTIVITIES ON A WORLDWIDE BASIS GENERALLY INVOLVE POLICY MATTERS, STRATEGIC PLANNING, BASIC PRODUCT PLANNING, FUNCTIONAL GUIDANCE TO LINE GEOGRAPHIC UNITS, AND COORDINATION OF ACTIVITIES BETWEEN GEOGRAPHIC UNITS.

EXECUTIVES WITH LINE RESPONSIBILITY FOR ALL OPERATIONS IN A PARTICULAR GEOGRAPHIC AREA.

corporate headquarters retaining responsibility for worldwide strategic planning and control. (Strategic planning, in this context, includes such critical decisions as the businesses to engage in, the nature of the basic product line, and the location of major facilities. Adaptation of the basic product to meet local need is, in contrast, an area activity).

In the geographic form of organization, which has replaced the international division form today in many companies, both single-product-line and multiple-product-line, the United States has become simply one of a number of world markets. Producing and selling operations are grouped into geographic units. Sometimes the make-and-sell operations in a given geographic unit are self-contained, with most or all of the company's output in a given area being sold locally. Then again, sometimes there is a substantial flow of semifinished parts or fully assembled units from one area to another.

In the geographic form, responsibility for all products in a particular area is assigned to a single line executive who reports to corporate management. Policy, strategic and logistic planning, and major product development are handled at the corporate level.

Three examples will serve to illustrate the emergence of the geographic structure in varying circumstances.

Homogeneous Gamma

The geographic form has been commonly used by companies with closely related product lines—such as pharmaceuticals, farm implements, soft drinks, home applicances, or packaged food products—which are sold in similar end-use markets around the world.

Some years ago Gamma, Ltd., a huge international farm equipment manufacturer whose operations had been organized along regional lines, adopted an organizational structure built around a series of largely self-contained marketing and manufacturing *operations* units. This grouping is not regional; that is, it is not divided into broad areas (North America, Latin America, or Europe). Rather, it is centered on important individual markets (the United Kingdom, France, Germany, the United States, and Canada). Supplementing these units is an *export marketing* unit to cover sales in parts of the world where Gamma has no manufacturing operations.

Longer-range corporate strategy—determination of the basic worldwide product line, decisions on major facilities, and changes in the logistic product flow from production sources to markets—is set at corporate headquarters. But these decisions are heavily influenced by *operations unit* judgments and recommendations. Each unit is responsible for determining the product lines best suited to its local markets. Besides directing the logistic flow of components and completed machines between countries, corporate-level executives coordinate the operations unit product planning and make strategic decisions on the nature of basic Gamma product development. Then managers at the local level carry out the engineering and product development modifications needed to meet market requirements.

Diversified Delta

Less commonly, the geographic form is also used by companies with reasonably diverse product lines. One example is the Delta Company, a fairly diversified maker of electronics products, which has established a distinctive regional organizational pattern. Four *area* managers (North America; Latin America; Europe/Middle East/Africa; and Far East/Pacific) are fully responsible for day-to-day operations of all Delta units within their geographical assignments. Regional offices for both North American and Latin American operations are located in New York; for Europe, in Brussels; and for the Far East, in Hong Kong. And reporting to these regional headquarters are individual *country* organizations in more than 30 nations.

Because much of its activity had been carried on overseas for decades, Delta was able to move into the area form unusually fast. In 1959 foreign operating companies, which were previously more or less autonomous, were drawn together for tighter control and closer coordination. Corporate headquarters quickly assumed ultimate responsibility for long-range worldwide strategic planning, and began to exert much tighter direction over the foreign companies. Now both short- and long-range plans are developed locally, reviewed at the *area* manager level, then submitted to corporate management for review and approval. Thus, although planning clearly reflects local needs and requirements, corporate headquarters can closely control capital investments and make other strategic decisions.

The Delta Company, it should be noted, has a special need for local identification in the areas where it operates. Since much of its manufacturing output goes to local governments and telephone companies, Delta's individual country organizations must try to avoid the appearance of having foreign control. Moreover, their products must be adapted to meet varying local requirements and specifications. Its *area/country* type of geographic organization enables Delta to fit its sales efforts and product specifications closely to local market needs.

Major Oil Companies

Another kind of business enterprise that employs the geographic concept is the international oil company, where key decisions on concessions, refinery scheduling, and tanker fleet management are logically made on a centralized basis, with geographic units operating within that framework. Worldwide exploration is essentially a corporate activity, as are major investment decisions such as building new refineries and pipelines. Moreover, the supply and distribution function, which works out the worldwide logistic flow of crude to an international complex of refineries, terminals, and markets, can perform effectively only on a centralized basis.

Understandably, in different oil companies the geographic structure takes varying forms. In one, for example, the area manager exercises true line responsibility for operations in his particular geographic area. In another, the area manager functions essentially as a coordinator, with instructions emanating from strong functional departments at corporate headquarters. But despite such variations the formal division by geographic areas is a common organizational feature among the giant international oil companies.

Common Characteristics

Companies successfully using the geographic organizational structure share two significant characteristics:

(1) The great bulk of sales revenue is derived from similar end-use markets.
(2) Local marketing requirements are critical. (For example, Delta's communications equipment is marketed to telephone companies around the world; but since each foreign government establishes its own product specifications, this equipment is really produced and sold to highly individualized markets.)

The geographic organizational form is well suited to coping with these problems, since variations from market to market in a centrally developed basic product can be dealt with at close range. Normally, such adjustments require only modest technological skills that can easily be provided at the *area* level or below. When greater skills are needed, they can be supplied from corporate headquarters.

The geographic pattern also works well where the product is highly standardized but techniques for penetrating local markets differ. For example:

A major soft-drink maker ended the separation of its international and domestic operations almost a year ago, placing worldwide direction of marketing, finance, and research at the corporate level. To strengthen their contact with corporate management, the overseas operations have been organized into geographic divisions. Each division is headed by an experienced area manager located at corporate headquarters.

Problems & Disadvantages

The tasks of coordinating product variations, transferring new ideas and techniques from one country to another, and optimizing the logistic flow of product from source to worldwide markets frequently prove difficult for companies using the geographic organizational form, particularly those whose products are many or diverse.

One organizational response to these problems, though by no means a universally satisfactory one, has been the creation of a unique type of *product* manager at the corporate level who is assigned worldwide responsibilities for particular products or product lines. Each product manager follows the progress of his assigned product everywhere in the world, acting as an "exchange desk" to transfer successful developments from area to area and recommending worldwide strategy for individual products with respect to broad markets and basic design changes. But in this arrangement, although the corporate *product* manager's purpose in the organizational structure is easy to describe, his operating relationships with the line *area* managers are liable to be ambiguous.

PRODUCT STRUCTURE

The third basic organizational pattern, more recent in origin than the other two forms, assigns worldwide product *responsibility* to product group executives at the line management level, and coordinates all product *activity* in a given geographical area (see Exhibit 3) through area specialists at the corporate staff level.

Thus, overall goals and strategies for the total enterprise and for each product group are set at corporate headquarters. Within these corporate guidelines, strategic plans for each product group are drawn together by the product group executives for review and approval by top management. Each group, therefore, has primary responsibility for planning and controlling all activities for its products on a worldwide basis. Staff officers at the corporate level provide functional guidance (financial, legal, technical, and so on) to the worldwide product organizations.

Epsilon's Answer

A notable example of the product pattern is Epsilon, Inc., whose diverse product line includes man-made fibers, organic intermediates, and plastic resins. By no means a stranger to international operations, Epsilon established a fibers plant in Mexico in the mid-1940's and invested in extensive timber, cellulose pulping, and petrochemical operations in Canada in the late 1940's and early 1950's.

With substantial foreign operations, ambitious plans for further international activities, and a diverse, technologically complex product line, Epsilon outgrew the capabilities of its existing organizational pattern and sought a more appropriate form.

The geographic structure offered no real advantages. Practically all of Epsilon's existing foreign operations were in the Western hemisphere. Its products drew on a wide range of complex technologies and went into many different end-use markets. These complexities, top management believed, would seriously overtax either the geographic pattern or an international division form of organization.

The product form promised to be a more appealing alternative, since Epsilon had a group of relatively strong domestic operating companies, each of which could provide essential technological and marketing leadership to present and future affiliates. To be sure, there were reasons to hesitate:

Exhibit 3   PRODUCT STRUCTURE

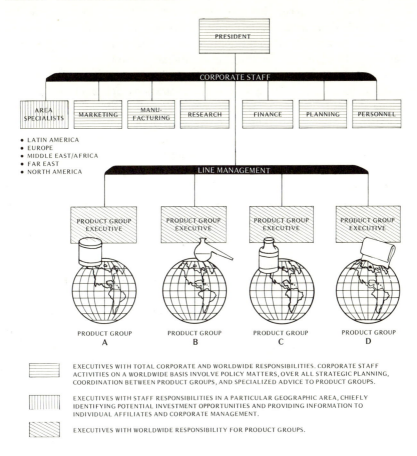

PRESIDENT

CORPORATE STAFF

| AREA SPECIALISTS | MARKETING | MANU-FACTURING | RESEARCH | FINANCE | PLANNING | PERSONNEL |

- LATIN AMERICA
- EUROPE
- MIDDLE EAST/AFRICA
- FAR EAST
- NORTH AMERICA

LINE MANAGEMENT

PRODUCT GROUP EXECUTIVE   PRODUCT GROUP EXECUTIVE   PRODUCT GROUP EXECUTIVE   PRODUCT GROUP EXECUTIVE

PRODUCT GROUP A   PRODUCT GROUP B   PRODUCT GROUP C   PRODUCT GROUP D

EXECUTIVES WITH TOTAL CORPORATE AND WORLDWIDE RESPONSIBILITIES. CORPORATE STAFF ACTIVITIES ON A WORLDWIDE BASIS INVOLVE POLICY MATTERS, OVERALL STRATEGIC PLANNING, COORDINATION BETWEEN PRODUCT GROUPS, AND SPECIALIZED ADVICE TO PRODUCT GROUPS.

EXECUTIVES WITH STAFF RESPONSIBILITIES IN A PARTICULAR GEOGRAPHIC AREA, CHIEFLY IDENTIFYING POTENTIAL INVESTMENT OPPORTUNITIES AND PROVIDING INFORMATION TO INDIVIDUAL AFFILIATES AND CORPORATE MANAGEMENT.

EXECUTIVES WITH WORLDWIDE RESPONSIBILITY FOR PRODUCT GROUPS.

First, the big domestic divisions had had relatively little contact with their foreign counterparts, so most of the executives who would be the logical choices to assume worldwide product responsibility had only modest experience with foreign operations and problems.

Secondly, Epsilon's ambitious expansion program was already taxing the executive group heavily, and it was not certain whether the international activities would receive the attention they would need.

But the promise of the product organizational form clearly outweighed these considerations, and so the new pattern began to take shape early in 1963.

The transition was eased by establishing an export sales organization to operate in markets where Epsilon had no production facilities. At the outset, export sales was set up as a strong operating unit, since the various world product groups had not had much international orientation and needed a good deal of assistance. However, as soon as individual managers in the operating divisions acquired sufficient experience, responsibility for export sales was to be transferred to the appropriate product group. In effect, export sales was to function as a "wasting" international division.

Since Epsilon's large and diversified domestic operations overshadow their foreign counterparts, the new group organizations are built around the existing domestic companies. At the heart of each worldwide group is the domestic operation. The group executive is the principal contact and channel of communication between the corporate operations committee (Epsilon's top decision-making body) and the individual foreign subsidiaries and affiliates within his product group. Each product group has a vice president-international, who acts as a deputy for international matters, with as much responsibility for managing the group's foreign operations as his group executive chooses to assign. Functional and technical advice are provided by appropriate staff at the domestic operating company level or the corporate level.

To coordinate the various product-group activities in major world markets, Epsilon has established area managers at the corporate staff level. Each area manager is responsible for keeping corporate management and the product groups informed about economic, political, and social developments in his assigned area. He is also responsible for identifying potential investment opportunities, for stimulating and assisting strategic planning by both corporate- and product-group management, and for developing an *area* plan for all Epsilon's products in a given geographic area to complement the worldwide *product* planning of the groups.

Further Examples

Certain international oil companies active in the petrochemical business have adopted another form of the basic product organizational pattern. This consists of two worldwide groups—one petroleum and one chemical—operating with considerable autonomy under top corporate management. In one international oil company, the petroleum operations are organized geographically, with all strategic and logistic decisions controlled at the corporate level. Its chemical operations, however, are divided into worldwide product groups.

A large electrical equipment manufacturer, Zeta, Ltd., which is one of the oldest of the true world enterprises, has evolved a unique form of the product organizational structure, embodying some features of the geographic form. This pattern comprises a corporate management group that provides a full range of corporate staff services; 13 major product divisions; and 56 separate national subsidiaries.

Each of Zeta's so-called product divisions is responsible for planning the development of its product line throughout the world. That is, each division acts much as a "worldwide product manager"—thus ensuring that steps are taken to penetrate important world markets for its particular product line.

Unlike the product groups at Epsilon, however, these product divisions do not have worldwide operational responsibility. First, they bear manufacturing responsibility only for operations in the home country. Secondly, although Zeta's product divisions carry certain responsibilities for marketing their products on a worldwide basis—such as in the home country and in export markets where no production facilities exist—much of the selling must be done through the national subsidiary companies. In fact, these subsidiary companies have primary responsibility for planning and managing all Zeta's businesses in their assigned countries. Once a subsidiary company undertakes production of an item, for example, it assumes full responsibility for marketing it as well. Thus, the product divisions, which have no line authority over the subsidiary companies, review relevant parts of subsidiaries' operating plans; but ultimate approval of all plans rests with top corporate management.

Favoring Factors

One limitation of the geographic form is its inherent awkwardness in cases where product lines of great diversity or technological complexity must be sold to various end-use markets. In contrast, the product organization seems made-to-order for these situations. Specifically, there are two situations where the product structure is likely to be advantageous:

1. *The company's product line is widely diversified and the range of products go into a variety of end-use markets.* (Bulk chemicals, for example, are sold on a specification basis to industrial users around the world. On the other hand, fibers require a highly specialized merchandising capability to reach from textile manufacturers to ultimate consumers.)
2. *High shipping costs, tariffs, or other considerations dictate local manufacture of the product, and a relatively high level of technological capability is required.* (Compare, for example, the technology involved in the production of Nylon 66 with that required for the manufacture of a standard product, such as bar soap, that can be made with comparatively little difficulty.)

At Epsilon, the product organization has brought the foreign operations into close contact with the latest technology in every product field. The foreign operations have gained a tremendous stimulus both from this contact and from the cognition that the domestic organization is really alert to their problems and needs.

Problems & Disadvantages

Perhaps the most important problem faced by companies adopting the product organization is the risk involved in turning worldwide product responsibility over to executives whose working experience has been largely domestic and who may either lack sufficient understanding of international problems or be disinclined to devote enough attention to them. Nor is the problem confined to the corporate and product group level. It also applies to key functional managers within the existing domestic operating companies, who are also called on to exercise judgment on international problems and to provide leadership for the foreign activities.

In the multiproduct company, for which the product structure has the strongest appeal, this problem is generally more serious than it is in the predominantly single-product business (automobile, oil, and others), where top management is invariably involved to some degree in worldwide planning for the total enterprise. In the diversified company, top management cannot plan effectively for each of these businesses; the prime responsibility for their direction must be divided into manageable assignments.

Another problem inherent in the product form is coordinating the moves of various product groups in any given part of the world. At Epsilon, where careful provision was made for this situation, there is still the problem of developing satisfactory working relationships and clearly drawing the lines of responsibility between the line product-group executives and the area managers at the corporate level.

DECISIVE VARIABLES

Clearly, there is no one right way to organize and manage any large-scale enterprise, particularly one that is worldwide in scope. Successful companies, as we have seen, are using various organizational patterns effectively in managing true world enterprises. Yet, despite the innumerable circumstances which affect the details of any such decision, the choice or organizational pattern has historically been largely determined by a small number of key variables.

Company History

The rapidity with which an emerging world enterprise moves toward a basic organizational structure is inevitably influenced by its past experience. As we have seen, a company that has operated overseas for decades and possesses a top management experienced in dealing with worldwide problems, as well as a large cadre of executive manpower able to assume international responsibilities, will approach organizational change very differently from a company which is a comparative neophyte on the international scene.

Management Traits

Some managements are bold, others cautious. Some make major organizational changes frequently, others only when absolutely necessary.

Some set high and ambitious growth targets, while others move more slowly to expand. Thus, management traits and limitations profoundly influence a company's approach to organizational change in the world enterprise.

Again, the capabilities of key individuals differ widely from company to company. At least over the short run, any sound organizational plan must be geared to these variations in the capabilities and personalities of key executives.

Nature of the Business

Perhaps the most significant influence on basic organizational structure is, or should be, exerted by the nature of the business itself. Certainly, a worldwide aggregation of different businesses with different end-use markets and highly technical production processes calls for a pattern quite different from that needed by a single-product world enterprise whose production process is simple and whose marketing requirements are not overtly involved.

Consider these pertinent variables:

What kinds of management decisions are really critical to the success of the enterprise?

How often must they be made, and at what organizational level?

How large are the international operations relative to domestic activities; and what structure will provide the management attention needed?

Is the over-all corporation too diverse and complex to permit effective planning in detail by top management?

How much control can and should corporate headquarters exercise over planning decisions for individual businesses around the world?

Only a searching and realistic analysis will permit a company to answer these questions—and the answers are crucial to choosing a sound organizational pattern.

Long-Term Strategy

A company that is committed to increasing its market position, or diversifying its operations on a worldwide scale, can cripple its organizational planning by failing to consider its *future* objectives and the most desirable strategy to achieve them. Unless it does so, it may find itself with an organization which is well adapted to what the company is today, but hopelessly unsuited to what the company will be tomorrow.

Sound forward planning is essential to the determination of the rate of international expansion, the strategy by which it will be effected, and the organizational pattern best suited to realize its benefits.

CONCLUSION

To successfully bring about fundamental change in a company's basic organizational structure, even in a purely domestic operation, is no easy accomplishment. In a truly world enterprise, however, it takes on special complexities—just as other management problems do. For this reason alone, it would be unwise to pass general judgments on the three broad organizational patterns that are currently dominant among emerging world enterprises. Even to categorize them as ultimate or transitional forms would presuppose a knowledge of the nature and behavior of world enterprise that we do not as yet possess.

However, one observation does apply with equal force to all the organizational patterns we have examined:

The really decisive point in the transition to world enterprise is top-management recognition that, to function effectively, the ultimate control of strategic planning and policy decisions must shift from decentralized subsidiaries or division locations to corporate headquarters, where a worldwide perspective can be brought to bear on the interests of the total enterprise.

The decision as to how tight that control should be, and how deeply top corporate management should become involved in planning for the individual businesses, obviously depends on the nature of the enterprise.

Below this top decision and control level, it should be noted, the four decisive variables just discussed—company history, management traits, the nature of the business, long-term strategy—stand as the basic determinants of corporate choice in selecting an organizational pattern to cope with the complexities of operating as a world enterprise. It is easy, unfortunately, to overlook the fact that only the latter two variables have permanent validity as criteria of the best ultimate organizational pattern for a given company. Indeed, many of the problems we have observed in working with world enterprises can be traced directly to a single mistake—that of allowing the corporation to remain locked in an organizational form originally chosen in the light of company history and current management limitations.

Inevitably, these are often important constraining factors at the time when organizational change becomes necessary—and the requirements they impose may *at that time* be entirely in harmony with the immediate objectives of the corporation. The difficulty arises only later, when new corporate objectives and external conditions may begin to chafe against the rigidities of a once-appropriate organizational pattern. Unless top management is keenly aware of this likelihood, it may continue to cling to an outgrown organizational form until the costs of inaction, in time and unexploited opportunities, have mounted dangerously high.

Indeed, no company that has embarked on the route to world enterprise can safely rest in the assurance that the organizational form originally chosen will indefinitely remain adequate to meet its growing needs. Rather, it is up to top management to periodically appraise its organizational structure, to evaluate its compatibility with the nature of the business and with long-term corporate strategy, and to take thoughtful action when the need for change becomes apparent. No top-management responsibility, it can safely be said, bears more directly on long-term corporate effectiveness and profitability in the global arena of world enterprise.

REFERENCES

1. *Business International*, June 12, 1964, p. 1.
2. Throughout this article, fictitious names have been assigned to the companies whose organizational structures are discussed. Otherwise, no facts have been altered.

ORGANIZATIONAL STRUCTURE AND THE MULTINATIONAL STRATEGY

LAWRENCE E. FOURAKER
and JOHN M. STOPFORD

Organizations that have a single or a few related product lines and a high degree of vertical integration tend to be capital intensive, and to be organized in a centralized, functionally-departmentalized structure. Organizations that have a diversified product line tend to have a decentralized, divisional structure. This paper indicates that the first type tends to concentrate on domestic markets, while the second type accounts for most of U.S. direct investment abroad. Expansion abroad requires diversification, reorganization, and the training of general international managers. The evidence suggests that the organizations that have been most successful in meeting this new challenge have been those that had previously acquired the ability to develop general managers capable of controlling and guiding a heterogeneous, diverse enterprise.

One of the landmark studies in the field of business administration is *Strategy and Structure* by A.D. Chandler, Jr. A central proposition in Chandler's book is that the strategy of diversification led to organizational problems and eventually to the emergence of a new corporate structure. The purpose of this article is to see if Chandler's proposition is useful in examining recent organizational changes in the international field.[1]

International business activity is a form of diversification that has become increasingly important for many large American companies in the last two decades. In some sense, this development may be considered a replication against which Chandler's thesis may be tested. That is, this new form of diversification should be dominated by firms with experience in managing diversified activities. Furthermore, the new diversification should lead to new problems of organization and, finally, to different structural accommodations.

MODEL

Chandler states: "Historically, the executives administering American industrial enterprises have followed a recognizable pattern in the acquisition and use of resources."[2] This process consists of a developmental transition through several distinct phases: "Thus four phases or chapters can be discerned in the history of the large American industrial enterprise: the initial expansion and accumulation of resources; the rationalization of the use of resources; the expansion into new markets and lines to help assure the continuing full use of resources; and finally the development of a new

From *Administrative Science Quarterly*, June 1968, pp. 47-64. Reprinted with permission of the authors and publisher.

structure to make possible continuing effective mobilization of resources to meet both changing short-term market demands and long-term market trends."[3] These four phases produced three fairly distinct organizational structures:

Type I. The organization is an extension of the interests, abilities, and limitations of its chief executive, who is often the creator and owner of the organization. This structure is generally limited to a single product line and often emphasizes one function (e.g., production) more than others. It is also constrained by the sequential decision-making pattern that characterizes a single problem solver. This is the entrepreneurial business organization, which serves as a building block for most economic models.

Type II. This is the vertically integrated, functionally coordinated enterprise. Generally such an organization continues to be limited to one or a few related product lines. The emphasis is on rational use of resources, efficiency, and coordination of functional activities.

Yet the dominant centralized structure had one basic weakness. A very few men were still entrusted with a great number of complex decisions. The executives in the central office were usually the president with one or two assistants, sometimes the chairman of the board, and the vice presidents who headed the various departments. The latter were often too busy with the administration of the particular function to devote much time to the affairs of the enterprise as a whole. Their training proved a still more serious defect. Because these administrators had spent most of their business careers within a single functional activity, they had little experience or interest in understanding the needs and problems of other departments or of the corporation as a whole.[4]

The type II structure might be enormously efficient in the production of some classes of products, but did not produce professional management.

Type III. The accumulation of resources by a successful type II firm often led to diversification of product lines, (*1*) to avoid risk, (*2*) to ensure continuation of the organization after the major product had completed its life cycle, or (*3*) to sell outside the company by some divisions due to integrated production requiring plant facilities of varying capacities at different stages.

The strategy of product diversification caused many administrative problems. The functional approach of the type II firm required that the senior marketing executive coordinate the marketing activities for all the organization's products, even though they might utilize different forms of distribution, advertising, and sales effort. The senior production officer was confronted with similar complexity. These functional responsibilities could be delegated to subordinates, most appropriately on the basis of product assignments; but profit contribution of functional specialists could not be measured against performance, so control and comparison became even more difficult. The unavoidable problems of conflict and coordination at the lowest levels of the organization would frequently have to be passed up to the highest functional levels for adjudication. And some operating issues could not be settled there, but would have to reach the office of the chief executive.

Attempts to add product lines in such an environment could lead to organizational stasis because of the limited ability of the chief executive's office to cope with the new demands on its decision-making capacity. Management would then be confronted with a choice: either abandon the strategy of product diversification, or abandon the functional form of organization.

Many organizations chose structural reorganization. This reorganization took the form of a multidivisional product structure with many functional responsibilities delegated to the division general managers. The divisions were separated on a product basis and were relatively autonomous. Generally each division served as a profit center for control purposes; coordination and control from the central office was concentrated on finance and some general staff functions such as planning and research.

"Besides allocating decision making more effectively and assuring more precise communication and control, the new structure proved to have another advantage over the functionally departmentalized organization. It provided a place to train and test general executives."[5] This ability to produce general managers allowed the type III organization to operate successfully in unrelated product areas.

With great diversity of products, staff, technologies, and managerial talents, the type III decentralized organization could move simultaneously to exploit opportunities in a variety of independent areas. The management innovation of moving from a type II structure to type III began, in the United States, in the 1920's. As is often the case,[6] the type III structure developed independently in several organizations; du Pont, General Motors, Standard Oil, and Sears are given special attention by Chandler. Many other organizations imitated these pioneers, with most of the transitions being delayed by the depression of the 1930's and World War II, so that many companies undertook the transition in both strategy and structure in the 1950's and 1960's.

In the type III organization, new products can be added, or old ones dropped, with only marginal effect on the organization. Indeed, given the prospect of finite life expectancy for any commercial product, the management is committed to a strategy of research and development as a means of ensuring the continued life of the organization. This sort of activity is compatible with the diversity and independence of parts in a type III organization. "In fact, the systematizing of strategic decisions through the building of a general office and the routinizing of product development by the formation of a research department have, in a sense, institutionalized this strategy of diversification."[7]

Since the type III organization makes it possible to manage a variety of heterogeneous activities, it also makes it feasible for reseach and development activity to be incorporated in the structure. Burns and Stalker, in a study of electronic firms in England and Scotland, found that certain types of business organizations did not develop research and development departments; such activity could not normally be absorbed by their "mechanistic" structures, which closely resembled Chandler's type II organizations.[8] The organizations that were successful in establishing research and development departments ("organic" structures) were described in terms that seem characteristic of Chandler's type III. These results are reinforced by the field work of Lawrence and Lorsch.[9]

This connection between research and development, product innovation, and organizational structure is important for the thesis of this paper, because the innovative capacity may be an important source of competitive advantage in foreign markets. Vernon and others have argued that the United States tends to export products developed for the U.S. market that are not being produced abroad, and this monopoly position in world markets offsets high labor costs in the U.S.[10] Furthermore, at some point the organization will invest in plant and equipment abroad in order to protect its export market, particularly if that market has grown to a size that is consistent with the most efficient current productive techniques.

The result of this chain of arguments is that type III organizations can be expected to dominate foreign direct investment. The initial structural response to this strategy of diversifying direct investment around the world is to establish an international division in the type III organization. Such a division reports to one man. This focuses responsibility and control for foreign operations and economizes on the need for general managers with broad international experience (who are inevitably in short supply when the organization first expands its foreign operations).

The international division is at the same organizational level, and will tend to receive the same general treatment, as the product divisions. This same general treatment tends to create stresses that will make the international division a transient form. It is not a product division, but is rather less autonomous, for it depends more on the cooperation and assistance of the product divisions than they typically depend on each other. As a result, the product division manager is subjected to stresses and conflicts that are not always in the best interests of the organization. The product division manager, who is judged against domestic measures of performance, is therefore somewhat motivated to (1) fill his domestic orders before extending assistance to foreign markets; (2) assign his best employees to domestic tasks and shunt the others to the international division; and (3) argue for a larger domestic share of the capital budget.

These are natural responses that may be quite costly if foreign markets are growing faster than domestic markets, which has often been the case in the postwar period. In many organizations, top management has responded to these lost opportunities in several ways. First, it has given product and functional managers more international experience and eventually more responsibility. Second, it has replaced the international division with some new organizational structure; for example, worldwide product divisions, world-partitioning geographic divisions, or some combination of these, perhaps retaining an international division for some purposes, or setting up a separate international company. Indeed some companies moved directly to these new structures, avoiding the problem of a conflict of interests between product divisions and the international division, and the possibility of a coalition of product divisions against the international division. This is most common where the vehicle for growth abroad has been merger with other organizations whose foreign interests are in different product lines.

Each of the possible alternative forms of the organization of international activities has distinct characteristics. The international division is the sole profit center for foreign operations, requiring only one general manager with international expertise. The manager of the international division and his staff become the repository of all the organization's international experience, causing problems of capital allocation, transfer pricing, and especially communication.

The worldwide product division structure avoids many of these problems by containing the areas of potential conflict within each division. The division manager is responsible for the profit performance of his product line throughout the world. This structure requires at least as many international general managers as there are product divisions operating abroad.

The geographic divisions partitioning the world also require an increased number of international general managers. The predominant characteristic is that the area divisions (of which the U.S.A. or North America is one) are headed by general managers of equal status in the structure. Each has the profit responsibility for an area, regardless of the produce lines involved. Typically, this structure is associated with those organizations that have mature, standardized product lines for which marketing, rather than production or technology, is the critical variable.

The mixed structural form is a combination of two or all of the above forms, adapted to the particular needs of a firm. A food company diversifying into chemicals might retain its international division for all the food products and establish the chemical division with worldwide responsibilities.

The separate international company is usually a response to lack of success abroad or to an unwillingness on the part of top management to become more involved abroad. Typically, this move precedes the sale of all or part of the foreign operations. It should be noted that this response does not necessarily include the incorporation of the international division as a separate subsidiary, since such incorporation is normally used as a method of reducing taxes.

The structures that have been adopted to replace the international division may not be stable. As the foreign business grows and diversifies, further structural changes may be required. Operations within the U.S. require a balance between product and functional management, with area requirements relatively unimportant. However, once the organization operates abroad to a significant degree the benefits to be gained from both regional and product line control or coordination may become large. This has led a few organizations to adopt a "grid" structure, where product, area, and functional responsibilities are linked in what may be viewed as a three-dimensional organization structure. There are serious problems associated with this form, but the ability of an organization to learn to operate within such a structure may be the key to the maintenance of the flexibility of administration necessary for continued growth and prosperity abroad.

DATA

Chandler classifies the 70 largest American industrial companies in 1959 into three categories: (1) industries consisting of companies that tended to remain as type II organizations: steel and nonferrous metal; (2) industries partially accepting the type III structure: agricultural processing, oil, rubber, and mass merchandising; and (3) industries consisting of firms that had generally adopted the type III structure: electrical, automobile (transportation), power machinery, and chemicals.

The last four industries have clearly played a prominent role in the economic processes that we have been discussing. They are quite diversified, supporting Chandler's thesis that diversification leads to the adoption of the type III structure.[11] They are leaders in research and development activity, supporting the Burns and Stalker propositions.[12] They are the source of most of the U.S. export strength, as indicated by Gruber and others.[13] And they are among the leaders in foreign direct investment in plant and equipment.

A crude measure of aggregate diversification is the number of manufacturing employees outside the primary industrial activity in which the firm has been classified. Of the 17 manufacturing industries of interest,[14] the five leaders are shown in Table 1. It should be noted that this is a measure of

Table 1   EMPLOYMENT OUTSIDE PRIMARY INDUSTRY AND IN RESEARCH AND DEVELOPMENT; EXPORT SURPLUS AND DIRECT FOREIGN INVESTMENT FOR MAJOR INDUSTRIES

Industry (and SIC number)	Number of employees		Export surplus 1958-1964 (millions of dollars)†	Direct foreign investments 1959-1966 (millions of dollars)‡
	Outside primary industry 1958*	For research and development 1958*		
Transportation (37)	474,095	27,094	493.6	4.870
Primary and fabricated metals (33-34)	342,284	—	—	1,962
Electrical (36)	265,473	36,305	486.3	1,401
Machinery (35)	254,160	4,526	2,063.0	2,698
Chemicals (28)	170,875	14,667	752.7	4,130

*U.S. Bureau of the Census, *Enterprise Statistics 1958* (Washington, D.C.: Government Printing Office, 1963).

†Trade Relations Council of the U.S., *Employment, Output, and Foreign Trade of U.S. Manufacturing Industries, 1958-1964/65,* (New York, 1966).

‡U.S. Department of Commerce, *Survey of Current Business* (Washington, D.C.: Government Printing Office, various dates).

domestic diversification, and that Chandler's four industries are among the five leaders.

Table 1 also shows an aggregate measure of research and development activity provided by total employment figures for people placed in these categories by their employers. Chandler's type III industries dominate the research and development activity of U.S. manufacturing establishments. The leading manufacturing contributors to the U.S. trade balance are also identified. Eight of the seventeen manufacturing industries had export surpluses on an industry basis; nine had deficits. Chandler's four represented 96.4 percent of the total export surplus by industry category of the U.S. in 1964. This is consistent with the Vernon position, as is the evidence that these same industries tend to follow their trade advantages with direct foreign investment as shown in Table 1.[15]

The evidence is summarized in Table 2, which relates the four industries Chandler identified as having generally accepted the type III structure and the four activities under discussion. The numbers in the body of the table indicate the rank of the organizations in these activities among the 17 industries.

From these two tables, it seems evident that the American manufacturing company with extensive international interests is likely to be: (1) diversified in its domestic busines activities; (2) type III in organizational structure; (3) a leader in research and development; and (4) a major exporter from the U.S. These propositions can be investigated in greater detail by using relative measures and data on individual companies.

Chandler distributed the 70 largest industrial companies (1959) in his three categories. Joan Curhan,[16] under the direction of Raymond Vernon, compiled a list of 170 companies that were in the 1964 or 1965 *Fortune*[17] classifications and that had manufacturing subsidiaries in six or more foreign countries at the end of 1963 where the parent company owned 25 percent or more of the subsidiaries. The Curhan list represents most of the American-controlled manufacturing activity abroad.

Comparison of the Chandler and the Curhan lists shows that only 35 percent of Chandler's first group (predominantly type II organizations) were also on the Curhan list. The only steel company on both lists was the most decentralized of the steel companies. In Chandler's mixed second group, 45

Table 2   RANK OF CHANDLER-TYPE III INDUSTRIES (OUT OF 17) AS TO DIVERSIFICATION, RESEARCH AND DEVELOPMENT, EXPORT SURPLUS, AND FOREIGN INVESTMENT

	Chemical	Machinery	Electrical	Transportation
Diversification	5	4	3	1
Research and development	3	4	1	2
Export surplus	2	1	4	3
Foreign investment	2	3	5	1

percent of the companies were also on the Curhan list, (54 percent if merchandising was excluded from Chandler's group of companies were all on the Curhan list except for one company which had gone out of existence through merger.

The mechanism by which this relationship is maintained was examined in more detail. The 170 companies of the Curhan list were sorted into the following categories: (1) type II organizations, (2) type III with an international division, and (3) type III with the other forms of organized international activity that were described earlier. This sorting was done on the basis of annual reports, interviews, and secondary sources.[18] The large sample size made it inevitable that most of the information was gathered from published material. As a result, the classification reflects the formal structure and ignores possible discrepancies between the analyses from published materials and the evidence gained from the interviews with a limited number of the companies. Therefore, the classification may be considered to be sufficiently accurate for the purposes of this paper. The main possible source of error is for those companies in transition between the categories, since the formal organization may often lead or lag behind actual administrative practices. This, however, was not considered a serious source of error.

The classification of each company on the basis of only a few structural forms was aimed at recording the central tendency of the structure observed. Various rules were developed to allow for the many possible minor variations in the control procedures. The most important of these rules were:

1. Foreign mining, agricultural, or service operations were not considered to be part of the manufacturing activities and were therefore ignored for the purposes of the structural classification.
2. Given an international division, the presence of one or two foreign joint-ventures reporting directly to a product division and accounting for an insignificant volume of the foreign business did not constitute a "mixed" form.
3. The international division did not have to control exports from the U.S.
4. Canadian subsidiaries were classified as part of the U.S. operations.

Each company was also classified by the two-digit Standard Industrial Classification number of its largest product line.[19] The result of these classifications is summarized in Table 3 which shows that only 18 of the 170 companies in the sample have type II structures. This finding immediately suggests that foreign investment is dominated by type III organizations, which is the thesis of this paper.

From Table 3 a structural index for eight industries was calculated as follows:

1. A ratio of the number of type II companies to all type III companies was calculated and normalized by assigning the value 1.00 to the industry with the largest proportion of type II companies.

Table 3 STRUCTURAL CLASSIFICATION OF COMPANIES BY INDUSTRY

Industry SIC number	Number of companies in sample	Stage II	Stage III with international division	Stage III with other forms of international structure
			Structure	
20	28	5	16	7
21	1	—	1	—
22	2	—	2	—
25	1	—	1	—
26	5	1	3	1
27	1	—	1	—
28	41	1	21	19
29	8	—	2	6
30	5	—	5	—
31	1	—	1	—
32	7	1	5	1
33	8	4	2	2
34	8	1	4	3
35	19	4	9	6
36	17	1	8	8
37	11	—	4	7
38	5	—	4	1
39	2	—	1	1
Total	170	18	90	62

2. A ratio of the number of type III companies with an international division to all type III companies was calculated and normalized, with a value of 1.00 assigned to the industry with the highest ratio.

3. The two normalized ratios were summed to form the index which is shown in Table 4. Low values of this index indicate the predominance of type III structures, particularly type III with some relatively complex form of organized international activity. Low values of the index therefore indicate the relative abundance of both general management in the United States and international general management.

This method of calculating a structural index is purely arbitrary. It is clear from Table 3, however, that any index reflecting the proportions of the structures of the sample of companies within an industry will provide approximately the same ranking as that shown in Table 4.

Also to be found in Table 4 is an index of diversification as calculated by Michael Gort.[20] Gort's index is derived from a sample of 111 large manufacturing companies, drawn from the 200 largest companies in 1954. This particular index (Gort does present other measures of diversification) represents the ratio of domestic employment in the primary two-digit SIC industry divided by total domestic employment, adjusted for employment associated with vertical integration.[21] These relationships tend to be stable over time, so that they should retain some relevance for the present problem; also the time

Table 4 STRUCTURE AND DIVERSIFICATION; FOREIGN INVESTMENT,
EMPLOYMENT IN RESEARCH AND DEVELOPMENT, AND EXPORT/IMPORT
RATIO IN MAJOR INDUSTRIES

Industry (and SIC numbers)	Index of structure	Gort's index of diversification*	1959-1966 Direct foreign investment relative to domestic†	Research and development employees as percentage of central administrative employment ‡	Export/ import ratio 1968- 1969§
Food (20)	1.175	.933	13.2%	3.10	.79
Paper (26)	1.300	.893	16.7	2.21	.31
Chemicals (28)	0.580	.752	27.7	22.49	2.79
Rubber (30)	1.000	.697	41.3	16.46	1.19
Primary and fabricated metals (33-34)	1.545	.810	20.3	6.37	.67
Machinery (35)	1.188	.807	21.8	12.56	6.37
Electrical (36)	0.638	.667	23.7	47.00	3.85
Transportation (37)	0.364	.728	35.3	34.32	1.49

*Michael Gort, *Diversification and Integration in American Industry* (Princeton, N.J.: Princeton University, 1962), Table 8, p. 33.
†U.S. Department of Commerce, *Survey of Current Business* (Washington, D.C.: Government Printing Office, various dates).
‡U.S. Bureau of the Census, *Enterprise Statistics: 1958* (Washington, D.C.: Government Printing Office, 1963).
§Trade Relations Council of the U.S., *Employment, Output, and Foreign Trade of U.S. Manufacturing Industries, 1958-1964/65* (New York: 1966).

difference is in the direction required for Chandler's thesis. The eight industries in Table 4 are those for which data are available on foreign direct investment. This implies that they are the leading manufacturing industries in this respect, since the others have too little foreign direct investment to be reported separately. Gort's diversification index for SIC 33-34 is an average of his figures for those two industries, weighted by their respective employment sizes and representation on his sample.

Table 4 discloses some relationships immediately; that is, the four most diversified industries are four industries with the lowest structural index: chemicals, rubber, electrical machinery, and transportation. The four least diversified industries are four industries with the highest structural index: food, paper, primary and fabricated metals, and machinery. The Spearman coefficient of rank correlation between diversification and structure is 0.64. This result provides additional support for Chandler's thesis that there is a relationship between diversification and structure.

Table 4 also shows the importance of foreign direct investment in plant and equipment relative to domestic direct investment in plant and equipment, for the period 1959-1966. Again a relationship is apparent; that is, the four industries with the greatest relative direct foreign investment are the four most diversified (also with lowest structural index): chemicals, rubber, electrical machinery, and transportation. The four industries with the least foreign investment are the four least diversified (also with the highest structural index): machinery, primary and fabricated metal, food, paper. The coefficient of rank correlation between the relative direct investment measure and Gort's diversification index is .86; between the relative direct investment measure and the structural index it is 0.69.[22]

A relative measure of research and development activity is shown in Table 4 for 1958. The four leading research and development industries are those that are the most diversified, have the lowest structural indexes, and are the most international in their investment practices. The coefficient of rank correlation between research and structure is 0.81; between research and diversification it is .90. The relationship between research and diversification is also apparent when the analysis is made at the more detailed three-digit SIC industry level. The median specialization ratio for organizations with research and development employees is .814 in 1958, and .939 for organizations without research and development employees. The specialization ratio measures the number of manufacturing employees classified in a primary three-digit SIC industry divided by total manufacturing employment in that industry.[23]

The export/import ratio for 1958-1960 is also shown in Table 4. Here the four leading industries are the same as in the case of the trade balance (rubber ranks fifth and is replaced by machinery among the leading four). The coefficient of rank correlation between the export/import ratio and structure is 0.52. The correlation between the research and development measure and the export/import balance is .71, which is consistent with the findings of Gruber and associates.[24]

CONCLUSION

It may now begin to appear that the evidence would support *any* hypothesis about the industry characteristics of the organizations that have led the movement abroad, simply because those industries are outstanding on all relevant scales for measuring business and performance. This is not the case, however. Consider the not unusual statement that it is the largest, most capital intensive and most integrated organizations that dominate foreign activity. If size is measured by assets per organization, this view is not supported by census data.[25] The rank correlation between assets per organization and the structural index is .40; between assets per organization and relative importance of foreign direct investment the correlation is .33. Gort also found that there was little association between size and diversification, as measured by the ratio of primary to nonprimary employment.[26] The correlation between the measure of size used here and Gort's diversification index is .29.

The measure of integration, taken from Gort, has a *negative* correlation with foreign activity, diversification (which agrees with his results), and decentralization for the eight internationally important industries.

Finally, the ratio of capital per production worker is negatively correlated with relative foreign activity (-.14). There is also a negative correlation between capital per production worker and the export/import ratio (-.40), as first suggested by Leontief.[27] The negative relationships carry over to the measures of structure (-.21) and diversification (-.36) used here. U.S. strength in international competition is concentrated in products with a relatively large labor content—probably the highly skilled technical labor required for product innovation and development, according to Vernon.[28]

The organizations that are left at home may be among the largest, most integrated, most capital intensive, and most profitable firms in the economy. Furthermore, they are not as likely to have problems of organization, management recruitment and training, staff-line conflicts, or of identifying what business the organization is really engaged in, or should be engaged in.

So, in the end, the question of the characteristics of the organization is a question of management's choice between sets of problems. Some business leaders have decided to make their organizations more cohesive by making them more integrated, capital intensive, and often more profitable. They have retained type II structures, and have tended to concentrate on domestic markets. Other business leaders have undertaken the difficult task of transforming an institution, of moving from a type II to a III structure. Many problems arise in this transition; for example, new systems of evaluation, reward, and control must be constructed. A critical aspect of the transition is teaching men to accept new roles—in this case roles as general managers. Once the organization had developed this educational capability, it could continue to diversify in an effective and efficient manner. It may be that the same pattern is being repeated in the international field: when the company has small foreign interests, it economizes on competent international management by having one man coordinate foreign activities. The growth of foreign markets and opportunities requires diversification, reorganization, and the training of many more general international managers. The organizations that have been most successful in meeting this new challenge have been those type III organizations that had already developed the ability to produce general managers capable of controlling and guiding a heterogeneous, diverse enterprise.

REFERENCES

1. A. D. Chandler, Jr., *Strategy and Structure* (Garden City, N. Y.: Anchor, 1966). We have received, and greatly appreciate, the help of J. Berman, C. R. Christensen, J. H. McArthur, B. R. Scott, and R. Vernon. This research was financed by a grant from the Ford Foundation for the study of the multinational corporation.

2. *Ibid.*, p. 478.

3. *Ibid.*, p. 479.

4. *Ibid.*, p. 480.

5. *Ibid.*, p. 385.

6. A. L. Koreber, *Anthropology: Race, Language, Culture, Psychology, Prehistory* (Revised ed.; New York: Harcourt, Brace and Company, 1948), pp. 445-472.

7. Chandler, *op. cit.*, p. 490.

8. T. Burns and G. M. Stalker, *The Management of Innovation* (London: Tavistock, 1961).

9. P. R. Lawrence and J. W. Lorsch, *Organization and Environment* (Boston, Mass.: Division of Research, Harvard Business School, 1967).

10. R. Vernon, International Investment and International Trade in the Product Cycle, *Quarterly Journal of Economics*, 80 (May 1966), 190-207; C. P. Kindleberger. *The Dollar Shortage* (New York: Wiley, 1950); Staffan Burenstam-Linder, *An Essay on Trade and Transformation* (Uppsala, Sweden: Almqvist & Wicksell, 1961).

11. Chandler, *op. cit.*, pp. 16, 17.

12. Burns and Stalker, *op. cit.*

13. W. Gruber, D. Mehta, and R. Vernon, The R&D Factor in International Trade and International Investment of United States Industries, *Journal of Political Economy*, 25 (February 1967), 20-37.

14. There are 21 two-digit Standard Industrial Classification (SIC) manufacturing industries. However, the Department of Commerce presents data for foreign direct investment on a combined basis for primary and fabricated metals industries (SIC numbers 33 and 34), excludes petroleum from manufacturing, and provides foreign trade data that omit petroleum and furniture. We have comparable data for 17 two-digit industries. These are: 20 (food), 21 (tobacco), 22 (textiles), 23 (apparel), 24 (wood products), 26 (paper), 27 (printing), 28 (chemicals), 30 (rubber), 31 (leather), 32 (stone, clay, and glass), 33-34 (primary and fabricated metal), 35 (machinery), 36 (electrical), 37 (transportation), 38 (scientific and similar instruments), 39 (misc.).

15. Vernon, *op. cit.*

16. J. Curhan, Private communication.

17. *Fortune*, The 500 Largest U.S. Industrial Corporations, (June 1965 and June 1966).

18. For example, E. B. Lovell, *The Changing Role of the International Executive* (New York: National Industrial Conference Board, 1966).

19. The source of this classification was the Securities Exchange Commission, *1965 Directory of Companies Filing Annual Reports with the Securities Exchange Commission* (New York, 1966).

20. M. Gort, *Diversification and Integration in American Industry* (Princeton, N. J.: Princeton University, 1962).

21. Gort's index is based on data in U.S. Bureau of Census, *Company Statistics: 1954 Census of Business, Manufacturing, Mineral Industries* (Washington, D. C.: Government Printing Office, 1958), Table 2.

22. The structural and diversification indexes were ranked from the lowest to the highest values, so that the "most diversified" industry was given first rank on that scale.

23. U. S. Bureau of the Census, *Enterprise Statistics: 1958* (Washington, D.C.: Government Printing Office, 1963).

24. Gruber, *op. cit.*

25. *Enterprise Statistics, op. cit.*

26. Gort, *op. cit.*, p. 74.

27. W. Leontief, Domestic Production and Foreign Trade: The American Capital Position Re-examined, *Proceedings of the American Philosophical Society 97* (September 1953). pp. 332-349.

28. Vernon, *op. cit.*

A COMPARATIVE ANALYSIS OF CORPORATE-DIVISIONAL RELATIONSHIPS IN MULTI-UNIT ORGANIZATIONS

STEPHEN A. ALLEN, III

Introduction

"The language of organization," wrote Alfred P. Sloan, "has always suffered from some want of words to express the true facts and circumstances of human interaction. One usually asserts one aspect or another of it at different times, such as the absolute independence on the part, and again the need of coordinating, and again the concept of the whole with the guiding center."[1] In the early 1920s, when Sloan was grappling with these issues of centralization versus decentralization, they were a problem for only a few large enterprises such as General Motors, Dupont, Standard Oil, and General Electric. Today they represent a crucial top management issue for the multiproduct, multinational enterprises and the large public institutions which have become the dominant organizational form of our society.

In this paper I wish to discuss some of the findings and implications of a recently completed study which was aimed at developing and testing a set of concepts to aid in understanding and affecting the behavior of upper-level managers in multi-unit organizations. This study, conducted by Professor Jay W. Lorsch and me, focused on corporate-divisional relationships in six diversified industrial enterprises.[2] Four of these enterprises were highly diversified (or conglomerate) firms, while two were vertically integrated paper companies. Comparative field survey techniques were employed to examine the behavioral issues of both operating in diverse industrial environments and managing the interdependence required between the headquarters unit and its product divisions. A total of 22 individual corporate-divisional relationships was intensively studied in the six firms.

Rather than attempting to reiterate all of the findings of this study, which will be reported in a forthcoming monograph, I plan to dwell on the following topics:

The conceptual scheme which was developed to study corporate-divisional relationships and how it differs from prior research in complex organizations.

The basic pattern of corporate-divisional relations suggested by our findings.

The impact of the differing environmental requirements faced by conglom-

Prepared for a meeting of The Institute of Management Sciences College on Organization, March 22-24, 1971, Washington, D.C. Reprinted with permission of the author.

erates and vertically integrated firms on their organizational design and internal workings.

The major implications of the concepts and findings for practicing managers and students of organization.

As a point of departure, I wish to briefly review the practical issues faced by the top management of multi-unit firms and to set down the reasons I feel these managers have secured only limited help from management theory and the behavioral sciences.

MANAGEMENT ISSUES AND LIMITATIONS
OF PRIOR RESEARCH

The basic issues faced by the executives who manage multi-unit firms are (1) how to constitute major organizational sub-units (e.g., divisions) so that they can most effectively engage their particular industrial environments, and (2) how to achieve the necessary coordination between these sub-units and the headquarters unit around the key issues of business planning, budgeting, and the allocation of the firm's resources. In attempting to deal with these issues, managers must come to grips with a number of difficult and seemingly amorphous questions. How much autonomy should a division have? How do you balance this autonomy with the need to maintain control over corporate earnings and funds flows? What services should be centered at the corporate headquarters, and in what major areas should the corporation set policy? What sorts of budgeting and reporting requirements should be developed for the divisions, and how do these formal systems affect managers' perceptions and decision making? What sort of reward system will insure that division managers' goals and interests will be consistent with those of the total corporation? This list of questions is intended to be illustrative rather than exhaustive; it could probably be extended for several pages. The point is that these issues are both complex and rather abstract; and what managers need is a mental map which can at once capture the crucial aspects of these questions, help make some sense of them, and point toward appropriate means of coping with them.

Organizational theory and the behavioral sciences would seem a logical place for managers to turn for help in getting a firmer grasp on problems like the ones I have outlined. Unfortunately, these disciplines at best have provided only fragmented assistance. I feel there are several reasons for this dearth of insight. First, those who have spent the most time on issues of centralization versus decentralization—namely, the classical organization theorists[3] and the bureaucratic sociologists[4]—have focused almost solely on the issues of formal structure and the delegation of authority. Furthermore, they have tended to devote their attention to deriving universal principles regarding these issues. While formal structure and delegation of authority are certainly important, an over-concern with then has tended to obscure some equally important factors, such as the cognitive, informational, and interpersonal issues which underlie inter-unit relationships in organizations. Also, the search for universal principles denies—either implicitly or explicitly—the importance of the differing environmental and economic characteristics of organizations.

Some recent studies, drawing mainly on prior work by psychologists and social psychologists, have provided important insights into the issues of interdepartmental coordination and conflict management.[5] These studies have been quite useful for middle management and particularly those directly concerned with the ongoing operations of single business units. However, these studies have never extended to the problems of multibusiness enterprises; and each one has tended to ignore the role of either environmental requirements, economic factors, or (you guessed it!) formal organizational devices. In summary, I feel that most organizational research has failed to speak to the top management of large institutions both because it seldom has focused on the total firm as its unit of analysis and because, where it has so focused, it has never considered the range of environmental, economic, and behavioral variables necessary to develop an adequate model of the situation.

A BEHAVIORALLY-BASED SYSTEMS APPROACH

The conceptual scheme which Lorsch and I developed views the multi-unit organization—or any large-scale organization—as

a complex adaptive system that seeks to survive and grow by coping with changing external conditions and by dealing with its own recurring internal conflicts and performance deviations.

This definition, which draws heavily on the theoretical insights of general systems theory,[6] had at least three important consequences for the way we conducted the research. First, we hypothesized that each of the firms and divisions studied would differ in their internal workings as a function of both their specific environmental requirements and the organizational assumptions and devices employed by their management. Second, we focused on describing the *interrelatedness* of organizational sub-units with one another and with their particular segments of the firm's total environment. More specifically, we sought to operationally define and measure the goal-seeking behavior, cognitive and interpersonal processes, and communications nets which form this interrelatedness. Finally, we sought to explain our finding not simply as a set of point-in-time correlations, but as a "snapshot" of a dynamic, emergent process. Indeed, we hoped to move away from the traditional view of an organization as a set of position descriptions and formally defined relationships and to adopt the cybernetic definition of *organization as a process which emerges from the dynamic interrelationships of the parts of a system with one another and with the system's environment.*

Drawing most heavily on the prior work of Lawrence and Lorsch,[7] March and Simon,[8] and Thompson,[9] we developed the basic conceptual model shown in Figure 1. This diagram simply suggests that organizational choices can usefully be viewed as being made and continually elaborated on the basis of the environmental requirements faced by the firm as these requirements are filtered through the mental sets of the firm's top management. It also suggests that organizational choices are related to overall performance through their impact on the organizational states and decision-making processes which operate within the firm. Finally, the organizational choice process is viewed as dynamic in the sense that overall performance feeds back upon the availability of financial resources and upon top management goals, assumptions, and strategies.

While data were gathered on each of the factors shown in Figure 1, our main effort was devoted to quantifying environmental requirements, organizational states and decision-making processes, and performance. In terms of environmental requirements we were interested in (1) the uncertainty, time span of feedback, and dominant competitive issues faced by each division; (2) the diversity of these requirements faced by the firm as a whole; (3) the interdependence required among the firm's diverse environments; and (4) the financial risk associated with these requirements. Measures of economic performance were taken at both the corporate and divisional levels. Finally, we examined four factors of an internal/behavioral nature. *Differentiation* is the degree to which major organizational sub-units (i.e., headquarters and divisions) differ from one another in formality of management practices and in the goal, time, and interpersonal orientations of their members. *Integration* is the degree of collaboration and mutual understanding actually achieved between these units. *Integrative effort* is the amount of their working time managers devoted to achieving integration. Inter-unit decision-making patterns were examined in terms of several interrelated factors—e.g., patterns of influence among units, quality of upward and downward information flows, rapidity of the headquarters in responding to division requests, perceived character of reward systems, and behavioral modes through which conflicts were managed.

In this paper it is impossible for me to cover the complex set of interrelationships which we found among all these variables. Thus, I shall simply outline the general pattern of corporate-divisional relations suggested by our findings and consider how this pattern differed in conglomerate and vertically integrated firms.

Figure 1   MAJOR FACTORS AFFECTING INTER-UNIT RELATIONSHIPS

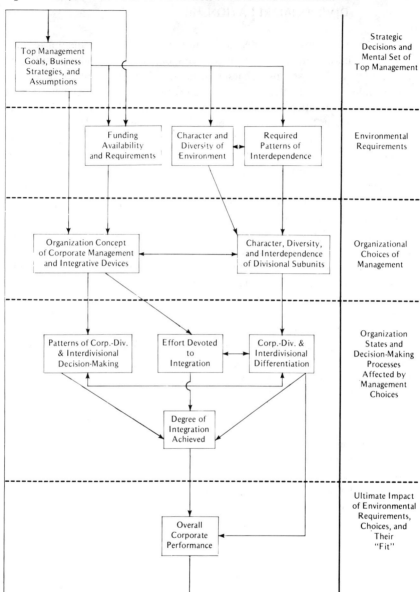

131

BASIC PATTERNS OF CORPORATE-
DIVISIONAL RELATIONSHIPS

Conglomerate firms face a unique set of environmental requirements. By definition, they face high levels of environmental diversity; yet,
paradoxically they are also characterized by relatively simple, required interdependence among their major organizational sub-units. The pattern of
inter-unit coordinative requirements which typifies these firms closely approximates what Thompson calls "pooled interdependence."[10] More specifically, the divisions enjoy a high degree of self-containment, the main area of
interdependence is between the headquarters and the divisions, and the
divisions are dealt with on a one-to-one basis by the headquarters unit.

When we began our study of the four conglomerates, we had several
hypotheses regarding the interrelationships we would find among environmental requirements, internal characteristics, and performance. First, we
reasoned that high levels of environmental diversity would tend to require
high levels of corporate-divisional differentiation. At the same time, we felt
that this high differentiation in practices and management orientations would
make it more difficult to achieve effective corporate-divisional integration.
Thus, we also expected that the higher the differentiation, the more effort
which would be required to achieve integration. We also reasoned that
performance factors would bear on these relationships in two ways. First, we
reasoned that low performing divisions would pose additional problems for
integration and thus require more integrative effort. Second, we hypothesized
that long-run corporate performance would be positively related to simultaneously achieving appropriate levels of corporate-divisional differentiation
and high integration.

Table 1 summarizes the overall patterns which we actually found. The two
high-performing firms were faced with high levels of environmental diversity
and achieved high differentiation. At the same time, however, they had high
levels of integration and relatively low levels of integrative effort. By way of
contrast, the two low performers were characterized by lower levels of
differentiation than their environmental diversity suggested was required. At
the same time, they were devoting considerably more effort to integration
but achieving lower integration.

These findings seem counter-intuitive. How could the high performers
achieve high integration in the face of high differentiation—and with less

Table 1 COMPARISON OF ORGANIZATIONAL STATES IN HIGHER AND LOWER
PERFORMING CONGLOMERATES

Organizational States	Two Higher Performers	Two Lower Performers
Differentiation	Higher	Lower
Integration	Higher	Lower
Integrative Effort	Lower	Higher

effort? Does this mean that the more effort a firm devotes to integration, the less integration it can expect to achieve? One explanation for the findings is that the pooled interdependence in conglomerates places both an upper and a lower limit on the benefits that can be gotten from integrative effort.[11] In other words, the lower performers seemed to have passed this upper limit; and, more specifically, this meant that they were overloading communication channels and also setting up internal requirements which were siphoning off the energies which their divisions might have focused on their own particular environments. This suggests the need to find a balance between requirements for diversity and interdependence and between internal organizational states and external requirements.

The foregoing explanation is somewhat abstract. To bring it down to earth, let's examine in more detail how a single, corporate-divisional relationship seemed to work. Figure 2 represents a general model of the operations of a single corporate-divisional relationship. This diagram describes the variables

Figure 2   BASIC PATTERN OF CORPORATE-DIVISIONAL RELATIONSHIPS

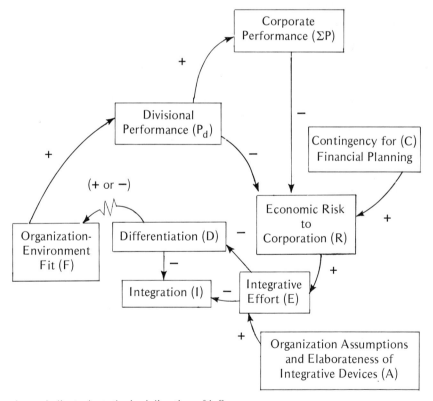

Arrow indicates hypothesized direction of influence.
Plus (+) indicates positive relationship.
Minus (−) indicates negative relationship.
Plus or minus (+ or −) and broken line indicates contingent relationship.

in the study as a set of mutual, causal relationships, some of which counteract one another and some of which feed back upon themselves. I should hasten to point out that this model is based on correlations among questionnaire data, and the directions of causation are inferred from interviews with the executives in the firms. At this point the model can be viewed only as one possible explanation of the findings; however, I am currently developing an industrial dynamics model based on these assumptions which will be tested with further field studies.[12]

The two factors which trigger the model are economic risk to the corporation (R) and organizational assumptions and integrative devices (A). We designed the study so as to be able to examine eight higher- and eight lower-risk corporate-divisional pairs. First, the lower-risk situation. If a division, through high performance (P_d) and/or low contingency for financial planning (C), posed a lower economic risk (R), this tended to lead to a lower level of integrative effort (E). Lower integrative effort seemed to permit higher differentiation (D) and also tended to be associated with higher integration (I). Although higher differentiation tended to create problems for achieving integration, these problems appeared to be counteracted by the positive effect that lower integrative effort had on integration. As noted above, this relationship between integrative effort and integration seemed to be based on the requirements posed by pooled interdependence in conglomerates. Now, let's close the loop. Any change in differentiation suggests a change in the orientations of divisional management. If higher differentiation for the high-performing division was still consistent with its environmental requirements— if it still maintained its organization-environment fit (F)—then performance would remain high and the whole relationship would tend to stabilize. So much for the successful situations.

A very different set of events seemed to emerge under high-risk situations. If a division were a low performer (P_d) this represented a greater risk (R), leading to higher integrative effort (E), which tended to reduce differentiation (D). At this point in the loop we encounter a contingent relationship. If lowered corporate-divisional differentiation led to a higher fit (F), this ultimately led to higher divisional performance; and the cycle tended to come to rest. If, however, lower corporate-divisional differentiation led to a lower fit (F), performance (P_d) would either remain low or decline further. This would lead to more integrative effort (E). Thus, the feedback loop can continue to amplify the very pressures which make it increasingly more difficult for the division to cope with its performance problems.

To carry this concept to the behavior of the firm as a whole, we added total corporate performance (ΣP) and elaborations of integrative devices (A). This helps to clarify the findings in Table 1. The two low performers had evolved much more complex integrative devices (e.g., intensive planning and budgeting exercises, large corporate staffs, more frequent top-down interventions). This corporate-wide set of organizational choices automatically raised the level of integrative effort. Also, the lower performance (ΣP) of these two firms placed additional pressure on the system via its effect on perception of risk (R).

While the model I have sketched is fairly general, I feel it begins to zero in on some of the crucial aspects of corporate-divisional relationships and how they operate. When applied in a specific conglomerate, it can help top management trace through the possible impacts of its organizational designs and intervention tactics. The model is particularly useful in considering the pitfalls which surround low-performance situations. In this vein, the findings may seem to paint a rather dismal picture of what can be done to improve matters. One thing is clear: simply more integrative effort and pressure for results not only may not improve things, but they may even trigger further deterioration. Further, integrative effort must be creatively managed.

There is something else that top management can do: focus on the quality as well as the quantity of integrative effort. In addition to the factors addressed in Figure 2, we found several qualitative aspects of corporate-divisional, decision-making processes which tended to facilitate appropriate differentiation and high integration. These included (1) intermediate orientations and high influence of managers in key coordinative positions, (2) maintaining an influence balance between the headquarters unit and divisional top management, (3) extensive use of problem solving (or confrontation of differences) to resolve conflicts, and (4) maintaining clear signals from the corporate office. In those low-performing situations where these factors were present, corporate-divisional integration and environmental fit did not tend to get into the self-defeating cycle which was discussed above.

So far my discussion has centered on the conglomerate firms. We found a very different pattern in the vertically integrated firms. The difference centered mainly around the interrelationships of differentiation, integration, and integrative effort. In these firms integrative effort again tended to reduce differentiation. However, higher integrative effort also resulted in higher integration. It appears that reduced differentiation tended to counteract the negative effects that integrative effort might have on integration. In terms of Figure 2, the relationships *D-I* appeared to exert a stronger force than the relationship *IE-I*. Why? Again the explanation seems to lie in environmental requirements.

The vertically integrated companies faced lower environmental diversity and more complex patterns of interdependence than the conglomerates. The pattern of interdependence which we found in these companies approximates what Thompson has termed "sequential and/or reciprocal" interdependence.[13] In other words, the division tended to be less self-contained; higher levels of both corporate-divisional and interdivisional communication were required; and the headquarters had to deal with several related divisions simultaneously. Thus, the lower environmental diversity and more complex interdependence of the vertically integrated firms required lower differentiation, more elaborate integrative devices, and higher integrative effort. One of the two firms which we studied met these requirements to a higher degree, and we found that it had both higher corporate-divisional integration and higher long-run corporate performance.

The differences which we found between the conglomerates and vertically integrated companies suggest that the range of feasible options for organizing and managing these two types of firms is quite different. Let's consider this issue of environmental requirements and organizational options in a bit more depth.

ENVIRONMENTAL REQUIREMENTS AND ORGANIZATIONAL OPTIONS

Table 2 summarizes the major differences we found between the high-performing conglomerates and vertically integrated companies with regard to environmental requirements, organizational choices, and resulting organizational states. Not only were the conglomerates faced with higher diversity and less complex interdependence, but they also had more overall environmental uncertainty and differing patterns of funds flow than the vertically integrated firms. Faced with the set of external requirements, the conglomerates had evolved a unique set of formal organizational arrangements—a higher degree of divisional self-containment, relatively small headquarters units which focused mainly on policy issues, and a less complex set of integrative devices (e.g., integrative positions, planning and budgeting procedures, and patterns of direct managerial contact). By way of contrast, the vertically integrated firms had lower degrees of divisional self-containment, larger headquarters units which exerted a direct impact on both policy and operating decisions (e.g., centralized Marketing and R&D functions for some parts of the business and centralized scheduling of paper mill output), and more complex integrative devices.

These differing patterns of organizational choice were associated with quite different organizational states and decision-making processes. For instance, the conglomerates developed higher levels of differentiation and depended upon less integrative effort. Divisional requests were acted upon more rapidly in these firms and the division general managers (three levels down in the organization) were the most influential level with regard to policy decisions. Also, these firms used much more formalized performance evaluation and reward systems. Both types of higher performers appeared to be well adapted to the particular set of environmental conditions which they faced. By way of contrast, it is interesting to note that the low-performing conglomerates had devised organizational approaches which tended toward those which would have been appropriate for a vertically integrated firm (e.g., larger headquarters units, more elaborate integrative devices, and direct corporate involvement in operating decisions). Similarly, the less effective vertically integrated firm appeared to be behaving more like a conglomerate (e.g., higher degrees of divisional self-containment and less elaborate integrative

Table 2 SUMMARY OF MAJOR DIFFERENCES BETWEEN CONGLOMERATE
AND VERTICALLY INTEGRATED FIRMS

Environmental Requirements	Patterns of Organizational Choice	Organizational States
Conglomerate Firms: Greater environmental diversity. Higher environmental uncertainty. Less complex required interdependence. Less intensive internal funding requirements. More uncertain patterns of funds flow.	Higher degree of divisional self-containment. Smaller headquarters units focusing mainly on policy issues. Less complex integrative devices.	Higher total differentiation. Lower integrative effort. Greater rapidity in responding to divisional requests. Influence peaks at a lower (division general manager) level. Performance evaluation systems with explicitly defined criteria, direct linkage between results and rewards, and heavier emphasis on financial/end-result criteria.
Vertically Integrated Firms: Lower environmental diversity. Lower environmental uncertainty. More complex required interdependence. More intensive internal funding requirements. More certain pattern of funds flow.	Lower degree of divisional self-containment. Larger headquarters units focusing on both policy and operating issues. More complex integrative devices.	Lower total differentiation. Higher integrative effort. Less rapidity in responding to divisional requests. Influence peaks at a higher (senior vice president) level. Performance evaluation systems which are more informally administered, without direct linkage between results and rewards, and balanced emphasis on financial/end-result and operating/intermediate criteria.

devices). It appears that these lower-performing companies had begun to move outside the range of feasible organizational options required by their environments.

What these findings suggest is simply this: the top management of every firm must develop or choose organizational forms to facilitate the overall control and coordination of the enterprise. This control and coordination is most effectively facilitated when top management chooses organizational forms which are congruent with the particular constellation of environmental factors faced by the firm. The conceptual scheme developed in this study provides one means of testing the environmental congruence of these choices as well as tracing through their impact on behavior within the firm. Let's consider the implications of this approach.

IMPLICATIONS FOR THEORY AND PRACTICE

In discussing the implications of our work for theory and practice, I do not wish to suggest a dichotomy between the two, for I believe they have strong common interests. Thus, I have argued that top management dearly needs a mental map—indeed, a theory—for dealing with the complexity of modern organizations. At the same time, I have been rather critical of much of the prior research in organizations because it has failed to model the range of variables which managers must consider in making organizational choices.

The implications for future organizational research are, therefore, that it should move more in the direction of developing multivariate, systemic models which can describe the complex interrelatedness of modern organizations. Such an undertaking requires the use of knowledge developed in diverse fields, e.g., economics, finance, sociology, psychology, political science, and (more indirectly) the physical sciences. In other words, the social and organizational problems we need to work on require an interdisciplinary approach.

While the study I have discussed represents one step in this direction, it is a very small step because it suffers from all the limitations of a point-in-time comparative study. To begin to gain the necessary insights into organizational design we must devise methods for determining how organizations change. It seems to me that this will require either longitudinal studies—which are time-consuming, expensive, and very difficult to design—and/or the use of simulation techniques. If and when we can begin to model the dynamics of interrelatedness in organizations, and between organizations and their environments, we will have a very powerful tool.

The conceptual model I have discussed can be useful to managers who are involved in designing complex organizations in several ways. First, it points to the importance of designing organizations in terms of their basic environmental requirements. The findings strongly support the contention that there is no single best way to organize a multi-unit enterprise. Second, the study points to a different way of looking at the issues of control and coordination. It suggests that the key issue is maintaining appropriate differentiation among sub-units as well as high integration between these units and the corporate headquarters.

Very often there is a tendency for managers to seize upon a single tool to solve their organizational problems, e.g., profit centers, long-range planning systems, or incentive compensation devices. Our findings suggest that it is necessary to trace through the behavioral impact of any single tool as well as coordinate its use with the full range of organizational devices employed by the firm. Indeed, it seems that it is the consistency of organizational devices with one another and with the firm's environmental requirements which is really crucial.

Although this study was designed to examine the particular organizational problems faced by multi-unit industrial enterprises, the management of sub-unit diversity and interdependence is an issue common to all complex organizations—both in the private and public sectors. As these institutions face increasingly complex and changing conditions, explicit organizational planning becomes a critical skill; and, thus, knowledge concerning the options for and potential effects of organizational design also becomes increasingly important. The concepts and findings I have discussed are aimed at providing a systematic analytical base from which administrators can identify organizational options and begin to gauge their behavioral effects.

FOOTNOTES

1. Sloan, Alfred P., *My Years With General Motors* (New York: Doubleday & Co., 1963), p. 53.
2. Lorsch, Jay W. and Allen, S. A., *The Whole and the Parts: A Comparative Study of Corporate-Divisional Relations in Diversified Firms* (Tentative title of manuscript in progress).
3. See, for example, Fayol, H., *Industrial and General Administration* (Paris: Dunod, 1925) and Gulick, L. and Urwick, L. (eds.), *Papers on the Science of Administration* (New York: Institute of Public Administration, Columbia University, 1937).
4. See, for example, Blau, Peter, and Scott, W., *Formal Organizations* (San Francisco: Chandler, 1962) and Gouldner, Alvin, *Patterns of Industrial Bureaucracy* (Glencoe, Ill.: Free Press, 1954).
5. See, for example, Blake, Robert, et. al., *Managing Intergroup Conflict in Industry* (Houston: Gulf Publishing, 1964) and Pondy, Louis R., "Organizational Conflict: Concepts and Models," *Administrative Science Quarterly*, September, 1967.
6. See, for example, Ashby, W. R., *Design for a Brain* (New York: Wiley, 1960), Buckley, Walter, *Sociology and Modern Systems Theory* (Englewood Cliffs, N.J.: Prentice-Hall, 1967), and von Bertalanffy, L., *General Systems Theory* (New York: George Braziller, 1968).
7. Lawrence, Paul R., and Lorsch, Jay W., *Organization and Environment* (Boston: Division of Research, Harvard Business School, 1967).
8. March, James D. and Simon, Herbert A., *Organizations* (New York: Wiley, 1958).
9. Thompson, James D., *Organizations in Action* (New York: McGraw-Hill, 1967).
10. *Ibid.*, pp. 54-55.
11. A similar pattern for individual and group information processing capacities has

been reported in Schroeder, Harold M., et al., *Human Information Processing* (New York: Holt, Rinehart & Winston, 1967).
  12. For a description of this technique see Forrester, Jay W., *Industrial Dynamics* (Cambridge, Mass.: M.I.T. Press, 1961) and Roberts, Edward B., *The Dynamics of Research and Development* (New York: Harper & Row, 1964).
  13. Thompson, *op. cit.*

ORGANIZATIONAL ARCHETYPES OF A MULTINATIONAL COMPANY

DAVID P. RUTENBERG

Decision premises, within which plans are made, should be formulated with an eye to the organization that will implement the results. This assertion seems especially relevant for multinational companies which consist of a headquarters with subsidiaries around the globe. Four archetypes of the relationship between a headquarters and its subsidiaries are presented. These are based on theory developed by Leavitt (executive-workers), and Churchman and Schainblatt (analyst-manager). Each archetype is developed by using existing literature to explore patterns of bounded rationality that would emerge in different organizational structures. After an example of a corporation illustrative of the archetype, appropriate planning guidelines are presented for investment discount rates, pricing policy, product design, planned managerial rotation, and liquid asset management.

Introduction

A multinational company does more than import and export from its U.S. home plant. It may do research in Germany, engineering design in Japan, and then manufacture in Taiwan, Italy, and Mexico to supply a hundred national markets, including the U.S. market in which its headquarters may be located. A number of multinational companies already move products, managers, capital, and research around the world, adjusting the rates of flow as local environments change. The ideal is to be rational on a global basis.

Current international management practice falls short of this ideal. There is very little sophisticated mathematical planning for international operations. For example, surprisingly few operations research models have been developed for international planning and coordination. Operations researchers object to the risks and uncertainties that cannot be assumed away, and to the confused problem statements. Risks and uncertainties constitute a weak excuse when one realizes that military planning is undertaken despite risks and uncertainties far greater than those ever encountered within a multinational company. In fact, mathematical analysis should offer a unique contri-

From *Management Science*, vol. 16, no. 6, February 1970, pp. B337-B349. Reprinted with permission of the author and publisher.

bution in environments of rapid inflation and great uncertainty, where U.S. business intuition may be quite inappropriate. Nevertheless there remains the objection to confused and contradictory problem statements.

One might conjecture that the degree of confusion in problem formulation would be linked to the industry and the formal organizational structure. Fouraker and Stopford [9] found a significant correlation between the extent of expansion abroad and Chandler's [2] organizational structure. Corporations with few related products (steel and nonferrous metals), organized by function, have not expanded to integrated operations abroad. Corporations with many product lines (electrical, transportation, power machinery, chemicals) generally have a product divisional structure, and have undertaken substantial expansion abroad. Chandler noted that some industries lay between these two clear-cut cases (agricultural processing, oil, rubber, mass merchandising) and are laced with dotted-line relationships between functional and product organization which, one might conjecture, would add ambiguity to problem definitions.

This may well be true, but there are ambiguous problem statements even in Chandler's clear-cut industries. In fact, unique statements of problems appear less possible as one looks in more microscopic detail at the statutory organization of a real company. There are technical licensing agreements with autonomous partners, intimate cross licensing in which know-how has been exchanged for some equity and the aspiration of more, various species of joint ventures, even management service contracts. Nor is there aesthetic refuge even among the wholly owned subsidiaries, for most have grown too fast and too unevenly. According to Lovell ([18], p. 85) "the lack of system in the organization charts of international management units is simply a reflection of the existing uneven state of development, and the different volume of activity within the various geographical areas, functions, and product lines." In an international company one might expect the formal organization to have even less relevance to the informal organization than in a domestic company subject to one set of laws. The reasons were explained a decade ago by Clee and diScipio [4].

For a number of reasons (e.g. local legal requirements, tax advantages, or need for financial control), a company creating a world enterprise often sets up a statutory corporate structure that differs from the more fluid and informal (though very real) lines of communication followed in the day-to-day operations of the business. The *statutory organization* is designed to put the pieces of the company together into a legal structure that optimizes cash flow for the overall corporation. The manner in which the company is actually coordinated and run involves a set of working relationships that are constructed to fit the managerial requirements of the company.... Recognizing the distinction between the formal statutory organization and the manner in which the total business is coordinated and managed dispels much of the fog that often surrounds all foreign operations.

The theme of this paper is that planning guidelines emerge as one studies the convictions of headquarters executives. Such men usually have firm convictions about the working relationships they shall have with foreign subsidiaries, and how the subsidiaries should regard headquarters. Clearly if two such executives have different convictions they will provide the planner with different (probably contradictory) decision premises within which to develop optimal plans. In this paper we shall delve into headquarter's behavioral patterns that appear to foster different convictions as to headquarters-subsidiary relationships. It is asserted that an appropriate combination of four archetypal patterns is very helpful in comprehending real problems, though naturally no archetype can encapsule the whole of reality. Thus an operations researcher could work through the implications of four sets of decision premises by formulating and solving his problem for each, and thereby gauge the significance of the political choice of premises being made around him.

To launch the taxonomy, we shall temporarily use a gross simplication of reality. We shall interpret headquarters as one person, and a subsidiary as another person. We can then invoke research into the interpersonal relationships between people two at a time. Clearly this is too gross a simplification, so we shall enrich each of the four archetypes with the insight of past investigators of organizational theory.

Leavitt ([16], Chapters 11-13), analysing relationships between people two at a time, focused on a person intervening in the affairs of another, both directly and indirectly. He devoted a chapter to each of authority, manipulation, and collaboration. Churchman and Schainblatt [3] analyzed the process one person might use to affect another, focusing on the question of whether each understood the other (understand was given the strong definition of ability to anticipate, teleologically, the other person's response). Churchman and Schainblatt devoted a section to each of communication, persuasion, and mutual understanding. Both taxonomies deal with people two at a time. Let one person be the headquarters, the other a subsidiary.

Clearly a specific problem must be in mind if these questions are to be answerable. Most headquarters intervene in major capital expansions of their subsidiaries, but few require central coordination of minor office supplies.

Figure 1   MULTINATIONAL CORPORATION INTERPRETATION OF THE
TAXONOMIES OF LEAVITT, AND OF CHURCHMAN AND SCHAINBLATT

| | | *Indirect intervention by headquarters?* *Headquarters understands subsidiaries?* | |
		NO	YES
Direct intervention by headquarters?		*Archetype 1* no intervention separate function	*Archetype 2* manipulation persuasion
	NO		
	YES		
Subsidiaries urged to understand headquarters?		*Archetype 3* authority communication	*Archetype 4* collaboration mutual understanding

Thus one company can occupy all four archetypes simultaneously, but on different problems. For a *given* planning problem, at a given time, this poses no problem. However, problems arise because different subsidiaries are treated differently. There is then a conflict between standardizing all subsidiaries, allowing a few exceptions, or grouping subsidiaries as to their most suitable archetype for the problem under consideration.

Easing people's transition between archetypes is central to the work of Perlmutter [22], [23], a social psychologist concerned with the way international managers impose boundaries upon the range of their awareness. Perlmutter's terminology has become popular in European discussions of multinational companies. Archetype 1 would be described as a polycentric headquarters with ethnocentric subsidiaries; there is no headquarters intervention, so there become as many corporate strategies as there are subsidiaries, and the awareness of each subsidiary is circumscribed by the borders of its nation. In Perlmutter's terminology Archetype 2 has a geocentric headquarters and ethnocentric subsidiaries as the headquarters manipulates and persuades the subsidiaries. In Archetype 3 the headquarters is ethnocentric and authoritarian, so the subsidiaries react by becoming xenophobic and resent the one-way stream of communication from headquarters. In Archetype 4 collaboration and mutual understanding are possible because both headquarters and its subsidiaries maintain geocentric world views. The focus is on interpersonal relations and convictions, rather than organizational structure.

The purpose of this paper is to evaluate the literature that might justify different planning decision premises within different archetypes of multinational companies. Decision premises are an acknowledgement of bounded rationality, a concept fundamental to the organization theory of Simon [26] and March and Simon [19].

ARCHETYPE 1

The separate function position, in which each subsidiary is a center of decision making for itself, occurs when:

(1) The legal owner is a holding company which has diversified its holdings over many countries.
(2) The legal owner of subsidiaries is a large U.S. company. Its headquarters International Division has not grown as subsidiaries evolved abroad, and it is clogged with work.

A corporation engaged primarily in domestic business cannot afford to have all of its executives keep up to date about changes in tariffs, foreign exchange regulations, and political ideologies. Howe Martyn ([20], p. 135) has described the evolution of ethnocentric subsidiaries when headquarters control is weak:

... The theory has been that [presidents of subsidiaries] need almost complete freedom to make the best use of their knowledge of local conditions and to take prompt actions. There has also been an unacknowledged readiness to shift some of the heavy weight of responsibility that burdens the top management of a large concern. Why should the parent company look for trouble? Let Jones, who is on the spot, follow his own way, which he says is the African or Australian way, so long as he makes profits.

The multinational company has a geographical diversified portfolio of investments, whose stream of total income should therefore be quite steady. Unfortunately, as relative business conditions change around the world, there is no adjustment mechanism to reallocate markets to plants, or otherwise to change the rate of flow of resources. Furthermore, because there is no strong central coordination, the bottom-up nature of planning in this Archetype will likely result in many small investments which otherwise might have been combined for economics of scale.

For the twenty years preceding 1948, the Ford Motor Corporation had a separate function relationship with its subsidiaries abroad. The stronger ones, such as British Ford, spawned subsidiaries of their own, adopted a local identity, and became entrenched in their independence. In the years after 1948 Ford gradually assumed control of these subsidiaries. The consequences at British Ford are criticized by Simmonds [28].

In this archetype no planning guidelines can be presented, for no operations planning is performed by the headquarters. The four illustrative problem areas that will be used for all archetypes are:

A. *Cost of Capital:* Each subsidiary will undertake its own capital expansions, using its own decision criteria. The marginal cost of capital will be the cost of any local borrowing that does not require headquarters approval.

B. *Pricing Policy:* Each subsidiary will set its own prices, bargaining for transfer prices on intercorporate imports without cognizance of worldwide production interdependence.

C. *Product Design:* Design standardization will be rare, and headquarters attempts to issue guidelines will be thwarted; such guidelines would impinge upon the autonomy of the subsidiary.

D. *Managerial Rotation:* Although individual subsidiaries may plan managerial development through rotation, there will be no intersubsidiary movement of managers nor will there be rotation to or from the headquarters.

E. *Liquid Assets:* Each subsidiary will manage its own portfolio of liquid assets, and there will be no mechanism by which a subsidiary in need of funds can obtain them from other subsidiaries.

ARCHETYPE 2

This archetype corresponds to Churchman and Schainblatt's [3] persuasion position. The headquarters has a geocentric viewpoint, understands the details of its subsidiaries, and how the subsidiaries interact. The subsidiaries are not urged to attain a similar geocentric understanding. In fact, as Leavitt ([16], Chapter 12) would see the interrelationship, the myopic ethnocentricity of the subsidiaries leaves them open to manipulation by headquarters.

Headquarters would be most likely to understand each national subsidiary if it is arranged into geographical divisions of formal responsibility. A contact officer mans a national desk, and all communication to the subsidiary is channelled through him. Clee and Sachtjen [5] have suggested that a geographical structure of formal responsibility is especially viable if only a narrow range of products is manufactured and marketed. It is also appropriate if the products are sold to nationalistic local governments. Robinson ([24], Chapter 8) calls this structure a multinational firm and emphasizes that it is psychologically viable only when more than 50 percent of sales are outside the headquarters nation. It may appear a little ironical to recommend gaining control over ethnocentric subsidiaries by creating a geographically organized headquarters. Yet this seems necessary if understanding (such that headquarters can teleologically anticipate the reactions of each subsidiary) is deemed a prerequisite for control.

The danger inherent in a geographically structured headquarters is that the contact officers may identify too closely with the subsidiary they are supposed to be controlling and become its proponent with headquarters. Some of the factors affecting group identification have been discussed by March and Simon ([19], Chapter 3).

March and Simon ([19], p. 68) suggest that similarity of background and similarity of position increase the perception of shared goals. Headquarters could recruit contact officers from the same graduate school of business, and by small group pressure encourage them to dress alike. On the other hand, the contact officer has some prior knowledge of, and probably empathy for, the nation he is supposed to control, and will identify with it.

The sharing of common goals and the satisfaction of an individual's needs within the headquarters group will tend to increase the frequency of his interaction with the group. This also works in reverse, and at a superficial

Figure 2 BASIC FACTORS AFFECTING GROUP IDENTIFICATION
(rearranged from March and Simon [19], Figure 3-8)

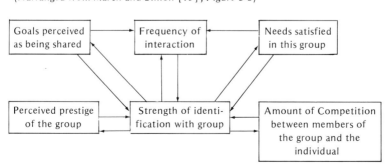

level calls for company dining rooms, cocktail parties, and social pressure to live in the same suburb. But if meaningfulness of interaction leads to group identification, there has to be a common language or planning framework in which to converse about the nebulous uncertainties of international business. On the other hand, the contact officer interacts with his subsidiary. He is exposed to a deluge of communication about the subsidiary, about government balance of payments policies, growth policies, commercial risks, and general political and social movements of the nation. His visits abroad are to the nation, and, in turn, he acts as host for visitors from the nation.

The more needs satisfied by a group, the closer a person identifies with it. A number of psychologists such as Maslow [21] have proposed hierarchies of human needs. The contact officer occupying a national desk in headquarters will have his physical and social needs satisfied by his pay check, fellow employees and family. Once these have been gratified, then a failure to achieve his ego ideal or his self-actualization in headquarters will appear most acute. He will identify with the subsidiary, and any desire for power in his ego ideal may well be satisfied by his relationship with it. He dominates the subsidiary and has autonomy of action to veto or censor messages sent to it. By linking this autonomy with the artistic subtlety of his job he can even satisfy his needs for self-actualization as he tries to make his part of the world into the image he desires.

There is a self-fulfilling prophesy to the contact officer's perception of the prestige of his headquarters. If the headquarters intervenes in the affairs of the subsidiaries then the contact officer will see the importance of headquarters, will tend to identify with it, and will therefore be more willing to intervene in the affairs of his subsidiary. Furthermore, he will likely strive to get promoted within headquarters, and this aspiration will weaken his identification with his subsidiary. The subsidiary itself may be prestigious. Prestige accrues to a subsidiary because of its size and its importance to the multinational corporation. But the general political prestige of the country will also influence the perceptions of the contact officer.

If an individual is in competition with other members of a group, then "in making a decision, he evaluates the several alternatives of choice in terms of their consequences for the specified group." (Simon [26], p. 205.) Competition helps him identify with the group; of course he will be scheming against the group if the competition becomes more serious than sporting. Each contact officer will identify with headquarters to the extent that he has an adequate conceptual framework to see that he is competing against other national desks for corporate resources. However, the contact officer is also in competition with his subsidiary. If the subsidiary employees are intelligent, an element of gaming in their responses is inevitable. So long as the contact officer retains his feeling of superiority then the more cunningly responsive the subsidiary the more he will be engrossed with it. There are a number of geographically organized companies depicted in Lovell [18]. Generally they are mature companies with mature product lines, so that marketing is their most important function. Clee and Sachtjen [5] describe a Massey-Ferguson like Gamma, Ltd.

Some years ago Gamma, Ltd., a huge international farm equipment manufacturer whose operations had been organized along regional lines adopted an organizational structure built around a series of largely self-contained marketing and manufacturing operations units. These are centered on important individual markets (the United Kingdom, France, Germany, the United States, and Canada). Supplementing these units is an export marketing unit to cover sales in parts of the world where Gamma has no manufacturing operations.

Longer-range corporate strategy—determination of the basic worldwide product line, decisions on major facilities, and changes in the logistic product flow from production sources to markets—is set at corporate headquarters. But these decisions are heavily influenced by operations unit judgments and recommendations. Each unit is responsible for determining the product lines best suited to its local markets.

In an extreme example of this archetype the pattern of interaction within the headquarters, and the relationships with the subsidiaries, would result in unambiguous planning guidelines within which a problem would be formulated and optimized. In a real geographically organized company, other views might prevail, but one would expect as strong sentiment for the following guidelines:

A. *Cost of Capital:* Especially if shares of each subsidiary are listed on its nation's stock exchange will each subsidiary remit a standard dividend to headquarters. This dividend will be adjusted only if inequities appear in the use to which retained earnings can be put. Thus the discount rate used in capital budgeting need not be identical in all subsidiaries, nor will it include the cost of taxes of repatriation back to headquarters.

B. *Pricing Policy:* Though joint production costs will be recognized in setting national prices, no pricing system will be imposed on the subsidiaries.

C. *Product Design:* Products will be designed or chosen to best suit each national subsidiary. If the company tailors design to each national requirement, it can get its products reclassified by customs inspectors so that they pay lower rates of import duty, can meet local safety and engineering standards, can use local grades and types of raw materials inputs, and can cater to local customer tastes. Tempering this on an *ad hoc* basis will be efforts to standardize some components so as to ease trans-shipments. Nevertheless the total number of designs will be quite high.

D. *Managerial Rotation:* Nationals will be employed in each subsidiary to the greatest extent possible, and only bilateral movements of managers will be planned. Nationals will be brought to headquarters to learn technical positions so that they can return to their homeland. In their temporary absence, Americans may fill their position.

E. *Liquid Assets:* Although each subsidiary will manage its own portfolio of liquid assets, dividend payments will be manipulated to get liquidity to subsidiaries in need. Some intersubsidiary loans may be arranged by the headquarters, but transfer prices and fee payments will remain unmanipulated.

ARCHETYPE 3

It sometimes happens that a prominent domestic company decides to expand abroad by building subsidiaries. It may have had an international division before, but its product managers were insulated from foreign business, and are now openly concerned about the instability of each foreign country, and suspicious of nationals as potential employees. They are ethnocentric. With the self-assurance of missionaries, their attitude is that "we (people of country A) are superior, and have greater resources, facilities and competence than you (people of country B). We will build facilities in your country if you accept our inherent superiority, and our methods and procedures for doing the job." (Perlmutter, [22]). Especially if the company has been successful domestically will it feel that its standard methods and procedures for problem solving represent a unique contribution that the alien company can make to the economy of the host country. The headquarters, therefore, requires that these standards and procedures be used by the subsidiaries. Product and professional specialists fly about the world educating their subsidiary counterparts.

The headquarters may not understand the environmental details of its subsidiaries. If it does not, it cannot tailor communications to the subsidiary but instead must urge the subsidiary to understand the way headquarters perceives the world, and implement communications in that way. Churchman and Schainblatt [3] call this the communications position, emphasizing its one-way flow. Leavitt ([16]), Chapter 11) would describe the behavior of the headquarters as authoritarian, for its intervention in the affairs of its subsidiaries is direct, rather than manipulatively indirect. If there are few products, the company can be organized by function: worldwide marketing, worldwide production, worldwide accounting, etc. Usually there are more products, and each product division can be given worldwide line responsibility, backed by functional staffs.

If the production process for a product is complex, each subsidiary production manager will tend to identify with his worldwide product. He will probably develop a loyalty to his product division and may view himself as only temporarily stationed in some particular subsidiary. Furthermore, his

Figure 3   FORCES LEADING TO STANDARDIZATION

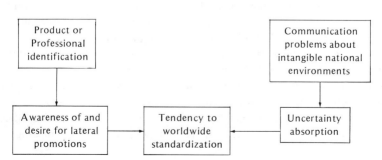

advancement is likely to be in the form of lateral moves, in the same product division, to larger subsidiaries. As a member of a group of professionals or product specialists, whether in headquarters or in the subsidiaries, he will be affected by norms of behavior. An individual whose recommendations transcend group norms will be eased out of the group. If a production manager recommends a non-standard design, tailoring products to a certain nation, he may find himself stuck at that plant for the rest of his working life. Perhaps this group identification is the basis for Martyn's observation ([20], p. 139) that:

It is a strict rule among the long-established international firms to manufacture the same products or to deliver the same services on which their home success was founded in as many countries as possible. If one of these products will not sell in a country for peculiar national reasons (soap with a carbolic smell was associated with brothels in France), the international concern prefers to withdraw rather than modify the product. Accepting variations would leave the company without consistent standards, which could disturb its accounting and its marketing, as well as its production arrangements.

A number of companies have been organized along product and professional lines so as to assure that the local subsidiaries will be run well but have then selected a local national president. The local president, assured that business is being well taken care of, is expected to make public appearances to refute the negative impression his (host) nation has of foreign corporations. He may not understand the language of each product and professional group, but he is likely to develop a well-founded suspicion that their decisions are not in the best interests of his subsidiary. But he can do little about it, because though he has formal authority he lacks professional authority (Etzioni, [7], Chapter 8). His reaction will probably be that of xenophobia—distrustful fear of foreigners, and their machinations.

One might expect the most vivid examples of product divisionalization to occur in the electrical manufacturing industry. Unfortunately, the example of General Electric is complicated by the indigestibility of Machines Bull of France, and the example of Westinghouse by its history of licensing agreements so that until recently foreign operations were minimal. Thus we shall use a Cellanese like example that Clee and Sachtjen [5] named Epsilon. This is a mature company that still maintains traces of its former geographical organization.

Since Epsilon's large and diversified domestic operations overshadow their foreign counterparts, the [product] group organizations are built around the existing domestic companies. At the heart of each worldwide group is the domestic operation. . . . Each product group has a vice-president-international, who acts as a deputy for international matters, with as much responsibility for managing the group's foreign operations as his group executive chooses to assign. Functional and technical advice are provided by appropriate staff at the domestic operating company level or the corporate level.

To coordinate the various product-group activities in major world markets, Epsilon has established area managers at the corporate staff level. Each area manager is responsible for keeping corporate management and the product groups informed about economic, political, and social developments in his assigned area. . . .

In a pure Archetype 3 relationship certain planning guidelines would rarely be questioned.

A. *Cost of Capital:* Financial resources are directed by the headquarters which is the only source of expansion capital. The discount rate used for capital budgeting will have to include the cost of taxes of repatriation. For reasons of control (though at an incredible tax cost) a few companies actually do repatriate profits each year, but most suffice with tight administrative control.

B. *Pricing Policy:* An item is sold at its U.S. price around the world, though the customer pays freight plus import duty. Performance evaluation is then more direct, and customers which are other multinational companies cannot buy in low-price nations for use in high price nations.

C. *Product Design:* The U.S. design will be sold in all nations, except where some law necessitates minor modifications. This policy will be justified by the cost of research and development, and thus the fixed cost of introducing another product. At a more sophisticated level, if a company manufactures identical products around the world it can achieve economies of scale, can benefit from the reliability of multiple manufacturing plants, can enjoy easier maintenance and can consider standardized marketing campaigns.

D. *Managerial Rotation:* Planning guidelines for managerial rotation will be quite explicit for Americans, who will be moved between subsidiaries and then back to headquarters. The acute shortage of local managerial talent will necessitate all local nationals staying within their subsidiaries, where their contribution is greatest.

E. *Liquid Assets:* The dividend rate will be set equal to earnings minus capital required for approved expansions. Any excess liquidity will be managed by the headquarters. If a currency is blocked, transfer prices and fee payments will be manipulated to get money out.

If the planning group can convince headquarters product executives of the appropriateness of their work, worldwide implementation is probable; the subsidiaries will succumb. This stands in contrast to Archetype 2 where implementation of a plan would be less likely.

ARCHETYPE 4

In the theory of this archetype of mutual understanding, headquarters not only understands the subsidiaries but also realizes that its maneuvers are understood by each subsidiary. Furthermore, it tries to encourage this understanding, for headquarter's ability so to encourage the subsidiaries is one measure of its own understanding of them. Leavitt ([16], Chapter 13), discussing collaboration, would have headquarters intervene indirectly in the affairs of a subsidiary so that the latter would recognize its areas of weakness and call in the headquarters for direct help.

Churchman and Schainblatt [3] eulogized mutual understanding, then described it in less than two pages. Leavitt ([16], Chapter 13) was reduced to using Alcoholics Anonymous as his example of collaborative organization. Similarly, Howard Perlmutter [22] depicted only the goal of a geocentric-geocentric organization, not the means. Although the previous archetypes have been descriptive of real companies, this fourth and final archetype is more conjectural. The first step to organizational design is to draw clear distinction between employees destined to remain always in their subsidiary (or their headquarters) and employees who will travel and live around all their lives. The latter group, the cadre of international managers, cannot be expected to accept pay differentials based on their original nationality. A pool of mobile managers is desirable for two reasons. First, the company would like to be able to adapt quickly to changes in business environments, and be able to move *some* people from a slack nation to a booming nation (this is in addition to the effective movement of people by the ability to have a worldwide engineering staff, in Japan perhaps, stop working on projects in the slack nation and turn to projects for the booming nation). The second reason for having this cadre is that they act as link pins ([17], 1961) to effect responsive communication and coordination between the following four dimensions of an organizational grid:

—area
—product
—function
—planning time horizon.

The dimension of different planning horizons is implicit in the ability to respond flexibly to environmental changes. The need for long-range planning is accentuated by the nationalistic reactions of host governments, and of local partners in joint ventures which make it difficult to back out of ventures. In this hypothetical geocentric-geocentric organizational design, the formal structure of authority shall be based on planning time horizon.

The multinational headquarters as a group is primarily engaged in strategic and entrepreneurial planning. This has been described for domestic companies by Ansoff ([1], p. 8), and must be done globally.

Extrapolative projections of the firm's present product-market position are supplemented by probing and far-ranging analyses of the firm's environment to discover threats and opportunities which may produce major departures from the extrapolative projections of performance and resources. . . .

The analysis involves studies of: economic and social forces which determine demand for the firm's products; the nature of the competitive forces which operate in its markets; and prospects for political and social changes which will affect the company and its environment.

Another new activity is a "strengths and weaknesses" analysis, which attempts to determine and project the firm's capabilities and skills. This includes estimates of both reserve and excess capabilities as well as distinctive capabilities possessed by the firm.

Massive information flows are implied, especially for information that cannot readily be reduced to unambiguous technical terms—reporting on possible government actions to further national development is appreciably more complex than reporting last month's production rate. March and Simon ([19], p. 164), emphasize that:

It is extremely difficult to communicate about intangible objects and non-standard objects. Hence, the heaviest burdens are placed on the communications system by the less-structured aspects of the organization's tasks, particularly by activity directed toward the explanation of problems that are not well defined.

Because a multinational company operates in many environments, and can thereby move resources from an adverse to a favorable national environment, it is all the more important that some group compare environments. This will not occur automatically. As Leavitt ([16]), p. 33) so clearly states: "People perceive what they think will help satisfy needs; ignore what is disturbing; and again perceive disturbances that persist and increase."

The various Area headquarters perform tactical planning and establish controls for the subsidiaries. There must be procedures and controls if production is to be coordinated, for this implies cross shipments of parts and subassemblies, coordinated inventories and production smoothing over all nations in the Area. Strongly centralized procedures and controls are also vital if transfer pricing between subsidiaries is to be used as an instrument of corporate financial-tax policy rather than be a hotbed of bitter acrimony. But the key difference between this and Archetype 3 is that now there are several Area headquarters. As soon as one Area adopts different norms and standards, an aware subsidiary elsewhere in the world realizes that it no longer faces an invincible wall of a single worldwide standard and is more likely to get procedures tailored to its local conditions. This possibility encourages a geocentric awareness by the subsidiary.

Though several corporations are close, there are not yet any examples of truly multinational, transnational, or global corporations illustrating Archetype 4. Shell Oil, and Standard Oil of New Jersey have historically developed very capable local managements in each subsidiary. These managements are now being urged to think globally and the use of third country nationals is becoming common. Nevertheless, perhaps Unilever is even closer to being geocentric except for its subsidiaries in the U.S.A. and in underdeveloped nations.

Most routine O.R. problems will occur in the Area headquarters, although their initial conception probably occurred in the planning group of the multinational headquarters. Thus it is still possible to propose guidelines consistent with the archetype.

A. *Cost of Capital:* Capital can be raised in many nations of the world, especially if it to be used locally, though capital can be moved between some nations. Thus the appropriate discount rate for a project in one nation depends on the strategic plans of the multinational company, for they determine the interest rates and tax liabilities.

B. *Pricing Policy:* In pricing a line of products for Archetype 4, an appropriate guideline would be to optimally determine the vector of one benchmark country (e.g. U.S.A.), and simultaneously calculate an optimal scale factor for each nation by which to multiply the vector of benchmark prices to obtain local prices. This scheme is simple enough to permit central coordination, yet is also responsive to overall market conditions in each nation.

C. *Product Design:* Non-price marketing considerations lead to a proliferation of tailored designs as described in Archetype 2. Product considerations tend to a single design to be marketed throughout the world. One rational approach to an optimum would be to modularize the design by subassemblies (and styling panels). Some modules would be standard around the world.

D. *Managerial Rotation:* In Archetype 4, multilateral moves, the use of "third country nationals" must be analyzed. The number of Americans and other foreigners who can hold executive positions in a subsidiary may be restricted by a host government, so it would seem that these slots should be allocated with care, being viewed as an opportunity to gain familiarity with that nation. The emphasis upon linking pins implies selecting personnel who can tolerate the role ambiguity such a position implies.

E. *Liquid Assets:* Dividends, intersubsidiary loans, transfer prices and managerial fee payments will be manipulated to get liquidity to subsidiaries when they need it, but in such a way as to minimize taxes paid to the world minus interest earned [25].

Conclusions

Once it has made a commitment in some nation, the foreignness of a multinational company may result in its having less flexibility than a native company. On the other hand, at the planning stage, until a commitment is made to a market name, a plant, or a work force, the multinational company has exceptional flexibility to set patterns for the movement of products, managers, money, and know-how. For example, the multinational company can establish a market in a nation long before it builds a plant, and then it can size that plant according to the number of national markets it is to serve. If the company is growing in a hundred nations, it faces many possible combinations of resource deployment patterns. The role of a headquarters planning group is to sift for the most promising ones.

On the other hand, it is not easy to plan in a multinational company. Data is lacking or irrelevant to the problem at hand, even for deterministic models, yet surely flexibility in the face of uncertainty should be achieved. Different interest groups have different perceptions of the same problems. Plans are not implemented, and planners become frustrated. Implicit throughout the paper is the viewpoint that to be effective a planning group must understand the positions within the multinational company, so as to implement from a Churchman-Schainblatt [3] persuasion position.

Four archetypes have been described, and for each appropriate planning guidelines have been put forth for a few problems. No archetypes encapsule the whole of reality; they merely provide a conceptual framework in which to hold problems of setting decision premises. At the very least, one has a mental check list to guide the discussion of ways to tackle a problem.

REFERENCES

1. Ansoff, H. Igor, *The Evolution of Corporate Planning*, Stanford Research Institute, Long Range Planning Service Report No. 329, Menlo Park, California, September 1967.
2. Chandler, A. D., Jr. *Strategy and Structure*, Doubleday and Company, Inc., Garden City, New York, 1966.
3. Churchman, C. West and A. H. Schainblatt, "The Researcher and the Manager: A Dialectic of Implementation," *Management Science*, Vol. 11, No. 4, (February 1965).
4. Clee, Gilbert H. and Alfred diScipio, "Creating a World Enterprise," *Harvard Business Review*, (November-December 1959).
5. —— and W. M. Sachtjen, "Organizing a Worldwide Business," *Harvard Business Review*, (November-December 1964).
6. Creelman, G. D. and R. W. Wallen, "The Place of Psychology in Operations Research," *Operations Research*, (January-February 1958).
7. Etzioni, Amitai, *Modern Organizations*, Prentice-Hall, Englewood Cliffs, 1964.
8. Faltermayer, Edmund K., "It's a Spryer Singer," *Fortune*, (December 1963), pp. 145-167.
9. Fouraker, Lawrence E. and John M. Stopford, "Organizational Structure and the Multinational Strategy," *Administrative Science Quarterly*, (June 1968), pp. 47-64.
10. Gulick, Luther and L. Urwick (eds.), *Papers on the Science of Administration*, Institute of Public Administration, New York, 1937.
11. Haire, Mason (ed.), *Modern Organization Theory*, Wiley, New York, 1959.
12. ——, E. E. Ghisselli, and L. W. Porter "Cultural Patterns in the Role of the Manager," *Industrial Relations*, Vol. 2, No. 2, (February 1963), pp. 96-117.
13. ——, ——, and ——, *Managerial Thinking*, Wiley, New York, 1966.
14. Hall, Edward T., *The Silent Language*, Fawcett, New York, 1959.
15. Kolde, Endel, *International Business Enterprise*, Prentice-Hall, Englewood Cliffs, 1963.
16. Leavitt, Harold J., *Managerial Psychology* (2nd ed.), The University of Chicago Press, Chicago, 1964.
17. Likert, Rensis, *New Patterns of Management*, McGraw-Hill, New York, 1961.
18. Lovell, Enid B., *The Changing Role of the International Executive*, National Industrial Conference Board, New York, 1966.
19. March, James G. and Herbert A. Simon, *Organizations*, Wiley, New York, 1958.
20. Martyn, Howe, *International Business*, Free Press of Glencoe, New York, 1964.
21. Maslow, Abraham H., *Motivation and Personality*, Harper and Row Bros., New York, 1954.
22. Perlmutter, Howard V., "L'Entreprise International-Trois Conceptions," *Review Economic et Social*, (May 1965), a translation appeared in the *Quarterly Journal of AIESEC International*, Vol. III, No. 3, (August 1967).

23. ——, "The Tortuous Evolution of the Multinational Corporation," *Columbia Journal of World Business*, Vol. IV, No. 1 (January-February 1969).

24. Robinson, Richard D., *International Management*, Holt, Rinehart & Winston, New York, 1967.

25. Rutenberg, David P., "Maneuvering Liquid Assets in a Multinational Company," *Management Science* (to appear).

26. Simon, Herbert, *Administrative Behavior: A Study of Decision Making Processes in Administrative Organization*, MacMillan, New York, 1957.

27. Steiner, George and, W. M. Cannon, *Multinational Corporate Planning*, MacMillan, New York, 1966.

28. Simmonds, Kenneth, "Multinational, Well, Not Quite," *Columbia Journal of World Business*, Vol. I (Fall, 1966).

29. Watkins, Melville H., *Foreign Ownership and the Structure of Canadian Industry*, Queen's Printer, Ottawa, 1968.

Cultural and Individual Differences in Managerial Values

PERSONAL VALUE SYSTEMS OF AMERICAN MANAGERS

GEORGE W. ENGLAND

The personal value systems of 1072 American managers are studied for their contribution to the understanding of managers and their behavior. A theoretical model for analyzing the impact of values on behavior is presented and utilized. Major results are explored with respect to the impact of personal values systems on the behavior of managers.

Thoughtful students of managerial behavior are beginning to develop the notion that an individual manager's personal value system makes a difference in terms of how he evaluates information, how he arrives at decisions—in short, how he behaves. William Guth and Renato Tagiuri, for example, recently presented a number of examples and case studies that illustrate the ways in which personal values influence corporate strategy choices.[1] Professor Tagiuri also has presented summary information on the measured values of nearly 1,000 executives, research managers, and scientists in terms of theoretical, economic, aesthetic, social, political, and religious values.[2] Robert McMurry has stressed the role of values in influencing behavior. He notes that many of the "people problems" such as 1) "the usually 'rational' owner who will liquidate his business rather than be forced to negotiate with a union," 2) "the scientist who, perhaps because he happens to be a misguided idealist, becomes a poor security risk," 3) "the labor leader who foments a long and costly strike simply to demonstrate his 'muscle,' " 4) "the hourly rated worker who welds pop bottles inside the body of the automobile he is assembling simply for kicks," and 5) "the intellectuals and politicians who advocate confiscatory taxes on the grounds that profits are

From *Academy of Management Journal*, March 1967, pp. 53-68. Reprinted with permission of the author and publisher.

unwarranted" all have their common denominator in the area of values and differences in values.[3]

I share, with these and other researchers, the belief that personal values are important in understanding managers and their behavior. The present study of personal value systems of American managers is directed toward furthering this understanding.

BACKGROUND FOR THE RESEARCH

The ideas and data presented stem from a long-term research project aimed at the description, measurement, and understanding of the personal value systems of managers and the impact of values on behavior. A personal value system is viewed as a relatively permanent perceptual framework which shapes and influences the general nature of an individual's behavior. Values are similar to attitudes but are more ingrained, permanent, and stable in nature. Likewise, a value is seen as being more general and less tied to any specific object than is the case with many attitudes. "Value" as used here is closer to ideology or philosophy than it is to attitude.

Managers of business organizations, vitally important in any industrial society, represent individuals whose values are of particular interest. The significance and importance of studying the value systems of managers is seen when one considers seriously the following reasonable assertions and their implications:

1. Personal value systems influence a manager's perception of situations and problems he faces.
2. Personal value systems influence a manager's decisions and solutions to problems.
3. Personal value systems influence the way in which a manager looks at other individuals and groups of individuals; thus they influence interpersonal relationships.
4. Personal value systems influence the perception of individual and organizational success as well as their achievement.
5. Personal value systems set the limits for the determination of what is and what is not ethical behavior by a manager.
6. Personal value systems influence the extent to which a manager will accept or will resist organizational pressures and goals.

THEORETICAL MODEL

The theoretical model underlying the present study is presented in Figure 1. Two major classes of personal values are recognized: *operative values*, or those that have the greatest influence on behavior, and *intended*

Figure 1   THEORETICAL MODEL OF SPECIFIC TIME-SPACE BEHAVIOR

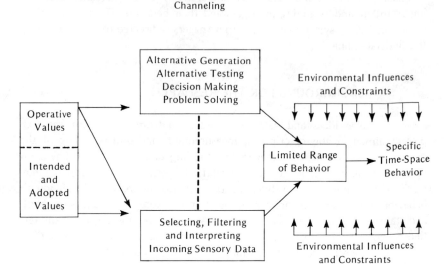

and adopted values, or those that may be professed but do not directly influence behavior to any great degree. The model also indicates the two primary ways in which values can influence behavior: *behavior channeling* and *perceptual screening.* Behavior channeling would be illustrated by the behavior of a manager who places a high value on honesty and integrity when he is approached with a proposition which involves deception and question-able ethics. His behavior would be channeled away from the questionable proposition as a direct result of his operative values. Behavior channeling represents direct influence of values on behavior as opposed to the indirect influence of perceptual screening. Examples of perceptual screening underlie the common expressions, "he sees what he wants to see," "he hears only what he already agrees with," and "you can't teach an old dog new tricks." The power of personal values to select, filter and influence interpretation of what one "sees" and "hears" is well known in common experience and in the scientific study of behavior.[4]

The model further indicates that the impact of values on behavior must be considered in relation to other environmental influences and constraints before specific statements can be made about an individual behaving in such and such a way at a given time and under certain conditions. Values are one part of the story, but not the whole story.

THE MEASUREMENT OF VALUES

The present attempt to "get at" a manager's values through the use of a carefully specified set of concepts was influenced by the work of Charles Osgood and represents an adaptation of his methodology.[5] Most of the research done by Osgood and his associates has been directed toward the development of an adequate measurement system for meaning. They have succeeded in showing that meaning has several dimensions which can be measured by using sets of bipolar adjectives such as good-bad, strong-weak, active-passive, to determine the meaning of a concept for an individual.

In the present study, we are concerned not with just any aspect of meaning of any concept or set of concepts. Rather it is necessary to specify a particular set of concepts and certain modes of the valuation process that are relevant to a personal value system for managers. The concepts in the Personal Values Questionnaire were selected from the voluminous literature dealing with organizations and with individual and group behavior. In addition, ideological and philosophical concepts were included to represent major belief systems. An initial pool of 200 concepts was reduced to 96 concepts through the use of a panel of expert judges. Preliminary findings with a pilot sample of managers further reduced the concepts to the current set of 66. These concepts are categorized into five classes: goals of business organizations, personal goals of individuals, groups of people, ideas associated with people, and ideas about general topics. Figure 2 lists the 66 concepts in the PVQ by categories.

The development of the PVQ was based on the rationale that the meanings attached by an individual manager to a carefully specified set of concepts will provide a useful description of his personal value system, which in turn will be related to his behavior in understandable ways. The theoretical importance of the meanings an individual attaches to concepts is at the root of a great deal of research aimed at a better understanding of human behavior. Attitude measurement, interest measurement, personality assessment, need assessment, and verbal learning experiments, for example, lean heavily on the assumption that modes of the valuation process for individuals provide predictive clues about their behavior. How concepts are grouped; valuation in terms of like or dislike, important or unimportant, and right or wrong; whatever reactions a concept elicits from an individual—all are expressions of what the concept means to the individual and have implications for his value system and for understanding his behavior.[6]

The PVQ uses four scales to represent four modes of valuation. The primary mode of valuation used was what might be called the power mode of valuation (important-unimportant scale). The rationale behind the use of this scale is similar to that underlying most value measurement—the general value of objects or ideas to an individual is largely a function of how important or unimportant he thinks the object or idea is. Because of concern about the

Figure 2 CONCEPTS USED TO MEASURE MANAGER'S VALUES

Goals of Business Organizations	Ideas Associated with people	Groups of People	Personal Goals of Individuals	Ideas About General Topics
High Produc- tivity	Ambition Ability	Employees Customers	Leisure Dignity	Authority Caution
Industry	Obedience	My Co-workers	Achievement	Change
Leadership	Trust	Craftsmen	Autonomy	Competition
Employee	Aggressiveness	My Boss	Money	Compromise
Welfare	Loyalty	Managers	Individuality	Conflict
Organizational	Prejudice	Owners	Job Satis-	Conservatism
Stability	Compassion	My Subordinates	faction	Emotions
Social Wel-	Skill	Laborers	Influence	Equality
fare	Cooperation	My Company	Security	Force
Organizational	Tolerance	Blue Collar	Power	Liberalism
Growth	Conformity	Workers	Creativity	Property
	Honor	Government	Success	Rational
		Stockholders	Prestige	Religion
		Technical		Risk
		Employees		
		Me		
		Labor Unions		
		White Collar		
		Employees		

behavioral effect of values, it was necessary to determine why individuals thought certain concepts were important or unimportant. To do this, three secondary modes of valuation were used. The pragmatic mode of valuation was represented by a successful scale; the ethical-moral mode of valuation was obtained through a right scale; and the effect or feeling mode of valuation was measured through use of a pleasant scale. It was reasoned that a combination of primary and secondary modes of valuation would be a better predictor of the likely behavior of a manager than would either mode alone. For example, if manager A were generally pragmatically oriented (e.g., when he said something was important, he was most apt to see it as successful as opposed to right or pleasant). His behavior would be predicted best by viewing it as a joint function of those concepts he thought were important and his pragmatic orientation as represented by those concepts he viewed as successful. On the other hand, individual B who was generally ethically-morally oriented (e.g., when he said something was important, he was most apt to see it as right as opposed to successful or pleasant) would behave in a way which is predicted by the joint function of those concepts considered important and right. In a more general sense, what is being suggested is that a manager's behavior (insofar as it is influenced by his personal values) is best explained by utilizing both those things he considers important and his personal mode of orientation. Symbolically, one could say $B_v f(I \Lambda PO)$.[7]

THE MANAGERS STUDIED

A national sample of 3042 managers was selected from Poors 1966 Directory of Corporations, Executives, and Directors on the basis of three stratifying variables (size of organization in terms of employees, level of the manager in the organization, and organizational function of the manager). A PVQ and an accompanying letter were mailed to each manager. After one follow-up letter, 1072 managers responded with useable data. Table 1 describes the 1072 managers in terms of personal and organizational variables. As seen in Table 1, the managers are a relatively diverse group in terms of organizational variables (type of company, size of firm, department or function, organizational level, and line-staff position) as well as in terms of personal variables (years of managerial experience), age, formal education, yearly income from their position, and job satisfaction. The personal value systems of these 1072 American managers is of primary interest here.

PERSONAL VALUE SYSTEMS OF AMERICAN MANAGERS

As a total group, managers' primary orientations are pragmatic; that is, when managers view some concept as important they also tend to view it as successful. As seen in Figure 3, thirty-nine (of sixty-six) concepts are rated by the total group of managers as being of "high importance"; twenty-nine of these are likewise seen as successful. The second part of Figure 3 shows that 562 of the managers (over half) assign more of the concepts to the "high importance-successful" cell than to any of the other eight categories. In short, these data indicate that as a group managers are best described as pragmatically oriented, and when considered as individuals more managers are pragmatically oriented than are ethically-morally oriented or are effect oriented. Figure 3 also shows that managers' secondary orientation is moralistic and ethical. Of the thirty-nine concepts rated "high importance," ten also are seen as "right." Individually, 276 of the managers (about one-fourth) assign more of the concepts to the "high importance-right" cell than to any of the other eight combinations.

The data shows that managers, whether considered as a group or individually, are not effect oriented; the concepts that are viewed as important by them are not viewed as pleasant.

The Value Profile of American Managers, as shown in Figure 4, allows interpretation of the responses of the 1072 managers to the 66 concepts in value terms with implications for behavior. When one considers managers as a group and utilizes the finding that managers are pragmatically oriented, the Value Profile would suggest the following:

1) The 29 concepts which are rated as "high importance" and are viewed as "successful" represent the operative values for these managers. They are

Table 1 MANAGER SAMPLE CHARACTERISTICS (N = 1072 MANAGERS)

Type of Company	%
Agriculture	2.1
Mining	.8
Contract Construction	1.8
Manufacturing	56.6
Transportation and Public Utilities	11.8
Wholesale and Retail Trade	7.0
Finance, Insurance, & Real Estate	10.0
Services (e.g., hotels & laundries)	.7
Other	8.0
No information	1.1

Size of Firm (No. of Employees)	%
Under 100	6.0
100-499	23.0
500-999	14.6
1000-4999	21.6
5000-9999	14.2
10000-29999	14.3
30000 and over	5.4
No information	.8

Department	%
Production	8.2
Operations	9.9
Sales/Distribution	9.0
Engineering	10.3
Finance/Accounting	6.8
Personnel/IR	15.5
Public Relations/Adv.	7.5
Research and Development	11.7
General Administration	17.0
Other	3.3
No information	1.0

Line Staff	%
Line	26.5
Staff	37.1
Combined	35.4
No information	1.0

Organizational Level	%
Director	1.5
President	4.6
Executive Vice President	4.0
Vice President	46.5
Levels reporting to VP	30.5
Two to Four Levels below VP	12.6
No information	.3

Managerial Experience	%
0-5 years	17.7
6-10 years	20.6
11-15 years	21.1
16-20 years	18.4
21-30 years	14.1
Over 30 years	6.3
No information	1.8

Age	%
20-34 years	9.0
35-39	12.5
40-44	18.6
45-49	18.6
50-54	15.8
55-59	13.2
60 or over	11.8
No information	.6

Formal Education	%
Some High School	2.4
High School Degree	5.1
Some College	19.0
College Degree	40.0
Post-Graduate Education	32.7
No information	.7

Yearly Income	%
Under $9,000	4.1
$9,000-11,999	8.7
12.000-14,999	12.3
15,000-19,999	16.0
20,000-24,999	15.3
25,000-34,999	18.1
35,000-49,999	13.5
50,000 or over	9.6
No information	2.4

Job Satisfaction (How well do you like your job?)	%
I hate it	.2
I dislike it	0.0
I don't like it	.7
I am indifferent to it	1.3
I like it	26.4
I am enthusiastic about it	50.2
I love it	20.4
No information	.7

Figure 3 GENERAL VALUE ORIENTATION OF MANAGERS (N = 1072)

As a total group, Managers' primary orientation is pragmatic
As a total group, Managers' secondary orientation is moralistic and ethical

Supporting data:

	High Importance	Average Importance	Low Importance	
Successful 1st Ranked	29	7	2	
Right 1st Ranked	10	11	0	
Pleasant 1st Ranked	0	6	1	
				66
Successful 1st Ranked	562	101	0	
Right 1st Ranked	276	87	0	
Pleasant 1st Ranked	12	29	5	
				1072

The 66 concepts are assigned to one of the nine categories (cells) by a joint modal frequency method for the total group of managers. For example, more of the total group of managers responded "high importance-successful" than in any other category of response to each of 29 concepts. Thus, 29 concepts are assigned to the "high importance-successful" category

Each of the 1072 managers is assigned to that category (cell) that contains the highest number of concepts for him. For example, 562 managers responded "high importance-successful" to more of the 66 concepts than to any of the other eight response categories.

considered important and fit the primary orientation (pragmatic) pattern of the group and should influence the behavior of the managers more than the ideas and concepts in any other cell in the Value Profile. For example, the fact that managers value the characteristics Ambition, Ability, and Skill more than they value the characteristics Loyalty, Trust, and Honor would be reflected in their own behavior and in their expectations about others' behavior.

2) The 9 concepts found in the cells labeled "Adopted Values—Situationally Induced" are those that have been observed as being successful in the manager's organizational experience but which he finds difficult to internalize and view as being of high importance. Managers seem to be saying, for example, that Labor Unions are successful (they do have a large impact on what goes on in organizations) but that they should not be considered as important as other groups such as Customers or Managers or Owners. The values represented by these 9 concepts would not be expected to influence the behavior of managers to the extent that operative values would, since managers are not as wholly committed to adopted values as they are to operative values.

3) The 10 concepts found in the cells labeled "Intended Values—Socioculturally Induced" are those that have been considered as highly important by the manager throughout most of his life but do not fit his organizational experience. Here the interpretation would be that managers, for example,

Figure 4 MANAGERIAL VALUE PROFILE (N = 1072)

	High Importance	Average Importance	Low Importance
Successful 1st Ranked	High Productivity Industrial Leadership Organizational Stability Profit Maximization Organizational Efficiency Organizational Growth Employees Customers My Co-workers Craftsmen My Boss Managers Owners My Subordinates My Company Stockholders Technical Employees Me White Collar Employees Ambition Ability Skill Cooperation Achievement Job Satisfaction Creativity Success Change Competition [Operative Values]	Labor Unions Aggressiveness Influence Power Compromise Conflict Risk	Prejudice Force [Adopted Values Situationally Induced]
Right 1st Ranked	Employee Welfare Trust Loyalty Honor Dignity Individuality Government Property Rational Religion [Intended Value Socio-culturally Induced]	Social Workers Laborers Blue Collar Workers Obedience Compassion Tolerance Authority Caution Conservatism Equality Liberalism	
Pleasant 1st Ranked		Leisure Autonomy Money Security Prestige Emotions	Conformity [Values with Low Behavioral Relevance]

have viewed "rationality" as an important criterion for behavior but that their organizational environment has not always rewarded "rationality." It is as if they were saying that we have always considered it important to be rational but don't see it as being highly useful in our organizational life. The complexities of organizational requirements do not square with individual notions of what is and what is not rational. These intended values where there is conflict between what one has learned to believe and what one sees in his accepted environment have been termed professed or talking values by a number of authors. Employee Welfare, for example, is viewed as highly important as an organizational goal by managers but it may not affect their behavior greatly because it doesn't fit their primary pragmatic orientation. It is a professed value but not one that is operative or directly influential of behavior to any large extent.

4) Finally, the 18 concepts found in the cells labeled "Low Behavioral Relevance" are those that would not be expected to influence a manager's behavior to any large extent since they are not considered important and do not fit the pragmatic orientation of managers.

Figures 5, 6, 7, 8, and 9 present more detailed information about each set of concepts. The columns of data in the figures represent 1) the percentage of the total group of managers who rated each concept as "highly important," 2) the percentage of the total group of managers who both rated the concepts as "highly important" and ranked "successful" as best indicating the meaning of the concept to them. As previously indicated, a useful general measure of the behavioral relevance of each concept for managers as a group is represented by the percentage in the third column of Figures 5-9. Analysis and interpretation of the data found in the figures suggest a number of conclusions.

With respect to goals of business organizations,[8] see Figure 5.

The eight goals clearly constitute four subsets of goals as identified by the horizontal lines. The first subset includes the goals Organizational Efficiency, High Productivity, and Profit Maximization. Both the high behavioral relevance score and the content of these goals suggest that they are what Simon

Figure 5 BEHAVIOR ANALYSIS OF VALUES (N = 1072)

Goals of Business Organizations	% High Importance	% Successful 1st Ranked	% High Importance and Successful 1st Ranked
Organizational Efficiency	81	71	60
High Productivity	80	70	60
Profit Maximization	72	70	56
Organizational Growth	60	72	43
Industrial Leadership	58	64	43
Organizational Stability	58	54	38
Employee Welfare	65	20	17
Social Welfare	41	8	4

calls maximization criteria.[9] They are the goals which managers attempt to influence by their actions, decisions, or behavior and are useful in generating alternative courses of actions or ways of behaving.

The second subset consists of the goals Organizational Growth, Industry Leadership, and Organizational Stability. The secondary position of these goals in terms of behavioral relevance and their content would suggest that they should be viewed as associative goals. They generally are not sought in and of themselves (actions are not usually taken to directly influence them); rather they are utilized in alternative testing. A manager may decide on a given action to influence the "maximization criteria" goals and then check to see what the impact is on the goals in this second subset.

The third subset of goals includes only Employee Welfare. The data suggest that Employee Welfare is a professed goal but one which will not influence managerial behavior to any great extent. Employee Welfare is considered "highly important" by 65% of the total sample, while only 20% view it as "successful." As previously indicated, Employee Welfare is an Intended Value which is socio-culturally induced but which has relatively low behavioral relevance.

The final subset of goals includes Social Welfare which is seen as neither important nor successful by managers. In other words, it is not important and does not fit the pragmatic mode of valuation characteristic of managers; thus it would be expected to have low behavioral relevance as is shown in column 3 of Figure 5.

With respect to ideas associated with people, ability, ambition, and skill are viewed as both important and successful and would be interpreted as operative values which influence a manager's behavior as well as the way in which he judges and evaluates other people.

Cooperation and aggressiveness represent moderately important values in

Figure 6 BEHAVIOR ANALYSIS OF VALUES (N = 1072)

Ideas Associated with People	% High Importance	% Successful 1st Ranked	% High Importance and Successful 1st Ranked
Ability	84	72	65
Ambition	75	73	57
Skill	70	75	55
Cooperation	78	46	40
Aggressiveness	42	76	33
Loyalty	80	19	18
Trust	91	18	18
Honor	86	12	12
Tolerance	39	18	12
Prejudice	11	36	10
Obedience	30	19	8
Compassion	29	10	8
Conformity	6	23	4

Figure 7   BEHAVIOR ANALYSIS OF VALUES (N = 1072)

Groups of People	% High Importance	% Successful 1st Ranked	% High Importance and Successful 1st Ranked
My Company	91	63	63
Customers	92	62	62
Managers	74	63	53
My Boss	73	52	45
My Subordinates	78	47	42
Technical Employees	63	55	42
Employees	84	44	42
Me	65	48	39
My Co-workers	67	37	32
Craftsmen	48	54	32
Owners	52	47	31
Stockholders	48	43	23
White Collar Employees	41	43	24
Blue Collar Workers	35	38	21
Government	44	29	19
Laborers	28	31	16
Labor Unions	21	42	15

terms of behavior of managers. It is interesting to note that cooperation and aggressiveness represent different types of values even though they have similar behavioral relevance scores. Cooperation is more of an Intended Value while Aggressiveness is an Adopted Value.

Loyalty, trust, honor, tolerance, prejudice, obedience, compassion, and conformity represent values with low behavioral relevance. It is interesting to notice that loyalty, trust, and honor have very high importance scores (80, 91, and 86 respectively) but are not viewed as successful by many managers (19%, 18%, and 12% respectively). This would suggest that these three value areas operate as intended Values which are socio-culturally induced and may have their primary effect on the behavior of managers through the process of perceptual screening as opposed to behavior channeling. It is possible, for example, that a manager is not influenced to any great extent in his own behavior by the notion of loyalty, but he may judge and evaluate associates in terms of the "loyalty" of their behavior.

With respect to groups of people, the set of concepts including my company, customers, and managers represents the highest level of operative values for managers and would be expected to influence their behavior most. The results indicate that managers make decisions and behave by using customers, managers, and my company as significant reference groups.

A second set of concepts including my boss, my subordinates, technical employees, employees, and me represents second level operative values. These also are significant reference groups in shaping managers' behavior but are less influential than the first group.

Concepts such as blue collar workers, government, laborers, and labor

Figure 8 BEHAVIOR ANALYSIS OF VALUES (N = 1072)

Personal Goals of Individuals	% High Importance	% Successful 1st Ranked	% High Importance and Successful 1st Ranked
Achievement	83	69	63
Success	70	64	53
Creativity	70	63	50
Job Satisfaction	88	41	41
Individuality	53	29	21
Money	28	46	20
Influence	18	47	15
Prestige	21	35	14
Autonomy	20	31	13
Dignity	56	20	13
Security	29	21	12
Power	10	52	9
Leisure	11	7	4

unions have low behavioral relevance for managers and do not represent significant reference groups.

With respect to personal goals of individuals, achievement, success, and creativity are the personal goals that represent high level operative values for managers. Since these goals are considered important and they also fit the pragmatic orientation of managers, it is suggested that they are keystones in the motivational structure underlying managerial behavior.

The idea of job satisfaction as a personal goal is seen as a second level operative value. Job satisfaction approaches being an Intended Value (88% saying it is of "high importance" but only 41% considering it "successful"). A theoretical inference would be that managers may be less influenced by striving to attain job satisfaction than by striving for achievement, but that they consider job satisfaction important for others. Job satisfaction, as a personal goal, may operate more through perceptual screening than through behavior channeling.

Individuality, money, influence, prestige, autonomy, dignity, security, power, and leisure are concepts that represent lower value personal goals. Individuality and money represent another example of different types of values even though they have similar behavior relevance scores. Individuality is an Intended Value while Money is more of an Adopted Value.

With respect to general topics, competition and change are concepts which represent operative values for managers and would be expected to be influential in shaping their behavior. The nature of these high value concepts suggests what might be described as an "action orientation" on the part of managers; doing is of primary importance.

Risk, rational, authority, and property are second level values for managers. Again, one sees concepts with similar behavioral relevance scores

Figure 9 BEHAVIOR ANALYSIS OF VALUES (N = 1072

Ideas About General Topics	% High Importance	% Successful 1st Ranked	% High Importance and Successful 1st Ranked
Competition	66	54	41
Change	45	50	31
Risk	36	62	27
Rational	58	33	26
Authority	42	39	22
Property	45	38	21
Compromise	19	41	13
Emotions	23	24	13
Force	11	55	9
Conflict	9	46	9
Conservatism	13	28	8
Liberalism	11	26	8
Equality	29	12	8
Caution	13	30	7
Religion	40	8	7

illustrating different types of values. Risk is an adopted value which has been organizationally rewarded but not highly internalized by managers, while Rationality is an Intended Value which was brought to the organization but is not always useful.

Compromise, emotions, force, conflict, conservatism, liberalism, equality, caution, and religion are values with relatively low behavioral relevance. It is interesting to note the Adopted Value nature of compromise and force as compared with the Intended Values represented by equality and religion. Both sets of values suggest areas of conflict for managers but with different consequences.

DIFFERENCES IN PERSONAL VALUE SYSTEM

The preceding discussion and analysis have been concerned mainly with the value systems of American managers as a group. We have been interested in the extent to which ideas, concepts, and values are important for managers in general. As would be expected, however, it becomes very clear that there is endless variation when we look at the personal value systems of each individual manager. Value systems are like most other human characteristics; individuals differ greatly with respect to them. While it is difficult to characterize these differences briefly, the following description of some ways in which value systems of managers differ from each other may be helpful and illustrative.[10]

As indicated earlier, the major orientations of managers differ. Some managers have a pragmatic orientation (important concepts for them are viewed as "successful"), while others have an ethical-moral orientation. For these latter individuals, important ideas and values are those which are viewed as "right." A very few individuals have an effect or feeling orientation.

Some managers have a very small set of operative values while others have a large set and seem to be influenced by many strongly held values. The operative values of some managers include concepts which are almost solely related to organizational life while other managers include a wide range of personal and philosophical concepts among their operative values. Some managers have what might be termed individualistic values as opposed to group-oriented values. Some managers appear to be highly achievement-oriented as compared with others who seem to value status and position more highly. Finally, it is clear that some managers have a personal value system that might be characterized as "hard." Their operative values include concepts such as Ambition, Obedience, Aggressiveness, Achievement, Success, Competition, Risk, and Force. Other individuals have value systems that are often thought of as "soft" and include such concepts as Loyalty, Trust, Cooperation, Compassion, Tolerance, Employee Welfare, Social Welfare, and Religion. Without attaching any personal judgment about what value system is best or most appropriate, one can appreciate the differences in behavior and in feelings of conflict that will arise because of these value differences.

SUMMARY AND IMPLICATIONS

The present paper presents empirical evidence about the nature of the personal value systems of American managers and a theoretical rationale for considering the impact of values on behavior. Additional study and analyses undoubtedly will clarify the role of values in understanding managers and their behavior. It does seem safe, however, to make the following generalizations which stem from this and related studies: 1) personal value systems of managers can be meaningfully measured even though they are complex in nature, 2) there is a general value pattern which is characteristic of American managers, as seen in the results of this study, as well as a great deal of variation in value systems from individual to individual, 3) personal values operate at the level of corporate strategy and goals as well as at the level of day-to-day decisions, 4) the personal value systems of individual managers influence the organization in both an indirect and direct manner at the same time that personal value systems are influenced by organization life, 5) differences in personal value systems help to explain the nature of conflict between individuals in an organization while similarity of value patterns is probably responsible for most accommodation among individuals, and finally and perhaps most importantly, 6) the study and thoughtful examination of one's own personal value system may well be helpful in the effort that all must make in the "strain toward consistency" between what one believes and what one is.[11]

REFERENCES

1. W. D. Guth, R. Tagiuri, "Personal Values and Corporate Strategies," *Harvard Business Review* (Sept.-Oct., 1965), pp. 123-132.

2. R. Tagiuri, "Value Orientations and the Relationship of Managers and Scientists," *Administrative Science Quarterly* (June, 1965), pp. 39-51.

3. R. N. McMurry, "Conflicts in Human Values," *Harvard Business Review*, (May-June, 1963), pp. 130-145.

4. See, for example, L. Postman, J. S. Bruner, and E. McGinnies, "Personal Values as Selective Factors in Perception," *Journal of Abnormal & Social Psychology*, XLIII (1948), pp. 142-154.

5. E. C. Osgood, G. J. Suci, and P. H. Tannenbaum, *The Measurement of Meaning* (Urbana: University of Illinois Press, 1957).

6. For a brilliant exposition of this point, see G. W. Allport, "Traits Revisited," *American Psychologist*, XXI, No. 1 (1966). pp. 1-10.

7. This expression would be read: the behavior of a manager, insofar as behavior is a function of values, is best indicated by the joint function of those concepts he considers important and those concepts which fit his primary orientation. For a pragmatically oriented manager, behavior is best predicted by those concepts considered important and successful; for a moral-ethically oriented manager, behavior is best predicted by those concepts considered important and right; while for an effect-oriented manager, behavior is best predicted by those concepts considered important and pleasant.

8. For a more complete analysis of goals of business organizations, see my "Organizational Goals and Expected Behavior of American Managers," *Administrative Science Quarterly* (in press).

9. H. A. Simon, "On the Concept of Organizational Goal," *Administrative Science Quarterly*, IX (1964), pp. 1-22.

10. See also R. Miles, "Conflicting Elements in Managerial Ideologies," *Industrial Relations* (1964), pp. 77-91.

11. For two excellent discussions of this point, see E. P. Learned, A. R. Dooley, and R. L. Katz, "Personal Values and Business Decisions," *Harvard Business Review* (March-April, 1959), pp. 11-120 and W. F. Bernthal, "Value Perspectives in Management," *Academy of Management Journal*, V, No. 3 (Dec., 1962), pp. 190-196.

THE EUROPEAN BUSINESS ELITE

DAVID HALL
H.-CL. DE BETTIGNIES,
and G. AMADO-FISCHGRUND

This study describes some of the characteristics of the men who run the biggest companies in Europe. The authors look at their careers, their companies, the kind of education they have received, and their family backgrounds. The European business leader is not a uniform type, for substantial differences are to be found among the six countries included in this survey.

"Who are the chief executives who run the largest companies in Europe?" There have been several interesting studies done on the managers of some European countries,[1] but none has yet attempted to compare business

From *European Business*, October 1969, pp. 45-55. Reprinted with permission of the publisher.

leaders from one country to another. This survey has been sponsored by INSEAD.

The international executive recruitment firm of Heidrick and Struggles has made similar surveys in the United States, and has been helpful in providing information about its research methodology and results. *We surveyed the chief executives of the biggest companies in six European countries,* namely France, Great Britain, Germany, Italy, Belgium, and the Netherlands. We thought it necessary to look at three major categories of information

First, what kind of company do they run? Second, what kind of career have they followed? Third, what are their social and educational backgrounds? We wanted to record the *mobility* of the chief executives, whether this was within or between companies, whether it was geographical or whether it was social; and we wanted to define their *personal* characteristics, such as their age, education, social class, language ability, and so forth.

The facts which are summarized in this paper should be seen by the reader as a temporary and slightly blurred picture of the situation that exists in 1968-1969. A given culture will affect the career pattern a businessman is likely to follow, as well as his personal and professional characteristics, and we shall try to specify some of the results of these pressures. They carry a number of sociological and policy-making implications, particularly with respect to the distribution and exercise of power in our European political and economic systems.

Research Design

We mailed a short questionnaire (23 items) to the chief executive of the 500 largest companies in France, Great Britain, Germany, and Italy, of the 250 largest in Belgium, and the 150 largest in the Netherlands.

Our overall response rate was 24%.

France and the Netherlands show the highest rate of return, 32.2% and 31.8% respectively. Less than 20% of the Germans and Italians replied. We think we have enough answers from each country to be able to make some fairly meaningful observations and interpretations.

THE COMPANIES

Although we were mainly interested in large companies, there is a considerable difference in size between the ten biggest companies in a country and those at the smaller end of a sample of 500. Moreover, the difference in company size varies significantly between countries, for the proportion of very large companies is greater in Britain and the Netherlands than in Belgium and Italy. It would be very difficult to match companies by size for the six countries under study.

Half of the sample of 576 companies which constitutes the basis for this report have annual sales of less than $40 million. 31% have annual sales between $40 and $120 million, and 19% are very large companies with annual sales exceeding $120 million.[2]

Nevertheless, all the companies in our sample are among the 500 biggest in their own country.

The variation in company size between countries is clearly reflected in Table 1 and we have not yet checked to see whether the sample from each country is representative of the country as a whole. But we can say at this point that the proportion of very large companies in the British, Dutch, and German samples is greater than in the French, Italian, and Belgian. The difference in proportion of companies with annual sales over $120 million for example is 35%, 23.8%, and 21.3% against 15.5%, 11.1%, and 2.0%, respectively. This disparity in company size between countries invites us to be cautious in making cross-cultural interpretations, particularly when we have evidence that the variable of size may be important.

Countries do not have identical industrial structures, and the variable "type of industry" may interact with company size further to distort our results. We could not match the distribution of companies by industry between countries given our basic constraint of looking at the largest firms. At this point in our analysis we shall ignore the effect of variations in type of

Table 1 SIZE IN ANNUAL SALES IN MILLIONS OF DOLLARS

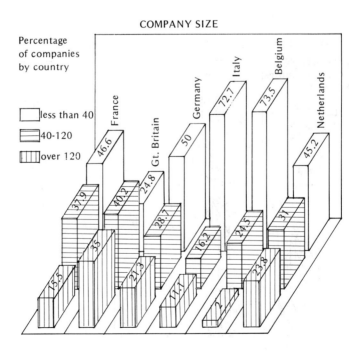

industry between countries. Our overall sample does cover practically every sector of industrial activity, although the industries which predominate are mechanical engineering (20.8%), chemicals (13.7%), and food (12.7%).

In summary, this report is concerned with 576 chief executives of the largest corporations in six European countries. Let us first take a look at their career patterns.

THE CAREERS

What did the respondents to this survey do before they joined their present company? In answering this question we shall try to describe the interfirm mobility of our chief executives, and the route they have followed to the top in their present company.

One third of our sample have had no experience in another company, and have spent their professional career with their present firm (Table 2). Interfirm mobility seems to be lowest in Great Britain and the Netherlands, for 45.9% of British chief executives and 40.4% of the Dutch have made their careers entirely in one company. The "company-made" chief executive is more likely to be encountered in bigger firms, and he is usually better paid than his more mobile colleagues even taking into consideration the greater

Table 2   NUMBER OF OTHER COMPANIES

NUMBER OF OTHER COMPANIES WORKED FOR IN CAREER

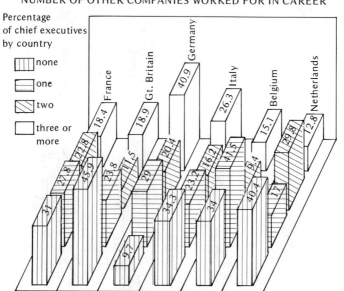

compensation given to the heads of larger companies. There seems to be some indication that the present system in Britain and the Netherlands tends more to reward the less mobile manager.

The high interfirm mobility of German chief executives is in marked contrast to this finding. Nine out of ten Germans have previously worked for at least one other company, and 40% have changed companies three or more times. Let us examine these mobile managers more closely.

Many of the chief executives brought in from outside have had prior experience in a company in the same type of industry. The overall figure is 63.6%, and the German figure is 72.9%. German respondents tend more to be specialists than their European colleagues, no matter which industry employs them. The situation is rather different in the Netherlands, where 50% of the mobile chief executives have not had prior experience in the same type of industry for which they now work.

We also find that those Germans (and this is true to a certain degree of the Italians) who have had prior experience in the same type of industry have had it in a larger company than their present one. Apparently, this experience in a larger firm of the same industry has helped in reaching a top position. 60% of the mobile German chief executives have held a senior post in the larger firm, whilst this is the case for only 30% of the Belgians. Generally, we observe that moves tend not to be made when one is in a middle management position, but rather when one is at the beginning of a professional career in a junior management position, or much later when one has already achieved a top position. Of mobile chief executives, 43% move early in their career, and 44% move much later. We can suppose that the motivation to leave will have been different in the two cases.

The German chief executives seem in some ways better equipped for their jobs than their European colleagues. They tend to have been more mobile, but in the same type of industry, and they often have had the experience of a senior post in a larger firm. Their careers have been mostly in business, whilst one out of four French chief executives was previously employed by a non-business organization (such as the civil service or the army). Not only does the German tend to focus on one industry, but he is generally more committed to his own company than other Europeans. 95% of French chief executives sit on the boards of other companies, and only 58.5% of the German. Very often the boards are those of smaller companies in the same type of industry.

Time to Reach the Top

A recent survey[3] of the presidents of the 700 largest U.S. companies showed that it took an average of seventeen years of work with his present firm before the president reached the top. Although this situation appears to be changing with the increased mobility of senior U.S. executives, it is nevertheless very different from what we observe in Europe. Taking

Europe as a whole, although there are significant differences between countries, the average chief executive is about 57 years old, joined his present company around 39, and usually reached the top job six years later. It seems that the presidents of U.S. companies have spent more time with their present firms, which they joined around 32, and trained for much longer before they became president. European companies on the other hand tend to hire more senior managers who have already had a good deal of professional experience, and to promote them to the top job in less time. Only 5% of our respondents became chief executives when they were over 60 (Table 3).

We should also mention that nearly 60% of the Dutch chief executives who are, with the British, less mobile between companies were appointed when they were under 40. Only 6.5% were appointed when they were over 55. Most of them did not have to wait long before succeeding to the top job, and half of them joined their company as members of the board.

Experience

As we remarked above, the average European chief executive spent six years with his company before being appointed to his present position. We sought to know what functions he performed during this period,

Table 3   AGE

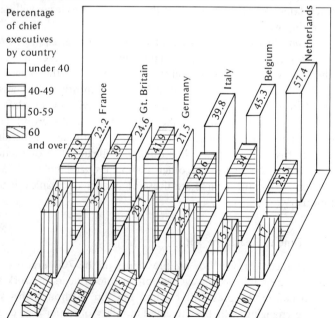

AGE BECAME CHIEF EXECUTIVE IN PRESENT COMPANY

what experience he considered the most useful, and whether he thought that certain kinds of experience would be more useful for future chief executives.

We should first stress that the replies to these questions apply to the experience obtained in the chief executive's present company, and not to any experience he might have gained elsewhere. In evaluating the usefulness of their own experience or that of future chief executives, our respondents were not necessarily relating their evaluations to that department of their present company in which they had previously spent the longest time.

Our data shows that European chief executives are likely to have been most concerned with General Administration prior to becoming the boss. 65% spent most of their time in General Administration, 12.6% in Marketing, 4.3% in Finance, and 12.2% in Manufacturing—which includes engineering. The category "Others" embraces all other departments such as personnel, legal, planning, and international. Only 3% of chief executives were previously concerned with an international department, and more than half of these were British.

It is not surprising that General Administration should dominate the other categories, since most chief executives will have been concerned with this kind of work immediately prior to their appointment to the top job. We can therefore anticipate that executives who change companies when they are already in a senior position will swell the category of General Administration, remembering our earlier remark that we are looking only at experience in the respondent's present company.

Approximately one quarter of our chief executives spent the most time in Marketing and Manufacturing, and under 5% in Finance. But we should be very careful in drawing firm conclusions from this data, since job titles and descriptions are not standardized in Europe. Although we can be tempted to say that relatively few top men seem to have been through departmental apprenticeships, the term *directeur adjoint* in France, for example, can mean something other than the General Administration under which we have to classify it.

Where did our chief executives gain the experience which they consider was the most useful to them? Again we find the category General Administration cited most frequently by just under a third of our respondents. Marketing is seen as the next most useful area, followed by Manufacturing and Finance. Almost 15% of our respondents replied "in all departments," which indicates that they attach some importance to the value of an all-round training.

Chief executives in Germany and France seem to rate Manufacturing as more useful than Marketing, whilst the reverse is true for Great Britain and particularly Belgium and Italy. The Italians indeed see Marketing as having been more useful than any other function. Belgium and the Netherlands see General Administration as having been more useful than do the other countries, with almost half of their chief executives choosing this category. The value of experience in all departments is seen to be greater in Britain, Germany, and the Netherlands than in France, Italy, and Belgium.

We asked our respondents whether they thought there was a specific·
department in a company which would best prepare a manager for the future
responsibilities of chief executive. Those who answered none to this question,
or who specified training in all departments, are classified under the category
All Departments.

Almost one half of our respondents replied that there is no specific
department which will best prepare a future chief executive for the responsibilities of his position. Only 18.6% chose Marketing as the best preparation,
and 13.7% chose General Administration. *We suggest that these replies reflect
the importance attached to a general management point of view, and the
increased role of marketing in European industry.*

This suggestion can be supported by examining the data for individual
countries. In France Marketing is seen as the best preparation for a future
chief executive, whilst all-round training is favored by all the other countries,
particularly the Netherlands, Great Britain, Germany, and Belgium. In general
France, Italy, and Belgium attach more importance to Marketing than Britain,
Germany, and the Netherlands.

There are certainly variations between countries in the perceived importance of different functional areas. It seems reasonable to assume that the
replies to our questions will have been broadly influenced by the problems
currently encountered in the different European countries. Thus we might
speculate that companies in Britain and the Netherlands are more concerned
with coordinating a wide range of activities, whilst France and Italy, seem
presently concerned with the problems of Marketing. Finally, we should
remember that replies to our questions are likely to be influenced by the
personal backgrounds of our respondents. Thus the importance attached to
Manufacturing in France may well be a reflection of the large number of
engineers who are chief executives in that country.

THE MEN

The way in which we describe the men who run such large and
significant enterprises is bound to be unsatisfactory. Statistics become individuals, and the "typical chief executive" grows out of the fantasy of an
individual reader. Our interest is in the similarities and differences found
between chief executives in European countries, and although we may speculate about them this is not an explanation.

In this section we shall concentrate on examining the social origin and
educational background of the men in our sample, and we shall look at other
characteristics such as age and present salary. Many methodological problems
are concealed in the very general presentation we shall make. For example,
comparisons between the educational systems existing in different European
countries are a nightmare. There is nothing similar to France's Ecole Polytechnique in the other countries, and most of Italy's university graduates hold

the title of Dottore. This is not the same as the German Doktor, the French Docteur, and the British Doctor. To add to the confusion these three themselves are not the same. The length of studies will vary between countries, and little agreement is found over the relative status of university graduates. Indeed the authors are themselves divided on this point.

Birthplace

Let us first begin with the easier comparisons. Table 4 shows where our chief executives were born. The category Big City embraces those born in one of the five biggest cities of the country concerned. Medium City means smaller cities and towns, whilst Rural refers to villages and the countryside. Some respondents did not specify the location within a country so they are to be found under the category In Country, and those born outside the country in which they are presently a chief executive are listed under Abroad.

The most even distribution of births is found for Great Britain, where it seems that there is no advantage to any particular birthplace. In direct contrast are France, Italy, and Belgium, where it is much more likely that a chief executive will have been born in one of the five biggest cities of the country. This is not particularly surprising for Belgium since a large proportion of the national population is to be found in cities such as Antwerp, Brussels, and Liège. Villages and rural areas are under-represented in the ranks of Italian chief executives, and again this is not surprising in a country where industrial development is very recent and where educational facilities are not nearly so evenly distributed as in Britain, for example.

France is rather misleading. 42% of French chief executives are found in the category Big City, yet of these 88% were born in Paris or its suburbs. This dominance of the capital city is not found in any other European country. Germany tends more to be the nursery of the man born outside the big cities, and Holland marginally favors those from the countryside over all others.

It is intriguing to see that 12% of all the chief executives in our sample were born outside the country in which they are presently working. One third of this figure is accounted for by Great Britain, which presumably was at the height of its imperial power when most of our respondents were born. Given the large number of upper and middle class families involved with imperial administration at this time, it is not very surprising that their children should rise to high positions in today's society. Foreign-born did not mean that one was foreign; it did imply family separation at an early age so that the children could go to public school in Britain. But Table 4 also shows that a good number of German, Belgian, and even Dutch chief executives were born abroad. We should point out that proportionately only one third as many presidents of the 700 largest U.S. companies were born abroad.[4] and this in what is supposed to be an immigrant society.

Table 4 WHERE BORN

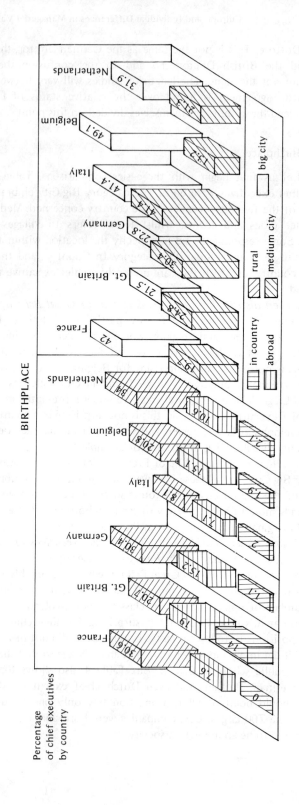

BIRTHPLACE

Percentage
of chief executives
by country

in country
abroad
rural
medium city
big city

France   Gt. Britain   Germany   Italy   Belgium   Netherlands   France   Gt. Britain   Germany   Italy   Belgium   Netherlands

30.6   20.7   30.4   18.1   20.8   34   42   24.8   30.4   41.4   13.2   31.2

7.6   19   15.2   7.1   13.1   10.6   19.7   21.5   22.8   41.4   49.1   31.9

1.4   1.7   2   1.9   2.1

0   7.6

Age

How old are our chief executives? Are there different age patterns between countries? Does the size of the company make any difference to the probable age of the boss? Table 5 answers some of these questions.

First, almost 40% of the men in our sample are aged between 55 and 64. There are more than two and a half times as many under 55 as there are 65 and over. In other words, a reasonably large proportion of European chief executives are relatively young. Italy has three times as many chief executives under 45 as does France, and slightly more than half as many 65 and over. The Netherlands has few top men under 45, but a significantly higher proportion than other countries between 45 and 54.

France is the country which appears to place the highest value on age. In this country, clearly, the older you get the more likely you are to be a chief executive. This may have a cultural explanation, in that once a Frenchman has acquired authority he cannot bear to let it go. Of the 5% of our chief executives who are over 70, almost half are French. It is interesting that Belgium, which has experienced a French cultural influence, also has a quarter of its top men over 65 and of this number more than half are over 70. Where Italy and Belgium do differ from France is in the number of top men under 45, for they have three times as many in this category. This we suggest is due to the smaller scale of industry in Belgium and Italy, and the greater probability of sons managing family businesses at a relatively early age.

Almost three quarters of the Belgian and Italian companies in our sample

Table 5 PRESENT AGE

YEARS

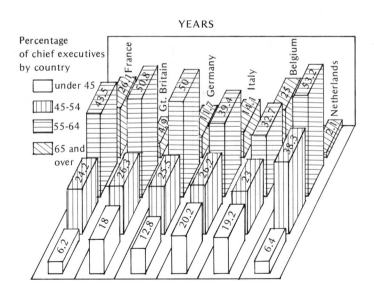

have less than $40 million in annual sales, whilst this is true of less than half of the French.

Social Class

We classified the occupations of the fathers, grandfathers, and fathers-in-law of our chief executives into a number of different categories, so that we could try to determine the social background of our respondents. Table 6 reports a grouping of these categories into what we shall call *upper, middle,* and *lower,* and we refer to these groupings as social classes. Obviously this is an arbitrary discrimination, but we feel that it does give some indication of our respondents' social backgrounds.

Upper in Table 6 refers to those chief executives whose fathers were either business owners, senior executives, or professional men such as lawyers, doctors, and university professors. *Middle* comprises those whose fathers were salesmen, schoolteachers, junior civil servants, office workers, clerks, and so on. *Lower* embraces farmers, and skilled and unskilled workers.

Most of our chief executives come from what we have called the upper

Table 6   CATEGORY

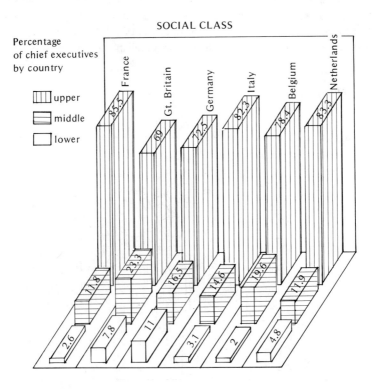

social class. More than three quarters come from this grouping, and slightly over 5% come from the lower social class. Evidently, social mobility is not very pronounced. This should not be surprising, for the advantages of a high status social background are not limited simply to the possession of wealth. They include the enjoyment of better education, not merely in select schools but also in the home itself, as well as the ease and confidence which come from familiarity with persons of influence and accomplishment.

What kind of differences exist between countries? Certainly Britain and Germany are the most mobile societies. This mobility may not be very great but it is there. More Germans are from the lower social class than in any other country. This may be accounted for by the devastation suffered by Germany in World War II, and the postwar economic miracle which perhaps provided more opportunities for mobility than in other European countries. France appears to have the most rigid society of all the countries in our study. Over 85% of chief executives come from the upper social class, and less than 3% from the lower.

Belgium has the highest number of top men from the middle class after Britain, although she falls back in the lower class. The Netherlands do better in the lower class but have the second highest number of men from the upper class after France. In fact, if we look at the lower class alone we can find a split between France, Belgium, and Italy, on the one side, and Britain, Germany, and the Netherlands on the other—although this is clearly rather weak as far as the Netherlands is concerned.

Educational Background

As we said in the introduction to this section, the difficulties in comparing European educational systems are great. We have been reduced to comparing whether our chief executives have been to a university or not (Table 7), and what general kind of training those who have been to a university have received (Table 8). We should point out that we have considered the Grandes Ecoles in France as university training in Table 7, and that we have included professionally trained men in Britain (chartered accountants and mechanical engineers) in the figures for Table 8. We have enough data to make a more sophisticated analysis, but difficulties of space will prevent us from doing so here.

First, it is clear from Table 7 that *France's chief executives are the most highly educated and Britain's the least.* We have previously reported that over one half of our French respondents are graduates of the Grandes Ecoles, and that half of these went to the Ecole Polytechnique, the grandest of the Grandes Ecoles.[5] We should note that the selection procedure for these schools is remarkably tough, and that children from lower class backgrounds stand very little chance of enjoying the educational opportunities that can help them pass through the successive screening procedures.

This is not in itself an exclusion by virtue of their class, but rather because

Table 7 UNIVERSITY DEGREE

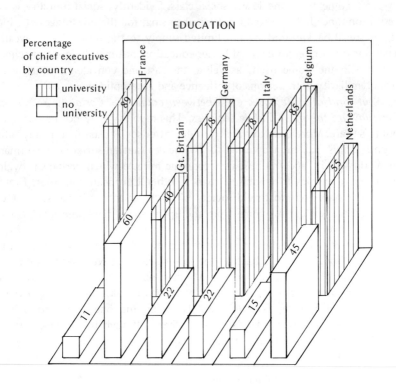

EDUCATION

Percentage of chief executives by country

▦ university

☐ no university

they lack the family environment which is so important in determining and stimulating educational achievement. Over time some very strong cultural effects have been produced, and a graduate of the Ecole Polytechnique is regarded as someone possessing both superlative and all-embracing intelligence. It is not therefore surprising that education should be regarded in France as the measure of man's worth, that most of the chief executives in our sample should have attended a university, and that almost one third of them have two diplomas.

Why should Britain have relatively few top men with formal higher education? Again we suggest that this is largely a product of the British cultural tradition. There is no educational elite in Britain comparable to that in France, and it is only since World War II that industry has made serious efforts to recruit university graduates. Mosson and Clark point out that younger managers in the chemical, engineering, and textile industries are formally very much better qualified than their elders.[6] We have indicated in an earlier paper that the basis for education of the present top managers is found in the public schools rather than in the universities.[7] Business experience tends to be regarded as the best qualification for a manager in Britain, and consequently the sooner he starts to acquire it the better.

Table 8 SUBJECT

FIELD OF STUDY

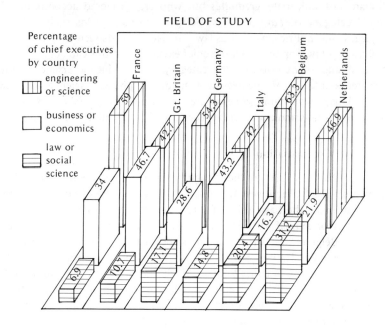

Over three quarters of German chief executives are university graduates, and more than half of these have the graduate degree of Doktor. Although there are twice as many top men in Germany without university education as there are in France, we can say that education plays an important role in career progress. The bigger the company the more likely is the German chief executive to be a Doktor. Of companies with less than $40 million in annual sale, just under one third have a Doktor's degree. This becomes 37% for companies of $40-120 million in annual sales, and 70% for those over $120 million. If one wishes to become the head of a very large company in Germany it seems that one would be well-advised to study for a doctorate first.

Most Belgian and Italian chief executives have been to a university, and Belgium seems to follow the French pattern with a strong emphasis on training in engineering and science (Table 8). More than three quarters of Italian chief executives are university educated and hold the title of Dottore. The Netherlands appear to be more similar to Britain than any other country, for only 55% of the top men have universtiy degrees.

Table 8 provides a rough picture of *the kind of studies followed by those chief executives who attended a university.* It is immediately plain that *Engineering or Science* are the most frequent fields of study followed by European chief executives, with over half of them graduating in these disciplines. Just under one third graduated in *Business or Economics,* and this proportion is swollen by the addition of 20% of the British chief executives who are not university graduates but who are chartered accountants. The general category of *Law or Social Science* embraces fields such as history, languages, and politics, as well as law. The Netherlands seem to place a heavy emphasis on law, for all the Dutch chief executives in this category studied it.

We should point out that the category Engineering or Science is much more representative of engineering than of the physical sciences or mathematics. This is reasonable since we are dealing with industrial companies, and 20% of our total sample are firms involved with mechanical engineering.

Compensation

Let us turn to the intriguing question of the financial rewards enjoyed by chief executives. We are aware that there are often fringe benefits which can make the basic salary figure unreliable. Nevertheless we feel that a comparison of annual salaries is interesting (Table 9). Top men in France, Germany, Belgium, and the Netherlands appear to be paid more than those in Italy and Britain. Italians are far and away the most bashful over revealing their salary, for more than 2 out of 10 did not reply to this question. One may wonder how far this accounts for their under-representation in the top salary bracket. Indeed the proportion of Italian questionnaires where the salary question was unanswered rises from 14% of the chief executives of small companies to over 43% of those running medium and big companies.

If we explore the difference between countries, it soon becomes apparent that *Great Britain falls behind most European countries in salary.* Approximately half of the French, German, and Dutch companies, and three quarters of the Belgian and Italian have annual sales of less than $40 million, whilst only one quarter of the British fall in this category. Yet more than 41% of the British chief executives managing companies in this category earn less than $24,000 per year, compared to just over 35% of the Italians and less for all other countries down to just over 35% of the French. Pursuing the argument, approximately 35% of the British companies on our sample have annual sales over $120 million, compared to 21% of the German. Yet three quarters of the heads of these companies in Germany are paid over $48,000 per year, and only one third of the British. Ten Dutch companies have annual sales over $120 million, and all but one of the chief executives receive over $48,000.

We can conclude that British chief executives are generally significantly underpaid for the responsibility they carry compared to their European colleagues.

Travel and Tongues

We thought it would be interesting to gather some data on the pattern of business travel of our chief executives, since this can give us some information on the number of cross-cultural contacts they enjoy.

Table 9   ANNUAL SALARY IN THOUSANDS OF DOLLARS

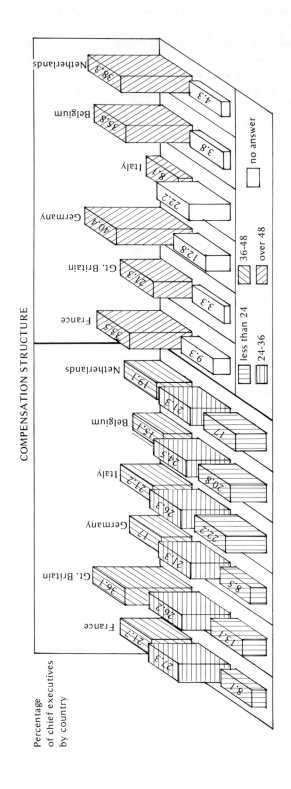

COMPENSATION STRUCTURE

Percentage
of chief executives
by country

less than 24

24-36

36-48

over 48

no answer

Netherlands 38.3   4.3

Belgium 35.8   3.8

Italy 8.1   22.2

Germany 40.4   12.8

Gt. Britain 24.3   3.3

France 33.3   9.3

Netherlands 19.1   31.3

Belgium 15.1   24.5   17

Italy 21.2   20.8

Germany 17   26.3   22.2

Gt. Britain 21.3   36.1   8.5

France 27.3   21.7   26.2   13.1   8.1

187

It is fairly clear from our data that European top managers do not make all their decisions sitting in a chair at head office. They move around a lot. Two thirds have travelled abroad on business more than nine times in the last two years. The Dutch are the most mobile; 80% of them have travelled this much, followed by the Germans (75.0%), the Italians (74.7%), the Belgians (66.0%), the French (64.0%), and the British (50%).

If we study the languages spoken by our chief executives, we find some rather interesting comparisons, although we did not unfortunately address a language question to the French. Less than 4% of the Germans, Italians, Belgians, and Dutch speak no language other than their own, but for the British the figure is 39% or proportionately ten times as many. Slightly more than 39% of the British chief executives speak one foreign language, and 21% speak two or more. The situation on the continent is very different. 97.9% of the Dutch, 79% of the Italians, 69.9% of the Belgians, and 66% of the Germans speak two or more foreign languages.

Two observations are striking. *First, the British are the most stay-at-home of all European chief executives, and second, they do not appear to have the gift of tongues.*

Conclusion

Although we do not claim that the results of this survey are by any means definite or conclusive, since the size of our sample and the problem of whether or not it is representative invite us to be prudent, we do think that they carry implications of relevance to European business.

Taken as a whole the European business elite turns out to be less different from the American business elite than we had expected, and this will be documented in a subsequent publication. In many cases, the differences between European countries are highly significant, and seem to be affected by the broad stream of cultural tradition in a given society. If we want to make sense of the data, we have to understand the cultural dimensions of the manager's job.

There is no "European chief executive" as such. In each country we encounter men with their own individual characteristics, some of which are shared by their colleagues in other countries. But we are struck by the contrasts which exist, even when we hold constant the type of industry and the differences in company size. The contrasts seem to us to place serious obstacles in the path of European economic integration. We think that corporate mergers across national boundaries are made more difficult when substantial disparities exist between the managers who must jointly develop common goals and objectives for the unified enterprise. And yet the variety of ideas that will be generated in overcoming these difficulties promises a new vitality in European business.

REFERENCES

1. D. G. Clark.—*The Industrial Manager: his Background and Career Pattern*, Business Publications, London, 1966.
    N. Delefortrie-Soubeyroux.—*Les Dirigeants de l'Industrie Française*, Lib. A. Colin, Paris, 1961.
    J. E. Humblet.—*Les Cadres d'Entreprises*, Ed. Universitaires, Paris, 1966. M. Maurice, C. Monteil, R. Guillon, J. Gaulon.—*Les Cadres et l'Enterprise*, I.S.S.T., Paris, 1967.
2. For the sake of brevity we shall refer to companies with annual sales of less than $40 million as "small," to those with annual sales between $40 million and $120 million as "medium," and to those with annual sales of more than $120 million as "big."
3. *Profile of a President*, Heidrick and Struggles, Chicago, 1967.
4. *Profile of a President*, Heidrick and Struggles, Chicago, 1967.
5. D. J. Hall and H. C. de Bettignies: "The French Business Elite," *European Business*, 19, October 1968.
6. T. M. Mosson and D. G. Clark: "Some Inter-Industry Comparisons of the Backgrounds and Careers of Managers," *British Journal of Industrial Relations*, July 1968, VI, 2, pp. 220-231.
7. D. J. Hall and G. Amado-Fischgrund: "Chief Executives in Britain," *European Business*, 20, January 1969.

SOCIOLOGICAL-CULTURAL AND LEGAL FACTORS IMPEDING DECENTRALIZATION OF AUTHORITY IN DEVELOPING COUNTRIES

GEZA PETER LAUTER

The concept of decentralization of authority as understood and practiced by managers in the USA tends to be of limited applicability in developing countries.

Decentralization of authority has long been one of the most cherished American management concepts. One management author, Peter F. Drucker, went so far as to write a whole book on the philosophy of decentralization in one company, the General Motors Corporation. On the basis of his study, Drucker summarized the advantages of decentralization of authority in the following manner:[1]

1. Speed and lack of confusion in decision making.
2. Absence of conflict between top management and the divisions.
3. A sense of fairness in dealing with executives.
4. Informality and democracy in management.

From *Academy of Management Journal*, September 1969, pp. 367-378. Reprinted with permission of the author and publisher.

5. Absence of a gap between the few top managers and the many subordinate managers in the organization.
6. The availability of a large reservoir of promotable managerial manpower.
7. Ready visibility of weak management through results of semi-independent and often competitive divisions.
8. An absence of "edict management" and the presence of thorough information.

This is quite an impressive list. It is probably not an exaggeration to say that it tends to include most of those characteristics which experts consider to be necessary for effective management in any formal organization. This conclusion can be supported by the fact that General Motors is certainly one of the most successful industrial enterprises in the world and that its success is largely due to its able management which operates on the basis of the philosophy of decentralization of authority.

As a result of General Motors' success and other firms' great achievements through decentralization of authority, this management concept, however, in recent years has tended to become a sort of cure-all. Its use has become so popular that any management not subscribing to it is generally looked upon as outmoded and backward.

As a consequence of this widespread attitude management experts of the American foreign aid organization, involved in the training of a new and efficient managerial elite in developing countries, tend to make the concept of decentralization of authority the cornerstone of all their efforts. In this they are strongly supported not only by the experience of General Motors, but also by many management theorists. Rensis Likert, Douglas McGregor, and Chris Argyris, to mention only a few of the major proponents of this concept, all argue for decentralization of authority through participative management, employee-centered supervision, and job enlargement as some of the most effective managerial techniques leading to a healthy and successful organization.[2]

Decentralization of authority, however, quite frequently turns out to be a specifically American management concept which, to a relatively high degree, is culture bound and which cannot be applied in the same manner in developing countries with differing environments. There are many examples in the history of the various foreign aid programs where the well-intentioned efforts of American management experts based entirely on the concept of decentralization of authority were doomed to failure because culturally they did not make sense; thus in the long run they would probably have resulted in less efficient managerial performance.[3]

It is interesting to note that there is a great deal of literature available on the organizational prerequisites for effective decentralization of authority.[4] Very little, if anything, however, has been published on the relationship between certain environmental constraints and the applicability of the concept of decentralization of authority in societies different from the United States.

This paper presents the major findings of a two-year empirical management study undertaken during 1966-68 in Turkey with respect to the applicability of the concept of decentralization of authority.

FOCUS OF THE STUDY

The focus of the study was twofold; first attention was paid to the possible impeding effects certain environmental constraints could have on the decentralization of authority in Turkey. Secondly, the question was explored whether or not the American educated and trained managers of U.S. subsidiaries in Turkey tended to decentralize authority more often and to a higher degree than the Turkish educated and trained managers of local firms. The American managers were products of a highly industrialized society where decentralization of authority is well understood and widely applied in practice. Thus it seemed reasonable to assume that they would probably attempt to decentralize authority to a higher degree than their Turkish colleagues. Such difference in managerial behavior would have implied that perhaps the efforts of American management experts with respect to the application of the concept of decentralization of authority through the intensive training of local managers could be successful within the foreseeable future.

Conversely, it was postulated that a uniform lack of decentralization or an insignificant difference in the degree of decentralization of authority between American and Turkish managers would imply the presence of very strong environmental constraints forcing even the American managers to adopt their behavior to the probably culturally conditioned expectations of their colleagues and subordinates. Such a finding, it was assumed, could imply that efforts designed to lead to a widespread and effective decentralization of authority through the intensive training of local managers were probably not enough and that perhaps a complete restructuing of sociological relationships and cultural values over a very long period of time was called for.[5] It could have also signaled the presence of very strong additional environmental constraints of other than sociological-cultural nature.

THEORETICAL FRAMEWORK AND METHODOLOGY

The theoretical framework used in the study was developed by Richard N. Farmer and Barry M. Richman in their book dealing with comparative management, and consisted of a set of hypothesized environmental constraints and a set of critical elements of the managerial functions of planning, organizing, staffing, directing, and controlling.[6] Among the critical elements of the organizing function the degree of decentralization of authority was explored in detail, because it was assumed that it forms the cornerstone upon which the performance of the critical elements of all the other managerial functions is based.

To obtain the necessary data eight Turkish and eight comparable American firms were selected on a judgment basis for the purpose of intensive study over a period of several months. The criteria of selection and thus comparability had to be limited to the nature of the product line manufactured, because the frequently employed standards of the size of capital investment and other financial indicators could not be used. At the time of this study Turkey did not have any financial disclosure laws; consequently, such information was not readily available. The size of the firms in terms of number of employees and other related characteristics was considered to be less important than the nature of the product line manufactured, because great differences in this respect could have seriously distorted the competitive position the firms faced and thus could have significantly affected managerial behavior. Minor differences in the nature of the product lines, however, had to be accepted.

The selected sixteen firms were drawn from eight different industries representing thus a reasonably good cross section of the industrial sector of the Turkish economy.

To determine the degree of decentralization of authority in the sixteen firms selected, all general managers, several departmental heads, and first-line supervisors were interviewed with the aid of a twenty-four page questionnaire related to the performance of the critical elements, as defined by Farmer and Richman, of the managerial functions of planning, organizing, staffing, directing, and controlling.[7]

These interviews lasted from two to two and a half hours and while all general managers spoke excellent English, when talking to most of the departmental heads and all first-line supervisors, the services of a professional translator were needed. Thus during this phase of the study, in particular, some of the relevant information could have been distorted or never conveyed.

In addition to interviewing departmental heads and first-line supervisors, their activities were also observed in as much detail as possible over a period of several days. The technique of observation was used to infer the degree of decentralization of authority from the general activities performed and types of decisions made by these employees. The results thus obtained were then crosschecked with the answers received from the general managers and the same departmental heads and first-line supervisors concerning the performance of the critical elements of the previously listed five basic managerial functions.

To discover the possible relationships between the degree of decentralization of authority in the firms and the impeding effects of certain environmental constraints with an acceptable degree of validity the political, legal, sociological-cultural, economic, and educational environment of Turkey was studied in detail in two successive stages.

During the first, exploratory, stage of this part of the study, secondary sources published by the Ankara Mission of the U.S. Agency for International Development, various other organizations, and individuals were evaluated. The information thus collected served as a general background for the second stage in which managing directors of the firms studied and representatives of the Turkish government, industry, banking community, and higher educational system, as well as the development experts of the Ankara Mission of US-AID, were asked to complete a questionnaire based on the Delphi-Technique.[8] Altogether ninety prospective respondents were approached. Seventy-three responded. Table 1 shows the distribution of the seventy-three respondents interviewed according to their fields of expertise.

The Delphi-Technique is a method which can be used for the purpose of developing a consensus of views about an issue which does not lend itself to a precise cause-and-effect analysis. While it does not give totally accurate information and while the results obtained through the application of this technique depend to some extent on the skill and imagination with which it is applied, it does represent a scientifically valid and reliable approach to the investigation of issues and problems which are otherwise very difficult to research.[9]

The questionnaire based on this technique used the Farmer-Richman framework of hypothesized environmental constraint categories, as, for example, political, legal, sociological, and cultural, and broke the same down into subelements, as, for example, the view toward authority, educational match with requirements, and trade restrictions. The selected respondents were asked to numerically weight the various environmental constraint subelements in terms of their impeding effects upon the performance of the five basic managerial functions in Turkey.

Table 1 SUMMARY OF EXPERTS INTERVIEWED BY THEIR FIELD OF EXPERTISE

Expertise	Institution Represented	Number of Respondents
Business Management	Firms Studied	33
Economics	Ministry of Finance, US-AID	12
Law	Ankara University	5
Management Development	Turkish Management Association, US-AID	5
Credit and Investment	Commercial Banks, Ministry of Finance	5
Political Science	Middle East Technical University	3
Education	Middle East Technical University	3
Sociology	Middle East Technical University	3
Labor Movement	Turk-is	2
Social Psychology	Middle East Technical University	1
Taxation	Ministry of Finance, US-AID	1
Foreign Aid Programs	US-AID	1
TOTAL		73

The complete procedure recommended in the literature for the use of the Delphi-Technique was not followed, because after the analysis of the answers to the first set of questionnaires, the information received converged to such an extent that a second set of questionnaires was not considered necessary.

From the answers received to the questionnaires, the average weight assigned to each particular constraint subelement was computed and then this average was used to identify the most impeding constraint categories and subelements. The results of this procedure were crosschecked very carefully with the experts of the Turkish Management Association, the Ankara Mission of the U.S. Agency for International Development, the members of the Department of Management and Economics of the Middle East Technical University, and the investigator's own experience gained during his three-year stay in Turkey.

FINDINGS OF THE STUDY

Decision-making authority in all sixteen Turkish and American companies was without exception highly centralized (see Table 2). Decisions related to all organizational activities, including most day-to-day operational problems, were made by a small group of managers at the top and then communicated down to all employees in the form of strict orders. Before any action could be taken, all subordinates, including middle managers, had to go through a tight series of reviews and signatures.[10] Frequently, such high-level approval extended to minor matters deserving the attention of a first-line supervisor at best. Underlying this high degree of centralization of authority was a control system which monitored actions at all organizational levels in a minute, legalistic manner. Standard operating procedures were looked upon as laws instead of guidelines and were treated as such by all employees.

Subordinates as a rule never attempted to make independent decisions even on minor matters and insisted on clearance from above every time they had to face a situation that was not provided for in the standard operating

Table 2 DEGREE OF CENTRALIZATION OF AUTHORITY IN THE FIRMS STUDIED

Firm Nationality	Planning Participation Below Top Management	Operational Decision-Making Authority	Use of Committees	Control Over Personnel	Supervisory Techniques Used	Nature of Communication Structure
Turkish	None	Top managers and some dept. heads	Limited to top managers	Very tight	Job centered	One-way: transmitting mainly orders
American	None	Top managers and some dept. heads	Limited to top managers	Very tight	Job centered	One-way: transmitting mainly orders

procedures. A first-line supervisor of a Turkish company, for example, explained that "decentralization of authority is undesirable, because if we do not send everything to the top, how do they know that we work well and how can they reward us?"

Contrary to expectations not even the U.S. educated and trained managers of American firms belonging to worldwide corporate systems found it possible, or desirable, to decentralize authority. Together with their Turkish counterparts in the domestic companies, they rationalized their behavior through a simple explanation; they claimed that all their subordinates were incompetent and could not be trusted to perform their jobs in a satisfactory manner.

The managing director of one Turkish company, for example, complained that his employees had a complete lack of ambition and discipline and did not conceive of time as an important factor in business life.[11] He explained that he had to spend a great deal of time calling in his subordinates to check the progress of work, because if he had not done so, his instructions would have been forgotten or carried out in the wrong way.

An American general manager was upset about the fact that even after sixteen years in Turkey, he would not get straight answers from his subordinates. He complained that every piece of information he received was couched in such a mass of words that in the end he never really knew what they wanted to tell him.

No doubt, these complaints were often more than justified, especially at the production level where workers were still not completely committed to the new industrial way of life. However, these complaints and explanations grossly oversimplified the situation and ignored the fact that most of the time managers were simply not willing to decentralize authority.[12] They were not willing and perhaps not able to do so because very powerful sociological-cultural and legal environmental constraints severely reduced managerial freedom of action in this respect.

The nature and approximate strength of these environmental constraints was determined through the Delphi-Technique questionnaire given to seventy-three selected respondents. The results obtained from the questionnaire pointed to the following environmental factors as the most negative constraints impeding decentralization of authority in Turkey during 1966-68.

The View Toward Authority

Historically the Turkish society has always been very authoritarian.[13] This authoritarian atmosphere permeated every phase of life from the family through the school to the government. It was probably the result of many divergent forces acting simultaneously. A Turkish psychiatrist, for example, hypothesized that overprotection and thus lack of independence in child rearing practices in the family could lead to passivity and dependence in adult life.[14]

During 1966-68 the educational system in Turkey was to a large extent still characterized by an emphasis on the memorizing of facts, rather than on the development of independent thinking and analysis. In addition to this, obedience to authority—as represented by the instructor and the books—was not usually open to challenge.[15]

At the time of this study ninety-eight percent of the Turkish citizens were Muslims. In the Ottoman empire Islam was the state religion. During the first years of the young republic of Ataturk, the situation, however, was basically changed. The practice of religion became a private matter. This resulted in an increase in the number of liberal-minded Muslims who did not closely observe the teachings and practices of orthodox Islam any longer. Thus the influences of Islam were far less than several decades ago. Its residual influence, however, could still not be ignored completely. Islam was not developed only as a religion, but as a comprehensive way of life, a mode for social and economic, as well as political, activities. While there were no Islamic ideals directly opposing economic development, there were elements in the social and legal practices of Muslims that needed careful reevaluation from this point of view. The behavior to which the believers were expected to conform and the final arbiter, the Koran, were established in the past. This resulted in a static way of looking at the world which could thus discourage departures from orthodoxy and thereby promote dependence on authority.

Finally, the government, both through setting the general tone of society and through the behavior of its officials, tended to create an authoritarian atmosphere. The government, although now working toward social and economic development, was historically organized for quite different purposes. It conducted warfare, maintained law and order, and collected the taxes necessary to support these activities. The patterns of organization, procedures, and general orientation today retain many features associated with these former tasks.[16]

The high degree of involvement of government officials with regulations and control, as exemplified by the great respect for laws, and with the prevention of abuses could be interpreted as a static view of the functions of the government which in turn tended to encourage passivity and obedience to authority.[17]

Thus for the average individual the socialization process in Turkey seems to have resulted in qualities such as respect for authority and being satisfied with things the way they are and an unquestioning acceptance of traditional wisdom. It is probably the result of this socialization process that the majority of the Turkish society seems to view authority as a natural right of all formal leaders in politics, the military, industry, and all other areas of activity. This socialization process thus seems to generate a type of subordinate who respects only a strong, domineering superior who issues orders and keeps discipline, but at the same time takes care of his subordinates in a paternalistic manner.

The Import Quota System

The balance of payments of Turkey has traditionally suffered from the fact that its exports have consisted mainly of primary products. The resulting need to protect the limited foreign exchange reserves of the country necessitated a very complex and burdensome import allocation system developed and administered by the government with the aid of the State Planning Organization. This system not only covered the importation of consumer goods and capital equipment, but also of raw materials and spare parts.

As a result of the legal implications of this system and the resulting resource uncertainty, top managers in all sixteen companies had to be continually informed of every small detail related to the importation of raw materials, equipment, and parts.

The general manager of one American firm, for example, complained that on the average he had to spend three to four days per week in the waiting rooms of various government officials in Ankara pleading for decisions or permissions related mostly to imported goods and raw materials. He said that very often he had to make managerial decisions together with his assistant on his way back from Ankara to Istanbul where his plant was situated.

The nature of this import system, based on a set of strictly enforced legal rules, strongly affected the decentralization of authority in all firms.[18] The continuous functioning of the firms depended on the availability of imported raw materials and equipment. Thus top managers were forced to get involved with every detail that in any way related to the import regulations. They had to be informed about the size of inventories, carefully watch the paper work involved, and spend a great deal of time with the Chambers of Commerce as well as the various government agencies to secure the needed foreign exchange allocations.

CONCLUSIONS

This study thus has shown that in Turkey during 1966-68 there were very strong environmental constraints of a sociological-cultural and legal nature present which tended to impede decentralization of authority to a high degree.

The resulting superior-subordinate relationship manifested itself in a paternalistic and rather strict and uncompromising attitude on the part of the managers, and a very respectful and unquestioning acceptance of this managerial attitude on the part of all subordinates. The result of this sort of relationship was an almost complete lack of decentralization of authority.

Contrary to *a priori* expectations it was significant to find that not even the American educated and trained managers of the worldwide U.S. corporate subsidiaries attempted to decentralize authority. While they rationalized their behavior in terms of the alleged incompetence and laziness of subordinates, it seemed more likely that the analyzed environmental constraints, the view toward authority, and the import quota system were so strong that they severely limited managerrial freedom of action regardless of education and general background. It appeared that U.S. managers were reluctant to change the established superior-subordinate relationships because they feared that this could easily upset the everyday operations of their firms. There also seemed to be some evidence to the effect that a widespread decentralization of authority could have been interpreted by many employees as a sign of weakness and indecisiveness on the part of management which under the existing sociological-cultural conditions could have led to a corresponding loss of work effort on the part of these employees.

Contrary to the reported empirical findings and various hypotheses of U.S. management theorists, this almost complete lack of decentralization of authority did not seem to disturb employees and apparently did not result in major organizational conflicts.[19] This finding strongly implied that the concept of decentralization of authority is to a relatively high degree culture bound and that before it can be applied with the same degree of effectiveness in societies different from the U.S., not only organizational, but also certain environmental conditions, would have to be changed.

This is not to say that an almost complete lack of decentralization of authority could not result in serious organizational inefficiencies. In the firms studied, for example, all top managers were swamped with minor details concerning almost all organizational activities and thus could not possibly fulfill all their managerial duties in a satisfactory manner. A meaningful evaluation of these inefficiencies, however, would have necessitated measuring them against the potential inefficiencies that could have been generated through a widespread decentralization of authority. Possible indecisiveness and lack of initiative on the part of employees who were not used to organizational power could have prevented these employees from effectively utilizing the delegated authority. Thus, under the existing sociological-cultural and legal conditions, widespread decentralization of authority was not only impeded by certain constraints, but was perhaps not even desirable from the point of view of overall organizational efficiency. This was a possibility which called for further research.

It could be argued that these conclusions can be applied only to Turkey. Strictly speaking this is true; however, the evaluation of the environmental constraints impeding decentralization of authority generated several observations which could safely be applied to many developing countries. Most of these countries have to limit imports both in the consumer and industrial sector of their economies. The resulting import regulations are usually complex and burdensome and tend to require the continuous and detailed attention of top managers. Most of them are also just now in the process of changing from a traditional to a modern society, and thus the prevailing sociological-cultural constraints tend to closely approximate those in Turkey.

REFERENCES

1. Peter F. Drucker, *The Concept of the Corporation* (New York: The John Day Co., 1946), p. 46.

2. For a detailed discussion of the possible relationship between decentralization of authority and participative management, employee centered supervision and job enlargement on the one hand, and successful managerial performance on the other hand, see Rensis Likert, *New Patterns of Management* (New York: McGraw-Hill, 1961); Douglas McGregor, *The Human Side of Enterprise* (New York: McGraw-Hill, 1960); and Chris Argyris, *Integrating the Individual and the Organization* (New York: John Wiley and Sons, 1964).

3. Andrew H. Whiteford, *A Reappraisal of Economic Development* (Chicago: Aldine Publishing Co., 1967), p. 177.

4. See, for example, Harold Koontz and Cyril O'Donnel, *Principles of Management* (New York: McGraw-Hill, 1966), ch. XVII; and William H. Newman, Charles F. Summer, and Warren Kirby, *The Process of Management* (Englewood Cliffs, N.J.: Prentice-Hall, 1967), ch. IV.

5. This is not to say that such a restructuring of sociological relationships and cultural values for the sake of perhaps improving industrial efficiency is desirable and would necessarily be acceptable to the Turkish society.

6. Richard N. Farmer and Barry M. Richman, *Comparative Management and Economic Progress* (Homewood, Ill.: Richard D. Irwin, 1965), chs. II, III, and IV. Among the critical elements studied were, for example, planning participation by employees, extent and use of committees, criteria used in promoting personnel, supervisory techniques used, degree of looseness or tightness of control over personnel, and the timing and procedure for corrective action.

7. The questions specifically asked for a statement as to the organizational level at which decisions concerning the critical elements of the five basic managerial functions were made. For a good discussion of a similar approach to the measuring of the degree of centralization of authority, see Jerald Hage and Michael Aiken, "Relationship of Centralization to Other Structural Properties," *Administrative Science Quarterly*, XII, No. 1 (June, 1967), 72-92.

8. A general description of the Delphi-Technique and a discussion of its scientific validity can be found in Olaf Helmer and Nicholas Rescher, "On the Epistemology of the Inexact Sciences," *Management Sciences*, VI, No. 1 (October, 1959), as cited and explained by Richman and Farmer in *Comparative Management and Economic Progress*, pp. 329-339.

9. The difficulties of doing empirical research in management using the environmental (ecological) approach are discussed in an insightful article by Hans Schollhammer. Mr. Schollhammer, however, did not mention the Delphi-Technique through which these difficulties can be overcome to at least some degree. No doubt the environmental approach, even with the Delphi-Technique, leaves room for the interpretation of relationships and findings by the investigator. This, however, holds true for almost any kind of research approach and does not necessarily, as Mr. Schollhammer claims, make the environmental approach "operationally defective," especially as long as social science researchers cannot approximate the laboratory conditions of the physical scientists. See Hans Schollhammer, "The Comparative Management Theory Jungle," *Academy of Management Journal*, XII, No. 1 (March, 1969), 86-87.

10. The need for a series of reviews and signatures at successively higher organizational levels, at times leading up to the general manager's office, for almost routine day-to-day operational decisions as, for example, the issuing of raw materials, served as an additional good measure of the degree of centralization of authority.

11. This manager strongly felt that the greatest contribution his foreign colleagues could make to industrialization in Turkey would be to teach the role of time as an element of cost to their subordinates.

12. By doing so the managers ignored the fact that as long as they were not willing to delegate any authority the abilities and loyalty of their employees could hardly be improved.

13. Nuri Eren, a former diplomat and now author, has this to say about his people

in this respect: ". . . until recently, Turkey remained essentially an authoritarian society in which individual rights never gained philosophic primacy even when they earned political recognition . . . , the Turks, in spite of their unreserved dedication to modernism, failed to lift man to the pinnacle of his inalienable rights, which protect his sacred worth and dignity." See Nuri Eren, *Turkey Today and Tomorrow* (New York: Frederick A. Prager, 1962), pp. 183, 251.

14. Dr. Orhan Ozturk, in a speech given to teachers as cited by Edwin Cohn, "Social and Cultural Factors Affecting the Emergence and Functioning of Innovators," in *Social Aspects of Economic Development* (Istanbul: Economic and Social Studies Conference Board, 1963), p. 98.

15. It has been the experience of this writer, as an instructor (1965-68) at the Middle East Technical University, the most progressive institute of higher learning in Turkey, that students tended to accept the texts and the words of the instructors as the "final truth." It was very difficult to generate discussions and to have students question the ideas and words of authors or instructors.

16. The Managing Board of the Central Government Organization Research Project came to the following conclusions in this respect: ". . . The particular conditions in Turkey necessitate acceptance of various public functions as central government functions, and in many cases, acceptance of decision making at higher levels. However, the acceptance of central government responsibility for these functions must not be considered a reason for continuation of extreme centralism which entails such handicaps as waste of time, bottlenecks, lack of personal development, and slowness." *Organization and Functions of the Central Government of Turkey* (Ankara: The Institute of Public Administration for Turkey and the Middle East, 1965), p. 360.

17. A recent study, however, found that today ". . . many civil servants express dissatisfaction with the excessively authoritarian atmosphere, the lack of thoughtfulness, and the lack of interest in ideas." Cemal Mihcioglu, *The Civil Service in Turkey* (Ankara: University of Ankara, 1963), p. 31.

18. Strictly speaking this finding could not be applied to all industrial firms operating in Turkey, because not all companies in every industry needed as many different types and as large quantities of imported materials and parts as the sixteen firms studied. However, as a result of the developing nature of the Turkish economy it is reasonable to claim that almost all of them had to cope with the import quota system to varying degrees and thus it seemed very likely that top management everywhere had to behave in essentially the same manner.

19. This conclusion was based mainly on observations and discussions with departmental heads and first-line supervisors. Thus, evidence of dissatisfaction and organizational friction may have been overlooked or never shown. The prevailing atmosphere in all organizations, however, seemed to support the above observation. The management theorists referred to are Chris Argyris, Douglas McGregor, and Rensis Likert.

Executive Selection, Training, and Development

THE SELECTION OF OVERSEAS MANAGEMENT

FRANCIS X. HODGSON

"It is better to know what a man thinks than to know his language."

The passage of the Trade Expansion Act, public discussion of the problem of balance of payments and the gold flow, and the formal declaration of economic warfare by Krushchev in January 1961 have created a steadily increasing interest in the role of American business, and of American business management overseas. It is hardly too much to say that our business manager abroad has become an agent of U.S. foreign policy.

The export of American capital and American personnel is not new. The United States has been an active participant in international trade since the days of the clipper ship. But today there is a fundamental difference. Heretofore, foreign investment and participation in international trade has been more the province of the private business sector. Now, however, our foreign economic involvement is related to national security. The Trade Expansion Act is essentially a security measure and calls for adjustment and sacrifice, on the part of domestic firms and the national work force, not unlike wartime adjustment and sacrifice.

For U.S. firms now engaged in international trade or planning to undertake it, there are many hazards. The spectre of nationalization lurks in many foreign areas. Moreover the return of profit to U.S. stockholders is frequently threatened. American marketing men must constantly innovate to adjust well accepted domestic products to the tastes and traditions of long-established foreign cultural patterns, and to combat foreign price-competition.

One frequently overlooked problem of overseas business participation is the matter of what types of Americans should be sent overseas. What are the

Francis X. Hodgson, The Selection of Overseas Management, *MSU Business Topics*, Spring, 1963, pp. 49-54. Reprinted by permission of the publisher, Division of Research, Graduate School of Business Administration, Michigan State University.

optimum characteristics required of those who are sent to foreign locations to manage the parent-company investment, to develop markets, or to supervise construction projects? Are the best available individuals selected?

HAZARDS IN SELECTION

Indications are that the selection of qualified members of over-seas management is pretty much a hit or miss affair. There are three major reasons for this. First, little thought is given to the fact that the manager is going to be doing business with people whose traditional beliefs are funda-mentally different from his own. Frequently his qualifications for assignment to a foreign post are based solely upon his management performance in the United States. The need for deep knowledge and understanding of foreign customs and traditions is taken for granted or ignored. In the second place, in the achievement-oriented status system which characterizes United States society, capable and ambitious men do not want to get too far away from the home office, and the most desirable candidates are often careful to decline overseas assignments. Thirdly, life is pretty comfortable here at home.

The Trap of Misunderstanding

The first of these problems is an outgrowth of our well integrated social system. The manager may have grown up accepting that fact that he and his family are referred to as "polacks," or the fellow in the next seat at school may have been called a Swede or a "wop." But at no time did these ethnic references ever imply that these individuals and their families were not true Americans in customs and beliefs. The United States is a nation of many subcultural groups. Insofar as is possible in a nation of its size, there has emerged from a diverse immigrant background a people with a fundamentally similar value system, particularly with regard to ethics, status, and human dignity.

When this same manager is sent overseas, he can fall into traps of mis-understanding, inefficiency, and even failure, unless he is specifically alerted to fundamental cultural differences. Because his assistant managers, some government officials and potential customers with whom he is associated frequently wear American-style clothes and speak passable English, the un-prepared U.S. manager in overseas operations will have a tendency to assume that these associates and other contacts are just Pete, or Ole, or Tony, in a different setting. He may miss completely the fact that his new associates are schooled in value systems which are considerably different from his own.

Depth studies have been made on this problem of cross-cultural differences by U.S. researchers in Japan, Mexico, and the Middle East. The untrained U.S. manager may, for example, conclude a discussion with his locally employed purchasing agent, believing that they have reached an agreement to switch to a new supplier who can furnish raw materials of similar quality at a lower price. A month later he is chagrined to find his company still buying from the original supplier; he did not realize that the supplier and his purchasing agent are brothers-in-law. The unalerted U.S. foreign manager may commit himself to expensive specialized training programs in the United States for select locally employed supervisors. But upon returning to the job, the recipients of the training manage to get transferred to positions which are unrelated to their specialized training. The reason is that the new positions command higher status in the local community. Errors of this type are extremely expensive in terms of operating costs, and in the achievement of employee and public relations.

Incentives and Ambition

The gay posters which encourage travel to glamorous lands and exotic foreign cities are not much of an incentive to many of the dedicated, hard working executives whom top management would like to see representing the firm overseas. Furthermore the capable manager is cagey enough to know that promotions in Chicago or Los Angeles can pass him by if he is working in Singapore or Paris. Sometimes the offer of overseas salary differentials or the prospect of a break on personal income taxes are believed to be sufficient to encourage the capable manager to accept an overseas assignment. But the qualified candidate realizes that such financial gain is extremely short run. When he returns to the United States the replacement and refurnishing of a home, the restocking of the family wardrobe, and the purchase of a car can dissolve the temporary increment of the bank balance.

Sometimes the experience factor is held out as an incentive. But let us assume that an executive has become highly skilled and experienced in installing supermarkets in Europe, or in negotiating trade agreements with the Middle Eastern sheiks. Where does this man have the greatest value to the firm?—in Europe and the Middle East, of course. The prospect of becoming a career expatriate is not appealing to most capable American managers.

The Comforts of Home

Life really is pretty good in the United States. It is not necessary to boil water before drinking. Lettuce can be eaten without disinfecting. There are no irritating language barriers. Some considerations are even more important. Is there an adequate hospital in the foreign location when the new baby is to be born? How about schooling for the children? The foreign-duty Englishman or Frenchman accepts separation from his teenage children when they are sent home for an education. The prospect of such separation is not acceptable to most American families.

The collective effect of these difficulties in discouraging capable members of management from accepting overseas assignments adds up to a single problem—there is a tendency to send second and third stringers overseas. Most U.S. companies follow the practice of staffing their foreign operations by offering transfers to members of their domestic organizations. Naturally, the transfer is offered first to the man whom the company feels will do the best job overseas. Frequently this man is a comer in the domestic organization. Often, for the reasons discussed above, he diplomatically refuses the offer on the grounds of family health or children's education. The offer is then made to successively less attractive choices, and it is not infrequently accepted by a fairly ineffectual man. But someone must be sent. It is not unusual for firms to have to go outside the company to find a man who is currently detached and willing to accept overseas employment.

A WAY OUT

As with most problems, there is an approach to overcoming these hazards. Capable management representatives can be encouraged to represent their firms overseas. However, a number of innovations are necessary. First, overseas duty for qualified members of U.S. management must be presented in its true perspective: as an experience and a sacrifice which capable men will accept for their own and their companies' growth. Foreign duty should be described for what it is, and the frustrations and discomforts factually presented rather than camouflaged with offers of subsidized travel and short-run financial gain. In addition the new approach would involve two other innovations: a change in some of the criteria of selection, and an adequate pre-departure training.

Integrating the Foreign Assignment

When top management offers foreign duty to the man who is believed to be most capable of filling the position abroad, there are a number of major considerations to keep in mind. Usually the individual is successful enough to afford personal vacation trips if foreign travel is of sufficient interest to him. Of greater import is the fact that a man with his qualifications has usually worked long and hard to prepare himself for promotion in the domestic organization. Also, aware of the mobility expected of executives, he is reluctant to refuse a transfer as a matter of principle. But leaving the United States is a much more drastic move than a transfer from the Midwest to the West Coast.

The problem can be attacked by integrating foreign assignments as a rotational experience in the company's management development program. This approach simultaneously achieves three objectives. It avoids presenting the selectee with the sudden prospect of divorce from the main stream of the parent company organization and the promotional pattern. At the same time it sets the stage for a candid presentation of the hazards and frustrations of overseas duty. And most important of all, from the viewpoint of achievement of company objectives, it precludes the need for top management to bargain with second and third stringers to accept the assignment.

IMPROVING SELECTION METHODS

To achieve the objective of placing the best possible candidate in an overseas management position, the adjustment required in the selection procedure is a shift in top management thinking. Proper selection of candidates for a foreign position requires other criteria than the fact that the individual has been successful in domestic operations. Some individuals have ingrained prejudices which do not manifest themselves in U.S. operations. Caution should be exercised in transferring an individual raised in the Deep South to an overseas position where his assistants are of negroid origin or have dark skin color. Equal caution should be used in regard to naturalized citizens from European countries whose early environmental training included a belief in their ethnic superiority to the national of Asia, Africa, Latin America, and other overseas areas.

In the past the sales approach used during the selection process has placed emphasis almost entirely upon advising the potential candidate of the amenities he will enjoy at his overseas post. Reasonable comfort and working conditions must be provided. But it should be borne in mind that if these amenities are ostentatious they have the immediate effect of inviting envy and criticism from the considerably less affluent local society. The American is usually a highly adjustable individual, and when the basic requirements of food, shelter, and health are provided, he can function satisfactorily overseas. It is of much greater importance that he be prepared psychologically to be accepted in the foreign community rather than to start his assignment in an environment of antagonism and envy.

Cooperation, Not Carpetbagging

Major emphasis should be placed upon selecting and placing overseas those Americans who do not accept the foreign assignment for purely selfish reasons. The type of representative needed is the one who sees his role as that of cooperator rather than a carpetbagger, and as that of a supervisor-trainer rather than an unapproachable manager.

The reasons for this are not centered in do-goodism but in cold economic fact. There are few business opportunities in foreign countries today, either established or planned, in which local participation is not required by law, or where rapid development of nationals into management positions is not required by contractual agreement. Furthermore, in the absence of such legal or contractual requirements the rapid emergence of a worldwide demand for personal and national recognition underlines the fact that a cooperative partnership-type approach is simply good business. The threat of nationalization can be partially withstood by admitting local employees to management positions.

The American who is sent overseas must therefore have the ability to subordinate his personal sentiments about ethnic and social relationships, and his personal ambition. Today it is not unusual for Americans abroad to be reporting to organizational superiors who are nationals of the host country.

PRE-DEPARTURE TRAINING

How can this new attitude of mind be achieved? It can be achieved by training. Because pre-departure orientation has heretofore been largely confined to convincing the overseas candidate that his personal goals and comfort are assured, little formal preparation has been provided. In a recent survey of seventy large and influential U.S. corporations with overseas operations, only three reported the existence of pre-departure training programs. Some of the firms do not even provide pre-departure literature. The reason usually given for the absence of orientation programs is that "our management people whom we send overseas have all demonstrated good performance in domestic operations, and we feel that no training is necessary."

The essence of pre-departure training is to provide an awareness of the basic cultural pattern of the host country, and the way this cultural pattern differs from our own value system. Is the host country characterized by a highly interpersonalized social system? To what extent is nepotism accepted and practiced? Is the status system based upon wealth, family name, or political achievement? Is the concept of delegation understood? What are accepted business ethics? Is the expectance of gratuities an accepted part of the income-compensation system? What is the situation with regard to racial integration?

These are some of the basic social norms which must be completely understood by the American manager if he is to function successfully in the foreign country.

Phases of Preparation

To provide this training requires up to eight weeks under the direction of qualified instructors. There are two phases to this training. The overseas candidate must first be instructed in the way a culture develops. Once he realizes that all of the social, ethical, and behavioral characteristics which constitute individual and national value systems are learned, just as reading and writing are learned, the American overseas will stand a chance of understanding rather than fighting the behavioral patterns of his overseas associates.

Training in Understanding

The achievement of understanding of the process of cultural development will help the American manager overseas to realize that beliefs and practices developed during a lifetime are extremely difficult to modify. As a guest in the host country, in order to achieve personal adjustment, satisfactory employee and public relations, and successful company operations, responsibility for most of the adjustment to local behavioral and attitudinal patterns will be his.

The costs in removing U.S. executives and supervisors from productive activity for training periods of up to eight weeks must be considered. However, research in overseas locations indicates that return on this investment in training will exceed expectations.

Foreign language study receives some emphasis in pre-departure orientation. Such training is useful from the practical viewpoint and valuable as a public relations tool. But since pre-departure orientation is costly, and language training can be accomplished at the job site, management will be well advised to give preference to training in the understanding of cross-cultural differences.

In conclusion, there is a Persian proverb which provides a guide line to management thinking in the face of increasing responsibility for the selection and preparation of men for overseas duty: *It is better to know what a man thinks than to know his language.*

DEVELOPING MANAGERS
IN DEVELOPING COUNTRIES

JAMES A. LEE

Training potential leaders in American-owned companies overseas calls for programs tailored to meet key environmental problems.

Foreword

Any attempt to identify, select, and train future business leaders in the developing nations of Africa, Asia, and South America must take into account the fundamental differences in management development conditions between the United States and the emerging world. Here, the author pinpoints five key environmental problem areas and suggests a straightforward program of techniques for coping with them.

Since World War II, U.S. direct investment abroad has increased to about $67 billion, of which almost a third is in Africa, Asia, and South America.[1] This has produced an unparalleled need for employing foreign supervisors and managers in American-owned companies in developing countries. Since there have also been increases in local pressures to nationalize the ranks of their management overseas, these companies will be required in the foreseeable future to identify and develop an unprecedented number of potential managers of different races, from different cultures, and with different language and educational backgrounds.

The numerous emerging nations, each trying to develop the business leadership necessary for the management of its new economic units, are discovering that a competent manager cadre is not an automatic byproduct of independence. They are also faced with the gigantic task of filling the leadership ranks of their own industries, government departments, and other institutions, which help deplete the small reservoir of potential managers by attracting a large percentage of the few college graduates produced in their new universities. Yet little has been written about the specific problems associated with developing local foreign nationals for management positions in American-owned companies abroad.

ENVIRONMENTAL PROBLEMS

This article identifies the five fundamental differences between management selection and development conditions in developing countries and in the United States, and suggests development techniques that take these differences into account. The key problem areas, which I shall cover in the course of this discussion, are:

1. Limited sources of managerial leadership potential.
2. Educational and technological deprivation.
3. Economic attitudes hostile to private enterprise objectives.
4. Divergent concepts of what an "ideal" manager should be.
5. Resistance to traditional American development approaches, such as face-to-face criticism.

An analysis of each of these will indicate, I believe, some techniques that are superior to "canned" American programs in producing effective results when selecting and developing managers in the emerging countries of Africa and Asia.

However, before examining these basic differences, let me say that while my own research studies have been conducted primarily in Pakistan and Ethiopia, there are similar problems in Latin America to which my findings apply. I know this generally from the literature[2] and from visits and personal contacts in many of those countries.

Limited Sources

Primarily because of low educational and economic levels, the sources of potential managerial talent remain extremely limited in developing countries. Consider Ethiopia, for example, with its estimated 7% adult literacy rate. There, only about half a million people have reached the minimum educational level of an average elementary school student in the United States. Moreover, that entire country of 22 million turns out less than 500 university graduates per year, all of whom have achieved an educational level roughly equivalent to that of a junior in an average American university. This is due, of course, to the cumulative effects of deprived home life, poor quality of primitive village-like schools, and substandard teaching at all levels. The secondary language (English, in Ethiopia) is used as a medium of instruction only from about seventh grade on.

This limited educational opportunity and cultural exposure produces few possible candidates for management development. Let us look briefly at the only pools of potential managers availabe in most underdeveloped countries.

Educated Elites. This tiny pool yields a very few candidates for purely professional (nonownership) management. Members of this group are generally well-educated, quite intelligent, and free-enterprise oriented. They often have real estate holdings and a family history of high-ranking government posts. Many members of this pool are partially educated in the United States or Europe, and their home environment has been modern and characterized by much hired personal service.

Ex-military Officers. This group, almost as small as the "educated elite," contains potential managers who hold many cultural values consonant with American management values. They are generally politically conservative, hardworking, reasonably logical thinkers, loyal, and quite reliable. They tend to be the most qualified source of technical management due (a) to the military selection and training system, and (b) to experience in supervision, logistics, equipment operation, and maintenance.

University Graduates. This pool, although generally too small and inadequately trained, is larger by far than the first two. Members of this group, however, are often hostile to profit and capital, and low in reasoning powers (more on this later) so necessary for business problem solving and planning. They are not motivated for decision making or economic growth planning. They tend to view their degree as an end in itself rather than to think of their higher education as a tooling up for solving challenging problems in their careers. This group contains a wide range of intellectual capabilities—from very low to very high—and most of the graduates possess what an American might term extraordinary talents for memorizing. Approximately half the members of this group aspire to work for their government on graduation.

University students in Ethiopia, for example, were asked to rank 11 occupations according to their status in society. Manager was ranked seventh and shop owner, ninth; while government official was ranked third and farmer, fourth.[3] The majority of these students see the government as the only agent to produce economic growth for their country.

High School Graduates. This group, although still small by U.S. standards, is by far the most numerous. Only a few, however, have the intellectual development potential for business management. Most of them have a reading ability in English about equal to that of an American sixth grader. Moreover, they have been exposed to few of the principles of the physical world. They, like the university students, habitually learn by memorizing and drill. Thus the transition to learning for problem solving can often be slow and tedious. There is one difference between this group and the university graduates: the high school graduates seem more highly motivated. Perhaps because they do not have the ultimate laurel—a university degree—they feel that they cannot rest so comfortably on lesser accomplishment.

Cultural Deprivation

The educationally and technologically deprived "raw materials" for management development in developing countries produce an intellectual profile very deficient in certain aptitudes vital to management performance. Most of their university graduates are seriously lacking (by American standards) in reading speed and comprehension, quantitative reasoning, and basic general science understanding. Their symbolic reasoning, numerical reasoning, and mechanical aptitude scores are usually comparable to those of Americans in the age 12 to 16 range. The use of ratios and indexes is strange to them, and consequently their decision-making habits do not usually include the use of many such tools.

Exhibit 1 shows the results of a five-hour battery of tests which I recently administered to 875 freshmen at the Haile Sellassie I University Testing Center in Addis Ababa, and to a group of 38 Ethiopians holding managerial job titles. The Ethiopian freshmen's results are comparable to those of a similar battery of tests I gave to graduate students in business administration in Pakistan in 1964. It is also interesting to note that the average English reading ability of 34 Pakistani senior managers I measured in 1967 came out at the same U.S. tenth-grade level as shown for the 38 Ethiopian managers.

Exhibit 1   INTELLECTUAL PROFILE OF ETHIOPIAN STUDENTS
AND BUSINESSMEN

Subject	U.S. School Grade Equivalent of University Freshmen	U.S. School Grade Equivalent of Business Managers
Verbal reasoning	9	11
Numerical ability (add, subtract, and so on)	14	14
Abstract reasoning	8	8
Clerical speed and accuracy (attention to detail)	8	8
Mechanical reasoning	6	8
Space relations	7	7
Spelling	13	14
Grammar	11	13
Reading speed/comprehension	8	10

Note: Grade equivalents over 12 and under 8 are estimates by extrapolation.

The often-heard argument that such American tests are not culture-*free* seems to me irrelevant in this case. The fact remains that they are reasonably culture-*fair*. And if foreign nationals are to perform a "Western" job—e.g., supervise the maintenance of a Boeing 707, oversee the production of pharmaceuticals, or manage the distribution of 4 million gallons of gasoline per month—a Western test is a better prediction instrument than any other tool available. There is no known way to Nigerianize or Indianize a Boeing 707 or the manufacture of antibiotics.

A Case Example

In 1967, I devised a selection procedure for an African airline to select African pilot trainees. The employement manager, himself an African, complained that it was unfair to hold the prospective trainees to the time limits of the various American aptitude tests. I argued that because all the ground instruction, pilot training, text materials, and aircraft were American, it was more appropriate to keep the time limits than to lose the value of the comparative standards. He persisted in his argument for "fairness" until I promised to double the time limit for the tests under one condition: that he go around the world and double the length of all the runways.

The 16 African pilot trainees finally selected by the employment manager from the 700 applicants *averaged* 94 IQ on an American test. Under the direction of three flight instructors, who were experienced American instructors, the trainees required 40 hours of dual instruction to solo (compared to 8 hours for a U.S. student pilot), suffered 6 accidents including the demolishing of an aircraft, and produced 6 pilots.

In my opinion, this difficult training situation was due purely to the educational and technological deprivation that severely reduced the number of applicants with flying potential.

Translation of such tests for managerial candidates into the native language is an unsatisfactory solution at the present time for two reasons: (1) each developing country usually has several languages, and (2) few if any of these languages are rich enough to make translation practical. Even terms such as "manager," "foreign exchange," "probability," "torque," and "capital" have no equivalents in most of the languages of the developing countries. Furthermore, the written versions of the languages of most developing countries are primarily sound-making systems rather than sense-making systems. Their system of absorbing new words is usually very inefficient. For example, Urdu, Hindi, and Amharic have absorbed the words "atom" and "atomic bomb" but the root "atom" changes its written appearance when the suffix "ic" is added.

In other words, while English (or some European language) is usually a second language for most managers or potential managers in developing countries, it also is often the official government and business language. Thus it is a most effective language for most nationals to use in learning what is necessary to become a manager.

The educational system in developing countries has also conditioned the foreign national to a rote-learning approach characterized by memorizing and drill. High school and university graduates are generally superior to comparable-age Americans in straight memorizing and in computational skills like addition, subtraction, multiplication, and division. But their lack of problem-solving practice has left them generally unable to decide *whether* and *when* to add, subtract, multiply, or divide.

The average reading comprehension and speed of an English-speaking foreign national management candidate in Africa or Asia—usually a university graduate—is approximately equivalent to that of a U.S. eighth grader. (About 70% of all candidates fall between the U.S. fifth and eleventh grades in reading ability.) He is not habitually a reader, and when he reads to learn, he often simply memorizes topic sentences and paragraph headings.

Hostile Attitudes

In most developing countries, the prevailing ideas of appropriate objectives of a business enterprise—whether governmental or privately owned —are that it be a provider of jobs and welfare. For nonowner managers and supervisors, the principle of efficiency as an economic unit is often considered a "foreign" idea, and one contrary to many of the values of the cultures of the developing countries.

There is also a general lack of economic understanding of where economic growth or new jobs come from. The role of profits, surplus, or savings is not usually understood by a large percentage of managerial employees or by the countries' opinion makers.

The results of an economic attitude survey I conducted suggest that such opinions represent the cultural values of most peoples of developing agricultural economies. *Exhibit 2* shows the responses to pertinent questions in the survey of Pakistani middle managers (PM) in a petroleum company, Pakistani graduate students (PS) at the University of Karachi, Ethiopian managers (EM) from Ethiopian Air Lines, African electrical equipment salesmen (AS) from seven African countries, and Ethiopian senior students (ES) in business administration at Haile Sellassie I University.

The socialistic attitudes reflected in this economic attitude survey—anti-private enterprise, overestimation of profits, belittlement of the role of capital, and so on—affect the "raw materials" attracted to management trainee posts. A foreign national department manager of an American overseas operations who believes that the wrong people own the company which he works for and that they are really profiteers is not likely to work very hard for its success. These attitudes, also held by many government officials, affect the freedom of the company to discharge "mistakes." Overall, these attitudes seriously affect the motivation of the foreign national manager to help the company achieve its primary objectives—return (to America) on investment and growth.

Managerial Concepts

Differences between concepts of the "ideal" manager held by American managers and those held by managers and students in emerging

Exhibit 2 SURVEY OF ECONOMIC ATTITUDES AMONG FIVE GROUPS IN DEVELOPING COUNTRIES

	Percent of group giving this answer				
Answer	PM (N = 62)	PS (N = 150)	EM (N = 51)	AS (N = 30)	ES (N = 54)
What percentage of (Ethiopia's) (Pakistan's) business and industry should be in the public sector (owned by the government)?					
0%	13%	5%	8%	0%	6%
25%	13%	15%	39	26	37
50%	24	26	20	33	30
75%	18	42	14	37	26
100%	32	13	20	3	2
Which of the following would you consider a capitalist in the most accurate sense of the word?					
A factory owner	45%	67%	33%	40%	57%
A taxi driver who owns his own taxi	10	6	0	7	0
A farmer who owns 2 acres of land, 5 oxen, a wagon, and a plow	10	5	12	27	0
The holder of a paid-up life insurance policy	0	4	12	7	2
All of the above	35	18	43	20	41
Which of the following is considered by experts to be one of the most important reasons why (Ethiopia) (Pakistan) has difficulty in world exports?					
Labor is too expensive	0%	2%	18%	26%	6%
(Ethiopia's) (Pakistan's) location	6	2	8	7	9
Shipping costs	6	14	12	3	17
Overpricing for too much profit	37	50	39	40	20
Trade barriers	50	32	24	23	48
What do you estimate is the annual percentage return on investment (after taxes are paid) in the textile industry?					
0%	0%	5%	0%	0%	0%
10%	8	17	18	27	7
15%	50	25	29	23	37
25%	24	35	21	43	43
50%	11	18	31	7	13
What do you think is the average capital investment per employee in the ten leading manufacturing companies in (Ethiopia) (Pakistan)?					
$100*	32%	25%	14%	23%	26%
$300	32	26	20	13	20
$500	8	25	51	33	30
$1,000	8	13	8	20	13
$2,000 or more	19	11	8	10	11

*Local currency equivalents were used in the original questionnaire.

213

countries point up some further problems involved in developing managers abroad. In 1966-1967, I asked managers from America, Pakistan, and Ethiopia to rank 15 qualities or characteristics—selected from American business literature—of the so-called ideal manager.

(In addition, business students from Pakistan and Ethiopia were asked to rank these same characteristics to determine something of the nature of their concepts of the ideal manager. Although their comparative rankings are not included in the accompanying discussion, I would like to point out that future managers—that is, new graduates—will be no closer to the American ideals. In fact, in my research the two most different groups are the American managers and Ethiopian business students. In other words, specialized rework of many of their values will be necessary before they can be given managerial responsibilities.)

Exhibit 3 shows the list chosen for the questionnaire and the abbreviated forms used in the accompanying exhibits and discussion. *Exhibit 4* and *Exhibit 5* compare rankings of the foreign national manager groups surveyed with American managers' rankings on each of the 15 ideal manager characteristics. Using median ranks, these characteristics are shown in order of ranking importance and connected to point up differences between American managers' rankings and those of business managers from Pakistan and Ethiopia.

It is clear from these comparative rankings that the foreign managers surveyed do not see the "name of the game" the same as do American managers. Those from developing countries indicate they expect a manager to be very sensitive to all kinds of requests from their own subordinates. This, in turn, can lead to dire economic consequences because the supersensitivities of the foreign national managers make it difficult to say no. For example, because his subordinates requested rest breaks, one foreign national manager gave away two daily 15-minute coffee breaks which cost the company the equivalent of U.S. $300,000 a year. He never even considered the cost.

The foreign managers do not expect from their managerial ideal the same incorporation of ethics in management behavior as does an American manager from his ideal. Also, they see an ideal manager as having less respect for his subordinates than an American sees him. This will no doubt affect their ability to develop their own subordinates.

(A rather astounding finding, in my opinion, was the overall agreement between divergent groups of American managers, who failed to see eye-to-eye on only 1 of the 15 characteristics. In other words, the American manager community is a subculture which is in close internal agreement on what a manager should be.)

Resistance to Criticism

The most common approach to developing managers for American-owned operations in developing countries is a mixture of coaching and performance appraisal. Both of these usually involve face-to-face criticism

Exhibit 3 RANKING CHARACTERISTICS FOR SURVEY OF WHAT THE "IDEAL" MANAGER SHOULD BE

As it appeared in questionnaire	Abbreviation
The concern for future planning and for future problem prevention.	Future planning
The recognition of one's superior both as the source of authority and as responsible for what his subordinates do.	Respect for authority
The patient and creative searching for quantifiable variables as both a basis for and measure of decision making.	Quantifiable variables
The capacity to respond to human needs and problems, and to be sensitive to the feelings of others.	Sensitivity to others' feelings
The recognition of the importance of personal friendships in achieving overall managerial effectiveness.	Personal friendships
The ability to make accurate and timely decisions based on unlike variables, incomplete information, and incompletely understood consequences.	Decision making
The willingness to apply religious and ethical values in the conduct of business activities.	Religious-ethical values
The steady desire to develop new methods and to take new actions which improve results.	Develop new methods
The recognition of the need for active cooperation with and support of government and its programs.	Support of government
The willingness to work hard and long hours to ensure the attainment of company objectives.	Hard work
The recognition of the importance of family obligations to one's overall management career success.	Family obligations
The respect for the need to maintain appropriate status differences between manager and subordinate levels of employees.	Maintain status differences
The willingness to take economic or career risks through bold decisions.	Risk taking
The capacity to be personally loyal to a company, organization, or work group.	Capacity to be loyal
A firm belief in subordinates' capabilities to initiate action and to maintain self-control in the performance of their jobs.	Belief in subordinates

which is often sufficiently depersonalized for an American subordinate to tolerate, but rarely impersonal enough for a foreign national. Because most of the developing world is characterized by highly personalized sensitivities, face-to-face criticism of *any* kind seldom accomplishes more than firing up various psychological defense mechanisms. Often the criticized foreign national reacts by narrowing his job responsibilities in order to prevent future error and thus to avoid more humiliation and ridicule.

Because it is not *his* (or his countryman's) company—and because he often resents this from the outset—his motivation to improve will not be the same. (In another research study, I found that only one out of eight Ethiopian and

Exhibit 4 COMPARATIVE RANKING OF ETHIOPIAN
AND AMERICAN MANAGERS

	Ethiopians *(N = 51)*	*Americans* *(N = 184)*
	Develop new methods	Develop new methods
	Sensitivity to others' feelings	Future planning
	Future planning	Decision making
	Quantifiable variables	Belief in subordinates
	Hard work	Capacity to be loyal
	Capacity to be loyal	Sensitivity to others' feelings
	Belief in subordinates	Quantifiable variables
	Decision making	Hard work
	Support of government	Respect for authority
	Respect for authority	Religious-ethical values
	Risk taking	Family obligations
	Personal friendships	Risk taking
	Maintain status differences	Maintain status differences
	Family obligations	Personal friendships
	Religious-ethical values	Support of government

Note: Black line denotes pair of ranking distributions found to be significantly different.

Pakistani business students are interested in future employment in a "foreign" company.)

Considering the foreign national's intellectual profile and his preference for concern with the present, his ability to anticipate or appreciate the consequences of performance errors cannot be expected to be the same as that of an American. Several Asian and African junior managers, in confidential conversations with me, have indicated that they interpreted criticism from their American bosses as an American peculiarity to live with rather than as a source of valuable information to aid them in improving their performance.

DEVELOPMENTAL APPROACHES

Given the five basic environmental problems we have been examining up to this point, the tailored approaches for selecting and developing managers in developing countries are almost self-indicating. Let us now turn

Exhibit 5   COMPARATIVE RANKING OF PAKISTANI
AND AMERICAN MANAGERS

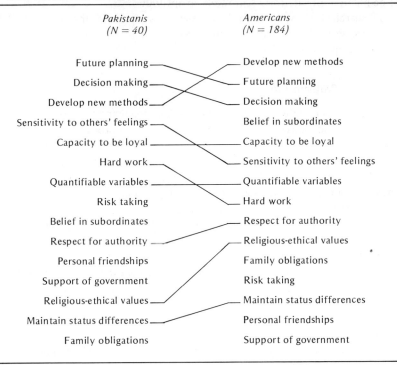

Pakistanis *(N = 40)*	*Americans* *(N = 184)*
Future planning	Develop new methods
Decision making	Future planning
Develop new methods	Decision making
Sensitivity to others' feelings	Belief in subordinates
Capacity to be loyal	Capacity to be loyal
Hard work	Sensitivity to others' feelings
Quantifiable variables	Quantifiable variables
Risk taking	Hard work
Belief in subordinates	Respect for authority
Respect for authority	Religious-ethical values
Personal friendships	Family obligations
Support of government	Risk taking
Religious-ethical values	Maintain status differences
Maintain status differences	Personal friendships
Family obligations	Support of government

Note: Black line denotes pair of ranking distributions found to be significantly different.

our attention to some of the more important courses of action open in each of these situations to American-owned companies overseas.

Problem One

The sources of managerial leadership potential are relatively few in the developing countries, as we have seen, primarily because of the limited educational opportunities and cultural exposure deficiencies. In tackling this problem, there are five courses of action:

1. Add a general aptitude test battery to the management trainee selection program.

2. Actively recruit from high schools and universities so as to increase applicant sample sizes.

3. Increase recruitment of military officers in the age 40 to 50 bracket if mature candidates are needed.

4. Give favorable consideration to applicants who have had only a high school education plus some relevant successful experience over applicants

who are the garden variety university graduate—provided the former appear to be highly motivated *and* score well on aptitude tests.

5. Search for experienced local managers more in the style of U.S. executive search consultants—through extensive personal contacts rather than by formal open advertising.

Problem Two

To counteract the effects of educational and technological deprivation, there are three techniques that will help to produce more effective results in the selection and development of foreign national managers:

1. American companies should consider offering a 100% refund for tuition, books, and supplies for evening extension or correspondence courses in physical science, mathematics, mechanics, logic, and engineering—whether or not these studies are directly job related.

2. In addition, American firms abroad could provide management potential with low-cost, high-interest informative reading materials at seventh- to tenth-grade reading levels, such as subscriptions to *Reader's Digest, Newsweek, Life, Look,* and *Time* magazines. Also, consider the distribution of special-level books on science and engineering that are printed in English.

3. Americans abroad should give maximum attention to explanations of simple mechanical and electrical functions when any explanation is necessary.

The cost per person for examples 1 and 2 just discussed would be approximately $200 to $300 per year if an employee is enrolled in one course at all times and receives three subscriptions. This would result in about 500 hours of classroom, reading, and study time for a cost per hour of learning of about 50 cents.

Problem Three

In this situation where the prevailing economic attitudes are hostile toward enterprise objectives, and where there is also a general lack of understanding, there are five possible approaches:

1. Screen applicants by means of questions on attitude toward or understanding of economics. (One inventory of such questions is provided by the economic attitude questionnaire I used in my research, which can be administered to seventh-grade-level readers and up. I will send a single copy free to anyone who writes me requesting it.)

2. American companies could well distribute booklets and pamphlets to managers and pre-managerial employees which explain the roles of profit and capital in economic growth in simple English with illustrations. (Two sources of such publications in the United States are the Economics Press, West Orange, New Jersey, and Good Reading Rack Service, 505 Eighth Avenue, New York City.)

3. Support more company memberships for foreign managers in local businessmen's organizations such as Rotary and Lions clubs. Personal contact with other managers will help soften Marxian views of the management class.

4. Issue news releases to communicate changes in the company's operations, appointments, and so forth, and to explain the role of business as a valuable instrument of local and national economic development.

5. Conduct economic-understanding training programs similar to those used in the steel and copper industries in the early 1950's in the United States.

Problem Four

Research studies have disclosed, then, that foreign managers do not see the "name of the game" in the same way their American counterparts do. In order to cope with the foreign national's different concepts of what a manager is and does, there are five courses of action open:

1. To help balance the supersensitivities of foreign nationals to requests from their own subordinates with organizational realities, American-owned companies can have their foreign managers practice "costing out"—that is, force them to look at the economic consequences of—various administrative decisions and policies. All fringe benefits should be costed by the foreign national managers. Extra effort should be taken to make sure that they know the approximate value of all capital equipment.

2. Incorporate, as a primary factor in any managerial performance appraisal system, the training and development of subordinates. Require periodic reports from the foreign national managers on their progress in these areas. Move in the direction of a modified management-by-objectives development program. The essential modification is that in the early stages the program objectives should be carefully "negotiated" with each foreign national manager, *beginning with a set of objectives prepared by him*.

3. Incorporate a "reliability" factor—that is, some incentive—in any performance inventory system used, and explain that the manager's reward will be based on his meeting performance deadlines and on his providing promised information or deliveries. Establish a climate of trust regarding money and valuables, but deal swiftly with clear cases of dishonesty and theft.

4. Spell out in some detail the ethics of managerial behavior as company policy. (For example, new employees will be selected from the many applicants on the basis of merit, rather than from the tribal group, ranks of relatives, or friends. The respective merits of such applicants will be determined not by rank favoritism, which is rampant today, but by as objective means as possible.)

5. American managers abroad must recognize the extensive role of local governments in economic development, and however clumsy these governments might appear to be, Americans should refrain from in-house "harping"

on local government interference. In such environments, to live and let live is not enough. Where possible, actively support government programs.

Problem Five

Resistance to traditional American development approaches can be effectively overcome in three basic ways:

1. Avoid *all* criticism in front of others. Private criticism should be depersonalized by focusing on methods, technical consequences, and company objectives.

2. Formal training sessions should either be concerned with the actual company problems or involve the small-team study of related business cases.

3. If not inconsistent with corporate policy, establish a management-by-objectives program in addition to the present company performance appraisal system.

IN SUMMARY

Five fundamental differences between the United States and the developing world in management development circumstances have been identified as key problem areas. Any attempt to develop managers in these environments should take into account the limited sources of management potential, intellectual deprivation, economic attitudes, concepts of what a manager is and does, and resistance to face-to-face criticism. The action program recommended is a straightforward approach to these problems. It consists essentially of more extensive candidate recruiting efforts, supporting further formal education, and assessing and dealing with hostile economic attitudes by disseminating information. Such a program will help to counteract divergent views of what a manager should be.

If certain of these approaches do not seem to fit a particular management development problem in Asia, Africa, or South America, the principle of assessing the local problem carefully and tailoring a solution to fit it should remain. Another principle which should serve well in this undertaking is that more than anything else development efforts will depend primarily on identifying the management potential accurately. The guiding principle here is simply that while bright, informed, eager people do not always make good managers, people who are stupid, ignorant, and hostile never do.

REFERENCES

1. Extrapolated from data given in Harlan Cleveland, et al, *The Overseas American* (New York, McGraw-Hill Book Company, Inc., 1960), and the U.S. Department of Commerce's Office of Business Economics News Release, April 21, 1967.

2. See, for example, "Management Problems and Opportunities for Management Training in Central America," a report by a survey team of Harvard Business School, Division of International Activities, December 1963; and *Elites in Latin America*, edited by Seymour M. Lipset and Aldo Solari (New York, Oxford University Press, Inc., 1967), particularly Chapter I.

3. Asnake Sahlu, "Opinion Survey of University Students with Regard to Business Professions in Ethiopia," *Ethiopian Business Journal*, June 1967, p. 59.

INCOMPETENT FOREIGN MANAGERS?

CAMERON McKENZIE

A common complaint of U.S. headquarters managements of companies new to international business is the incompetence of their foreign general managers (that is, the chief operating executive in the foreign country). The result is a high and costly turnover of foreign managers and, subsequently, among their superiors at headquarters.

For example, since 1957 a company with a new and expanding foreign operation has had three international division presidents and four vice-presidents; in each foreign country in which it operates it has averaged a new general manager every two years.

In one country, another company has had three general managers since 1959. This rate is only slightly higher than the over-all turnover rate for its entire foreign general manager staff.

In another company the manager in virtually every country is under heavy criticism.

Incompetent foreign managers? Perhaps. But a closer look may reveal that the overseas manager, whose function closely approximates that of a U.S. company president, is being judged primarily on details. His judges are experts in the details, to be sure, but they are novices when it comes to assessing how well a chief operating executive is performing. If this situation is reinforced by a control system that looks primarily at the operating details and not at how well he is meeting broader, top-level objectives, such as total profitability and use of assets, his being branded as "incompetent" is almost unavoidable.

This is not to suggest that real incompetence does not exist. Certainly it does. The problem, however, is to distinguish true incompetence from apparent incompetence.

An example was recently cited by one company with a manufacturing facility abroad:

From *Business Horizons*, Spring 1966, pp. 83-90. Reprinted with permission of the publisher. Mr. McKenzie is presently President, McKenzie & Associates, Inc., Management Consultants, Ponce, Puerto Rico.

Within a one-month period production had twice been paralyzed: once because the facility ran out of a basic raw material supplied to it from the United States and importable without restriction, and once because of local supplier manufacturing difficulties, signs of which had been seen for several months.

In the former case, the basic raw material had, through an oversight, simply not been ordered, even though the general manager had been specifically queried about his supply by both the president and international vice-president.

In the latter case the general manager had not taken the obvious, feasible precaution of importing sufficient material to ensure continued production, or having the supplier import it.

At first glance these occurrences seem to provide sufficient reason to begin the search for a replacement. But do they really? What would lead a rational man, who management must have assumed was qualified for the job when they hired him, to let these things happen? Unless utter stupidity is assumed (which is more a reflection on those who hired him than on the man) they can only be symptoms of more basic problems.

This article will suggest that such "incompetence" is often actually caused by a hodge-podge of controls that are imposed on the foreign operation by headquarters. It will postulate that such controls are the ultimate result of unrealistic performance criteria which, in turn, develop from the dual and incongruous nature of the headquarters management position, and will offer some suggestions for helping headquarters management to avoid being plagued with "incompetent" foreign managers.

COMMON SYMPTOMS

Foreign operations that complain of incompetent general managers usually have at least three things in common. *First*, they have overextensive control systems, that is, headquarters demands data that are useless for evaluating performance and for communicating its objectives to the local management or motivating it to reach them. *Second*, the manager really has no grasp of what is going on, even though his reports may be current and correct. A *third* common symptom is the irrational fashion in which the manager reacts to either verbal or written instructions. If such symptoms exist, management will be well advised to take a careful look at its control system before passing judgment on its manager.

Often the overextensive controls are justified by headquarters management as the logical result of having incompetent foreign managers. In other instances, the controls were established initially with the intent of removing some of them when the operation was "ready." When this never came about, the controls remained. In one company, headquarters demanded that a production facility abroad report to it *daily* the number of containers damaged at each point in the production process. In another company, headquarters demanded that, before a claim for a defective supply item costing $5.00 could be paid, it had to be inspected by a man from headquarters staff. In another, not even a clerk could be discharged without headquarters approval.

The receipt of such detailed reporting and control data triggers action at headquarters. Detailed suggestions, queries, and instructions flow back to the foreign operation. The inevitable result is that the onus of management shifts to the U.S. headquarters. Such controls take away responsibility in one area and deposit it in another. Ultimately the foreign general manager loses (or never develops) the sense of responsibility and proprietary interest that is essential for a chief operating executive to have. He becomes a man on a string, being pulled this way and that by headquarters demands, attempting to satisfy not the needs of the business but of his advisors. He is no longer managing a system on whose smooth and successful operation profit depends, but a series of disconnected functions. Under these circumstances the phenomena occur of forgetting to order a basic raw material or failing to react to supplier difficulties.

Certainly the foreign general manager, like any manager, must rely on his staff, and they may let him down occasionally. But for events such as those described to occur, *a sense of responsibility must be lacking throughout the entire local organization*. Thus, in the case of the "forgotten" raw material, neither the inventory clerk, the worker on the floor, the foreman, nor the plant manager was sufficiently motivated in the business of running a business to see that they had enough supplies to continue production.

In the case of the supplier difficulties, the receiving clerk had been rejecting an increasing number of shipments during the two months prior to the shutdown. Yet, again, neither he nor anyone else was sufficiently motivated to ensure that positive action was taken.

As such things occur, the natural tendency is to institute more controls to avoid such mistakes. Finally, the foreign manager has a disproportionately large staff and a vast framework of controls and reports, or he makes an inevitable series of blunders that cost him his job.

The second symptom develops from the first. Because of the demanded emphasis on individual functional aspects of his business, the manager is often unable to answer vital, but nonroutine, questions. Further, obvious and important changes in the business environment, such as increases in duties or local taxes, he may allow to escape unnoticed. Such occurrences tend to strengthen whatever doubts existed about his competence.

The third symptom can be illustrated by observing the following reactions to headquarters' suggestions. In one company, a request for a minor change in the accounting handling of one account brought cables from the general manager (with the support of the local consulting accounting firm) claiming many hours of work when the time actually required was less than one hour per month. In another company, a request for sales emphasis on a particular supply item brought concentration on it—to the virtual exclusion of other, and more profitable, items.

These instances may show a typical inability of the general manager to assess requests, suggestions, and instructions in the perspective of their usefulness in running the business. Instead, he will assess them on factors that are essentially irrelevant as far as the success of the business is concerned—factors such as the tone of the instructions and who has given them. Such reactions are symptomatic of a person who is shell-shocked from a bombardment of requests, instructions, and demands from headquarters.

Thus, suspected incompetence leads to excessive controls, which in turn verify this incompetence. This self-fulfilling prophecy seemingly leaves little doubt that a change of management is mandatory. This is the dilemma.

THE FOREIGN MANAGER'S DILEMMA

This dilemma has occurred because of a fundamental misunderstanding of the foreign general manager's role and because of the dual and incongruous position of the headquarters management as both operating expert and judge.

The foreign general manager's role is that of the president—in fact, if not in title—in the country in which he operates. His job is more nearly like that of the U.S. company president's than any other job in the headquarters staff.[1] Although the order of magnitude admittedly varies, he must perform nearly all the functions that the U.S. president does.

Even though he probably does not become involved with stock and bond issues and determination of dividends, he is faced with a host of equally difficult problems, which rarely trouble his U.S. counterpart. Issues of nationalism, tariff restrictions, legal restrictions on foreign companies, language and communication problems, political unrest, currency exchange problems, and conflicts between home office policy and local custom and law demand constant attention. He must operate with a local staff that must be taught to "think U.S." Their training is different—often technically not as good—and their thought processes are naturally somewhat different. Yet, the foreign manager must rely on these people to perform to acceptable headquarters standards. To make his job harder, he often finds himself in the role of a "doer" in at least one functional area.

It is useful to carry the analogy between the U.S. president's job and the foreign manager's job further. The U.S. president's board of directors is usually chosen for reasons other than its detailed knowledge of the business. It assumes that the president has this knowledge. His performance is judged on relatively few reports, most of which concern gross input-output comparisons. Within a few broad guidelines, he is usually free to run his business.

Contrast this situation with the foreign manager's situation. His "board of directors" usually consists of operating management, experts who, in total, have more technical know-how in every functional area of the business than he does. They usually know, from years of experience, the company's routine and corporate way of doing things. But, paradoxically, the chances are that very few, if any, of them have ever experienced the problems of either a chief operating executive or a board member attempting to assess the performance of its president.

The resulting problem can take different forms. In one company, over-all production efficiency of the foreign operation was equal to that of the U.S. plant, but the foreign general manager and the foreign plant manager were under heavy general criticism for a large variance in one area. In another, total sales expenses were down but out of line on one product—again extreme criticism was leveled at the foreign manager.

A clearly inequitable and incongruous situation exists, then, in that a man who is responsible for the over-all operation often is judged primarily on details, by those who are experts in the details, but novices when it concerns the job they are judging; namely that of a president. When viewed in this light it is hardly surprising that few foreign general managers are considered competent by their "board," and overcontrols develop.

This problem is difficult and insidious, since the foreign manager actually was responsible for those errors, and, if they had not been made, profits would have been greater. The point is that it is not the "board's" place to impose corrective detailed controls any more than it would be for the U.S. president's board to do so. Yet, because of its intricate knowledge of the operation, that is what often happens.

It is interesting to conjecture how many U.S. presidents would accept a job as a foreign general manager if they were to compare the problems they would face and the restrictions under which they would be expected to work to those they were accustomed to.

Headquarters management, because of its dual role as operating expert and judge, tends to impose extensive controls and restrictions on the new operation in a misguided attempt to reduce the risks and improve performance. And yet, the problems facing the foreign manager of a new operation generally cannot be satisfactorily assumed by headquarters any more than the U.S. board of directors can assume the problems of its president. The critical problems require on-the-scene handling, imagination, and freedom to act within broad guidelines. In other words, they require general management handling of the type that the U.S. board would expect from its president.

If U.S. headquarters management will recognize what the foreign manager's job entails, including the dual capacity in which it must operate, and if it will take an objective look inward at its own management philosophy and then plan the control of its international operations on the basis of what it finds, it will have gone a long way in avoiding "incompetent" foreign management.

PLANNING THE CONTROL SYSTEM

As an initial step, the operating executive in charge of foreign operations should determine to what degree operating responsibility and control *must* rest with headquarters. Such things as the U.S. president's style of leadership and the degree of centralization of decision making will help him to do this. Then he can decide what *will* rest with headquarters and devise his system. His best guide is to look at the U.S. company. Is decision-making authority vested in a few top executives, or is it widely spread? Do the top executives personally get involved with operating details at many levels, or do they leave the details to their subordinates? Do they demand to be kept informed of daily operating statistics or desire only to know about the exceptions? Do they generally consider that without their personal attention to all facets of the operation that it will not function properly, or do they feel that their subordinates are capable and willing to manage their functions without detailed checking?

In a smaller company, where the chief operating executive can become involved in the detailed running of the company, his management philosophy is often the controlling factor. If he is prone to get involved in the details and reserve decision making to himself, even at lower levels, an extensive control and reporting system will probably be necessary to satisfy his demands for information. He may well expect that solutions to foreign operating problems will be found by headquarters management, not by the foreign operation, and if the headquarters staff is unsuccessful, he will probably take action himself.

If decision-making authority is highly centralized and restricted to a chosen few, and if this is the result of the chief operating executive's predilection (the same result can come about because he leaves such matters to operating officers), then, from a pragmatic standpoint, it is probably unrealistic to expect that authority and responsibility can be delegated to the foreign operation to any great extent. With greater risks, more unknowns, and generally less qualified people abroad, the natural result will be a demand by him for more, not fewer, controls.

In this situation the head of international operations must accept the fact that the onus of management will rest with him and attempt to prepare for it. A complete control and reporting system must be established, extending to all the details of the business. Controls must be set so there is little room for discretionary action by the foreign operation. Reports must provide enough raw data so that interpretation and analysis can be accomplished by headquarters and detailed instructions for action be transmitted to the foreign operation. The foreign manager's performance must be judged, not on the basis of the success or failure of the operation, but on how well he has followed instructions from headquarters. Adequate travel and telephone and telegraph expense budgets must be provided to allow headquarters personnel to maintain constant contact and to make frequent visits. In short, the foreign general manager will be, and must be expected to be, only a medium for receiving and transmitting instructions. The responsibility for success or failure will be with headquarters and must be accepted.

Few headquarters find it attractive to accept such responsibility, but many have imposed such controls and restrictions. The tenet that control must be centralized as a company decentralizes its decision-making authority is well recognized. This does not refer, however, to detailed operating controls. Rather, it refers to broader, over-all systems controls at the policy and planning levels, consistent with the responsibility that has been delegated.

If, on the other hand, controlling management philosophy is such that responsibility and authority can be delegated, a specific timetable for this delegation should be established during the planning stages. This timetable should be established in terms of absolute dates as well as on performance criteria to assure that this delegation actually occurs.

It is natural and correct for a new operation, while it is feeling its way and gaining experience, to report in detail. Such reports serve several purposes: they provide the new manager reinforcement during the learning process, so that he can feel that headquarters management is sharing some of his responsibility and has not just left him to pioneer on his own. They give him the opportunity to see various control devices in action, to analyze their usefulness to his new operation, and to see possible advantageous modifications.

As the operation matures, the gradual removal of the headquarters reporting requirements is a useful way of transferring responsibility at the desired rate. It also proves to the manager that he is making progress.

If the reports have served a purpose and have helped the manager to do his job better, headquarters management need not fear that the reports will be discarded at the local operating level. The local manager will realize or soon find that he needs them.

AVOIDING THE REAL INCOMPETENTS

Some foreign managers are, of course, incompetent. A number of them clearly should never have been hired. Because otherwise responsible executives who are shrewd judges of domestic talent do not fully understand the foreign general manager's job, they seem to lose their sense of perspective when hiring foreign managers. Often, they choose an applicant because of his ability to present himself in the English language, because he is widely traveled, or because he knows certain influential people, not on the hard facts of previous successful experience, education, recommendations, and other factors, which would be of paramount importance if they were seeking a domestic executive.

One diversified manufacturing company picked a bandleader to run its English operation; it chose a public relations and publicity man, with no general management experience, as its general manager in Europe. A food processing company picked a perfume salesman to be general manager of its production-oriented foreign operation. Application of a few simple rules would have helped these companies avoid the obviously incompetent.

1. Pick a man on essentially the same grounds as his counterpart would be chosen in this country. He should have the background, education, and the experience required of a chief operating executive in the country in question.
2. Pick a strong man—strong physically, mentally, emotionally, and educationally. If possible, he should be a strong company man, or at least one who has proven his loyalty elsewhere.
3. More important, he should be a man that *everybody* has confidence in. If anyone in headquarters has serious doubts as to his ability, do not risk hiring him. It has become clear that a foreign general manager is extremely vulnerable. He will be made the scapegoat for errors made by those physically closer to the headquarters management. He will make mistakes —possibly serious ones—for he probably has not had experience in being a president before. He will be fighting the home office more or less continually on issues where he feels his judgment should prevail.

   For such a man to survive he must have all the characteristics described above; in the final analysis, the strongest factor will be that headquarters had confidence in him and uniformly respected his ability when he was appointed.
4. After he is hired, stick with him. Changing general managers in a new operation is time-consuming, bothersome, and costly. Since there is little routine, no traditional ways of doing things, and few, if any experienced assistants to carry on, continuity of operation is impossible while the replacement is learning the job. Also, if a manager feels he is going to be discharged, he usually is not much good in the months before the change.

If a manager does not do well even though headquarters had confidence in him when they appointed him, the chances are that the causes are factors over which he has little control. One must assume that he is capable of being taught how to overcome his difficulties. It is not probable that he has suddenly become incompetent and needs to be replaced. Until the problems can be isolated and corrective steps taken, the operation will manage to keep above water, and by strong support the company will almost surely eventually develop a good manager.

By doing so, management saves itself the task of finding, interviewing, bringing to headquarters, training, and perhaps relocating a new man; it is free to concentrate on other, probably more lucrative, aspects of its business.

PERFORMANCE MEASUREMENT

Perhaps the most important step that management can take in the planning stage to avoid the problem of "incompetent" foreign managers is to carefully define and put in writing the basis on which the manager is to be judged and by whom he is to be judged. This is essential in order to avoid the tendency to judge him on the knowledge that the "board of directors" has about the details of his operation.

The performance criteria to use vary with each company, but in a new operation the best criterion is usually performance against critical budget projections. Simple comparison against the previous year is generally subject to distortion.

In one company the principal basis for judging performance was profit and the basis on which bonuses were given was improvement over the preceding year. The company was, through a fortunate market freak, riding a sales curve which was increasing by 15 percent to 20 percent annually, and profits were correspondingly higher. However, the foreign manager had little to do with the sales effort. After being produced under his supervision, the product was sold by an independent agent.

Establishing broad criteria as the primary basis for judging performance requires to some extent the "closing of one eye" by headquarters management and cannot be wholly successful. However, consciously establishing what is critical to the operation, and reviewing performance only on the basis of such predetermined, and somewhat limited, criteria, will tend to keep performance appraisal in perspective. As a further aid in avoiding distortion, other top management personnel who are not involved with the operating details of the business can be asked to review the operation on the basis of only pertinent, selected data. If the president is of such a nature that he does not insist on daily detailed information, he is an ideal person, since he has firsthand experience in running, and being judged on the running, of a business. If the criteria are carefully chosen, poor performance cannot be hidden any more than good performance can be overlooked.

By realistically appraising the controlling management philosophy and establishing a reporting and control system consistent with it, management will remove many areas of conflict. If a rational set of criteria for judging performance is selected, consistent with that philosophy and with an awareness of the dual role that headquarters management must play, a reasonably accurate performance appraisal of the foreign general manager can be made. If the nature of the foreign manager's job is understood and qualified men are selected, incompetence need not plague the foreign operations.

A diagnosis of true incompetence may then be made with increased confidence. Management need not fear that bad performance was caused by a faulty selection system or by an inefficient system of controls.

NOTE

1. Although the foreign manager's job has often been likened to that of a U.S. manager of a decentralized division, there are basic dissimilarities. The division manager is working in an environment and culture well known by the experts judging him, his problems are generally more similar to those of other division managers than are those among various country managers, and he usually has appropriate historical decision criteria and tradition to guide him that the foreign manager may not have.

Compensation and Job Satisfaction

STRUCTURING THE INTERNATIONAL COMPENSATION PROGRAM: EQUITABLE PAY FOR OVERSEAS EXECUTIVES

JOHN L. LESHER
and RALPH E. GRIFFITH

Policies and procedures in the field of international compensation—for expatriates, nationals, or third-country nationals—are not clearly defined in most companies with interests abroad. The authors' observations on this subject are most pertinent to those companies that rotate their executives through domestic and foreign assignments. They have found, for example, that expatriates generally receive too many extras. Their primary recommendation is that compensation programs for domestic, expatriate, and foreign national managers should not be allowed to function separately, but should bear a well-defined relationship to each other. They feel that the trend today is toward true executive mobility despite national origin in large multinational firms and that compensation practices should be modified in order to accommodate this trend and not work against it.

The control and administration of compensation for international executives—whether they be expatriates, nationals, or third-country nationals —are subjects of great frustration for many U.S. companies with interests abroad. On the other hand, guidelines for the company's domestic compensation program are usually firmly established, and compensation policies and procedures are clearly defined. The result is that both top- and middle-management spend a disproportionate amount of time and effort on international compensation matters. Despite the increasing attention devoted to the matter, and the efforts and research of academicians and consultants, otherwise sophisticated companies are still wrestling with such questions as:

What amount and type of extras should the U.S. expatriate executive receive, and how should his total compensation package relate to that of his domestic counterpart?

What arrangements should be made for third-country nationals (a non-American employed by an American company outside his home country), including considerations of both the practices in his home country and the

From *Business Horizons*, December 1968. Reprinted with permission of the authors and publisher.

country to which he is assigned, and the compensation package of U.S. expatriates?

How should the international executives in regional organizations who are responsible for several countries be compensated?

What adjustments are necessary to establish policies and procedures for compensating foreign nationals as more and more of these executives move up the ladder and into the domestic headquarters organization?

These questions have been raised and discussed with numerous executives over the past two years in the course of carrying out assignments in the field of international compensation. Comments and opinions on these topics and the probable long- and short-term developments have been assembled. Hopefully, this material will help relieve some of the basic concerns of top management in this area and, at the same time, introduce some new concepts to guide the development of international compensation programs. Some of the principal conclusions we have reached in the process of working in the field are these:

Generally, U.S. expatriates receive too many extras; companies are over-compensating these executives and incurring unnecessary costs.

Third-country nationals are also compensated at rates much higher than the rates set for their home country counterparts. In fact, their pay levels are almost the same as those of U.S. expatriates.

The compensation of regional executives still reflects their home country practices, whereas it should probably be related to practices of the parent company.

Only a few leading companies have thought out a compensation program for nationals that is adjusted to the parent company's over-all management development and organization plans. This area will require more of top management's attention over the next few years if top talent is to be retained.

The details supporting these conclusions are described in the following material, along with some specific case examples.

FORMS OF BUSINESS ABROAD

U.S. business involvement abroad, to a significant degree, began at the turn of the century, commonly in the form of licensing or franchise arrangements with companies or sales agents already established in foreign markets. Thus, U.S. companies were usually exporters or licensers of foreign manufacturers and took little part in direct management of the foreign operation. As U.S. interests expanded, however, other forms of business, such as the joint venture, gained popularity; still, the management of the U.S. company was not directly involved with the foreign operation to any great degree.

Two world wars slowed U.S. business expansion abroad, which did not really begin to develop again until after the end of World War II. Since then, U.S. investment abroad has climbed sharply. Total private investments abroad were $19.0 billion in 1950. Direct long-term investment, the category most representative of U.S. foreign business activity, was then $11.8 billion; today, this figure has increased to approximately $60.0 billion. At this point, probably more than 4,000 U.S. firms today have some form of overseas operation.

This rapid expansion of U.S. business interests abroad was accompanied by several significant developments in the "way" in which they did business in foreign markets. To be sure, licensing, franchising, and joint ventures are still popular, but the most significant development centered around the more direct involvement of U.S. companies in the management of their foreign enterprises. This came about as U.S. companies began either to build their own organizations or to acquire complete or controlling ownership in already-established businesses. Thus, these organizations developed a more direct working relationship with the parent company, which in many ways was similar to the relationship between corporate headquarters and the traditional domestic division or subsidiary of the company.

This new arrangement produced changes in the ways in which top management filled key executive positions in these operations. In the past, many companies often used these positions as "dumping grounds" for managers who, for various reasons, had reached their peak in the domestic organization. This practice, however, has changed radically in recent years in several dramatic ways. *First*, as foreign investment increased and its contribution to total company profits grew more substantial, the parent company management recognized the importance of committing top domestic talent to overseas operations. Today, however, only a small percentage of foreign managers are U.S. expatriates. *Second*, these companies began to depend more on nationals or third-country nationals to staff their overseas operations. This practice had already been adopted by such foreign-based international companies as Unilever and Nestlé. *Finally*, foreign nationals have now begun to move into the top management posts at the U.S. parent company headquarters. Typical of this trend is the appointment by IBM of Jacques Maisonrouge to head its world trade organization.

Problems still remain in integrating international operations with companies' over-all programs for organization planning, manpower planning, and management development and compensation. This article is concerned only with the latter, but, in the long run, international compensation programs should be structured in parallel with other programs.

At this point we want to emphasize that not all companies have adopted the viewpoint that there should be increased executive mobility between their domestic and international organizations. In fact, many companies do just the opposite. For them, a commitment by an executive to take a foreign post is a career decision, not just a move up the organization ladder. The following observations are generally *not* applicable to companies that keep their executives on nearly continual overseas assignments. They are most pertinent to those companies that make a practice of rotating their executives through domestic and foreign assignments.

CONPENSATION FOR EXPATRIATES

Much has been published on the numerous adjustments that should be made in a U.S. executive's compensation package when he is transferred abroad. Many of these practices are based on the historical pattern set by U.S. petroleum companies, our first international companies of any consequence. The practices of the U.S. State Department have also been influential, especially in the area of cost-of-living and housing adjustments. The number and type of these adjustments have proliferated to the point where more managers and compensation administrators are frustrated and confused. As a result, most companies do not have consistent and systematic approaches to compensating their international executives, and tend to negotiate each case individually.

Clearly, two basic tenets of a sound expatriate compensation program have become obscured:

The executive should not suffer any loss of income if the transfer is truly a lateral move or a promotion. He should remain "whole," in the economic sense.

Whatever the compensation package, it should not stand in the way of an executive's future movement, either within the international organization or back into the domestic company or headquarters organization.

The basic types of adjustments that a company usually considers in structuring expatriates' compensation packages include tax equalization, cost of living, housing, hardship, dependents' education, and other adjustments, including the overseas premium. In addition, companies also usually consider such items as relocation and travel expenses, allowances for temporary quarters, automobiles, and club memberships. Most of these are one-time allowances, however, and do not affect the expatriate's permanent pay package. Finally, some arrangements are usually made for home leave and holidays.

From studies that have been conducted with clients of Booz, Allen, & Hamilton, data have been extracted to illustrate the net effect of these adjustments on a U.S. expatriate's compensation in comparison with his domestic counterpart. Typical expatriate compensation packages have been selected for various income levels and converted into U.S. dollar equivalents. Since almost all companies equalize taxes for expatriates to U.S. rates, figures were not converted to an after-tax basis, but considered on a pretax basis.

In addition, domestic and international jobs were related, using evaluation techniques similar to those used by many companies in their position evaluation programs. This means that the compensation of managers with similar responsibilities was compared, even though one might be located in the domestic organization and the other in the international organization. The results of this comparison—for executives in the total compensation range of $10,000 to $50,000—are shown in Figure 1. The general level of comparison for expatriate executives runs consistently higher than that of their domestic counterparts, ranging from 70 percent higher at the $10,000 base salary level to 40 percent at the $50,000 level. In most cases, the additional dollars available to the expatriate do not increase at the same rate as his base salary, so that the $10,000 expatriate receives approximately $8,000 in allowances while the $50,000 expatriate receives $19,000.

The finding that U.S. expatriates generally are compensated at higher levels than are executives in domestic organizations is obvious. The more important question is whether such a substantial difference should exist. To answer this question, the principal differences between an executive's domestic and international compensation package must be evaluated individually.

Essential Adjustments, All Cases

First, we shall review those adjustments that can be classified as essential to any expatriate compensation program—tax equalization and cost-of-living allowances. The basic purpose of *income tax adjustments* is, of course, to ensure that an executive does not suffer loss of after-tax income just because he takes on an assignment in a country with higher income tax rates. Income tax rates vary considerably among countries, so that expatriate executives with similar responsibilities and gross compensation could receive substantially different amounts of after-tax income in comparison to their domestic counterparts (see table).

Figure 1 COMPENSATION OF EXPATRIATE AND DOMESTIC MANAGERS (UNADJUSTED)

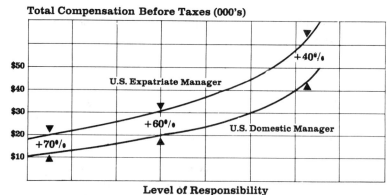

Total Compensation Before Taxes (000's)

Level of Responsibility

EFFECTIVE AVERAGE TAX RATES IN FOUR COUNTRIES*

Salary	France	Germany	United Kingdom	United States
$10,000	9.0%	20.8%	24.2%	13.4%
$20,000	17.2	30.6	34.0	18.8
$30,000	21.1	35.7	42.5	23.4
$40,000	25.6	39.2	51.3	27.9

*Husband, wife, two children, standard deductions.

Additional factors complicate this tax equalization question. Contributions to employee benefit plans are tax deductible in Europe but not in the United States. In France, pension annuities are taxed at ordinary income tax rates, but there is no tax on group life insurance. Other countries have adopted other variations.

Most companies' *cost-of-living adjustments* are related to U.S. State Department indexes. The purpose of these adjustments is to avoid reductions in after-tax purchasing power that can be caused by variances in the cost of living from country to country. The logic supporting this adjustment in expatriate compensation is inescapable, but one should consider domestic practices. Few U.S. companies, to our knowledge, make formal recognition of these differences in their base salary structure when transferring executives from one *domestic* location to another. The case for domestic adjustments is supported by a study prepared by the U.S. Department of Labor in 1966, which analyzed the city worker's family budget required to purchase comparable goods and services in various metropolitan areas. The study revealed, for example, that the family would need a budget 17 percent greater in the metropolitan New York area than in Dayton, Ohio, and one 25 percent greater in Hartford, Conn. than in Austin, Tex.

Furthermore, State Department indexes are not straightforward comparisons of purchasing goods in one market versus purchasing the same goods in other markets, but in many cases contain extras, such as a maid for the foreign location.

Essential, Case by Case

A second category of allowances can be classified as essential, but will probably have to be treated on a case-by-case basis. The 1966 Department of Labor study showed that *housing* budgets varied more from one metropolitan area to another than did total family budgets. For instance, the budget for shelter (including household operating costs) was 42 percent greater in the metropolitan New York area than in Detroit, Mich., and 71 percent greater in Boston, Mass. than in Atlanta, Ga. Once again, these variances would cover many adjustments made for foreign locations.

Hardship allowances originated in the petroleum industry for personnel in remote outposts and are doubtless still appropriate in such cases. However, in isolated instances, companies grant "hardship" allowances for locations such as Paris, where a hardship hardly exists.

The amount of adjustment for *schooling* for dependents depends on local educational facilities and individual family situations. The policy of providing "comparable quality" is probably the best that can be adopted. Domestic adjustments are not made, however, despite the differences in the quality of public schooling systems among U.S. communities.

Questionable Allowances

Finally, there is a category of adjustments where allowances are questionable, especially when assignments abroad are viewed as part of the company's normal promotion pattern and management development process. Companies should seriously consider foregoing such allowances as the three that follow.

Vacations or home-leave allowances sometimes exceed those given to domestic counterparts. It could be rationalized that the San Francisco branch manager, whose past business career had been in the East, should receive home-leave allowances comparable to those given expatriates.

The cost of *memberships* in country clubs or other social clubs should be borne by the expatriate, just as they are borne by the U.S. executive. This would not be the case, of course, for companies that provide club membership for their domestic managers. Automobile allowances should be treated similarly.

Perhaps the *overseas premium* should be the first allowance to go. The executive should view assignments abroad as an opportunity for advancement in the company and should not have to be lured by an overseas premium. Furthermore, the discontinuance of such a practice makes it easier for the company, in the long run, to move the executive back into the domestic organization.

Discontinuance of these allowances will substantially reduce the expatriate executive's total compensation. Figure 2 illustrates the effect of eliminating these questionable allowances and making more conservative adjustments for cost-of-living and housing allowances. In general, the levels for both groups are now nearly parallel, with some slight advantage remaining for the expatriate because of the remaining cost of living adjustments and allowances for schooling, shelter, hardship, and the like.

One other factor must be considered when evaluating the expatriate's compensation package. In most cases, a manager who undertakes an assignment abroad has been promoted, and has already received a salary increase— probably 15-20 percent—before extras and allowances are added. Granted, the executive has taken on new responsibilities, but the spread between what he received for his previous job and the one abroad has become unreasonably large when total compensation is considered.

Figure 2   COMPENSATION OF EXPATRIATE AND DOMESTIC MANAGERS (ADJUSTED)

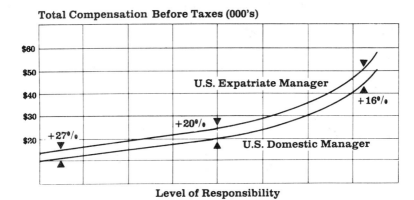

THIRD-COUNTRY NATIONALS

Many U.S. companies employ nationals in countries other than their home country, particularly companies that started their foreign operations in the United Kingdom or in Europe, and then expanded to Latin America or the Far East. For example, an Englishman may be found working in Brazil for a U.S. company. Aside from the fact that this executive has a different nationality and therefore has a different home country orientation, his organizational status does not differ basically from that of the U.S. expatriate. There is really no reason why the compensation program for this executive should be any different from that proposed for the U.S. expatriate.

In the limited number of situations examined, the compensation levels of third-country nationals have a relationship to their home country counterparts that is similar to the relationship of the U.S. expatriate to the domestic manager (see Figure 3). The only notable difference in this pattern versus the one shown in Figure 2 appears at the lower end of the responsibility scale, where compensation levels are almost equal. There is no apparent reason for this; perhaps it is due to the limited amount of data available for this comparison.

The figure also shows the relationship of U.S. expatriate compensation levels for the few cases in which a third-country national and a U.S. expatriate in the same country hold jobs that are equivalent to one held by another manager in the third-country national's home country. As can be seen, the compensation levels for U.S. expatriates and third-country nationals are roughly equal; the U.S. expatriate holds a slight edge. This relationship may not, however, be as equitable as it appears. These figures are presented on a pretax basis, and there is some evidence from our surveys, especially of foreign-based international companies, that tax equalization is not as universally practiced with third-country nationals as with U.S. expatriates.

Figure 3   COMPENSATION LEVELS, THIRD-COUNTRY NATIONALS,
U.S. COUNTERPARTS

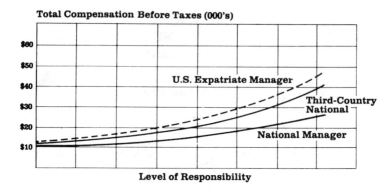

It appears, therefore, the the marketplace has forced near-equivalent pay levels for U.S. expatriates and third-country nationals. There is a slight gap, however, and this should be closely watched by top management and not allowed to widen. This pool of third-country management talent is limited, and the top performers are going to end up with the companies offering the most attractive compensation package.

REGIONAL AND HEADQUARTERS STAFFS

Up to this point, orienting the executive's compensation package to the levels paid in his home country has been offered as one of the cornerstones of a company's international compensation program. In two vital areas of the company's organization, however, this approach is becoming more difficult to apply: regional organizations that are responsible for operations in more than one country and are staffed with executives and managers from several countries, and parent company headquarters organizations in which outstanding foreign national executives become part of the top management structure.

The basic question facing companies in these two areas is how they can continue to compensate their executives at different levels, based on their country of origin, even though they hold positions of comparable responsibility. Today, this question is more pertinent to the regional organization employing as many as four or five executives of different nationalities, but it will become a major issue at the corporate headquarters as more and more foreign nationals move into top positions. Currently, U.S. compensation standards are the highest, and they will probably serve as the guidelines for the future in setting the salary structures at the regional as well as the corporate headquarters level. Other surveys over the years have disclosed a narrowing of the gap between U.S. expatriates and local nationals, holding comparable jobs, to the point where the premium is now only 10 to 15 percent. It can be anticipated that this gap will continue to narrow in the future and that eventually compensation levels will be the same.

Both of these developments—the growth of regional organizations and the appearance of more foreign nationals at the U.S. headquarters level—create pressures for the development of integrated compensation programs. Economics will dictate, for some time to come, that the compensation of local nationals continue to be tied to their home country levels and practices. Once an executive gets above this level in the organization, however, it appears inevitable that the compensation package must be based on the practices followed by the parent company. By adopting this approach, companies can assure themselves of internal equity and the development of a reasonable basis for administering the compensation of U.S. and foreign national executives who are working side by side.

PROJECTIONS

The developments that have been described argue for fully integrated compensation programs for today's international company. Even though complete integration is not feasible at this time, the current programs for domestic, expatriate, and foreign national managers should not be allowed to function separately, but should bear a well-defined relationship to each other. The principal advantages of such an approach are self-evident, but they bear repeating: it will ease the movement of executives throughout the organization; compensation programs can be more closely aligned with other related activities, such as manpower planning, management development, and organization planning; and the administrative task will be lightened, as the programs become company-wide and firm guidelines and policies are established.

The marketplace appears to be emphasizing the need for most international companies to move in the direction noted. Pay differentials between U.S. expatriates and local nationals have declined by over 50 percent in just the past few years. Differences in local economies and pricing structures will continue to be the principal obstacle, but these are being diminished by such developments as the Common Market.

Companies should begin to use the same evaluation plans and guidelines for international positions that they use in their domestic operations. Salary structures and salary grades should be aligned so that they parallel each other and can be easily integrated as general salary levels move closer together (see Figure 4).

Most companies could adopt two relatively minor administrative practices that would strengthen their programs in the short run. *First*, where extras are to be provided, identify them specifically, both in content and in amount, in a formal written agreement with the executive. Too many extras get folded

Figure 4   EXAMPLES OF PARALLEL SALARY STRUCTURES

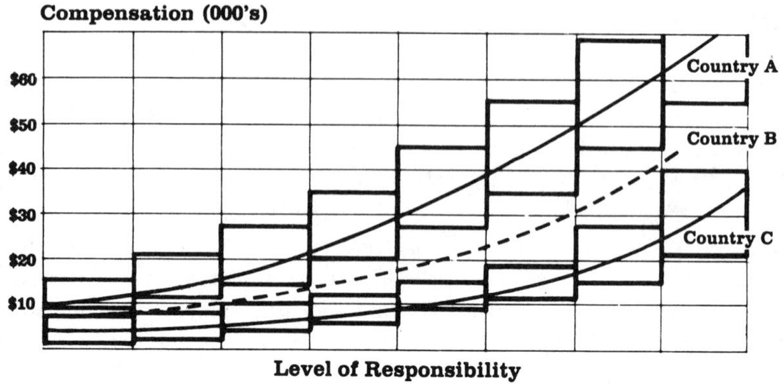

into the base salary and become lost. *Second*, pay extras separately and do not confuse them with base salaries or cash incentive awards. This eases the reentry step.

During this transitional period, the best policy appears to be to continue to relate the U.S. expatriates' or third-country nationals' compensation to their home country levels and practices. For regional organizations, the most appropriate yardstick at this time is a domestic U.S. orientation for executives of any nationality. This practice will ease the way as these executives are either promoted or transferred to the headquarters group.

Basic to all these approaches, however, is the recognition that assignments abroad will be offered to highly qualified personnel, and these assignments in many of today's international companies will be viewed as no different from a promotion or transfer from one domestic division or subsidiary to another. In addition, foreign nationals will be used increasingly, not only at the headquarters, but also at the divisional levels in these large international firms.

The trend is toward true executive mobility despite national origin in today's multinational firm. Management compensation practices and systems should not stand in the way of this mobility, but should be modified or developed to accommodate this trend.

REMUNERATION AND MOTIVATION IN LATIN AMERICA

CARLOS J. MICHELSEN TERRY
and JOHN M. VIVIAN

Latin American renumeration policies can be a labyrinth of confusion in their complexity. Management is advised to go beyond legal requirements, discover what motivates the work force and reward accordingly.

A top executive of a multinational firm operating in Latin America, asked to describe the program of total remuneration—wages, salaries, benefits, etc.,—received by his employees, would probably mutter something uncomplimentary about Social Security costs and too many laws. There is no question that programs of pay and benefits in Latin America are heavily influenced by a labyrinth of social legislation. Explanations are usually left to lawyers and technicians. It is a moot point whether the present maze is the cause or the result of past top management inattention to pay practices; what is important now is that management continuously review its remuneration policies and programs to make sure that they are appropriate to the rapidly changing Latin American business environment.

After slow beginnings, the Latin American economy is getting up steam. A vast system of mountain and jungle-breaching roads and railways is well under way; the Central American and Andean Common Markets will eventually develop continent-wide trade. In a more open and active economy, worker mobility will increase, skills will be more in demand than ever, and a pay program that effectively implements corporate manpower objectives will be obligatory.

Of equal or greater importance to the multinational firm as the indigenous economy grows stronger, will be a growing resistance to foreign investment. Foreign-owned and -managed firms which survive in the chauvinistic environment of Latin American nationalism will be those having the greatest market acceptance. One of the most effective media of communication between an enterprise and its host population is the weekly pay check and benefit program provided to the employee group. The pay program and related aspects of human resources management can easily spell the difference between a firm's ultimate success or failure in Latin America.

TRADITIONAL METHODS

In the past, remuneration policies of foreign companies operating in Latin America have typically taken one of two forms—both of them bad.

From *Columbia Journal of World Business*, January-February 1969, pp. 41-53. Reprinted with permission of the publisher. Copyright © 1969 by the Trustees, Columbia University.

Most obviously disfunctional is the importation of home-country attitudes and programs without regard for the differing economic and social values in the new operating locale. Complex, formal job evaluation and salary administration programs, or "actuarially sound" and profusely communicated pension plans, make little sense in a developing country which has no operating labor market and is experiencing chronic inflation. Indeed, such programs may be considered by the work force as just another *gringo* trick to exploit them.

Less obvious but equally dangerous is the error of attempting to maintain "local consistency"—a fancy term for copying the pay programs of purely local industry. These programs are characterized by low pay and productivity, high security and absenteeism and can be (charitably) described as paternalistic. Most foreign managers fail to realize that such traditional management is under tremendous pressure to change.

All classes of urban Latin Americans are increasingly giving the lie to the common stereotype—a "siesta/fiesta" attitude toward life and a "mañana" attitude toward work. They have embraced many of the material values of modern industrial society and are deeply committed to change and modernization of society and the economies. Latin American workers will be suspicious of a large foreign corporation which professes—explicitly through actual statement or implicitly through policy—to have a paternalistic interest in them. Such paternalism may be resented, but accepted, from a local employer; the foreign company attempting it will not be trusted. The foreign concern will be seen as failing to fulfill its opportunity to increase employees' independence and economic well-being and reneging on its promise to contribute to national economic growth. It will be accused of opportunism at best, exploitation at worst.

To grow—perhaps to survive—in the Latin America of the next few decades, a multinational corporation must devise remuneration and allied policies that synchronize with the rapidly changing social and economic structure, and that are sensitive to the attitudes and expectations of its volatile Latin hosts.

STATUTORY REMUNERATION

The introduction of labor regulations in Latin America goes back to the earliest *Conquistadores*, who reputedly carried instructions from the Spanish kings covering treatment of Indians working in gold mines. In the second decade of this century the independent republics began to enact more meaningful legislation. Peru was first in 1911 with a workmen's compensation law; the Mexican constitution of 1917 contained extensive social provisions; and today the nations of Latin America have the broadest programs of social benefits in the Western World.

We estimate (Figure 1) that the employer-paid costs of statutory remu-neration in Latin America have increased an average of 1% of base payroll each year since 1915; the present seven-nation average is nearly 65%. The rate of increase was greatest between the Great Depression of the early '30's and the first years of this decade. Our research indicates that statutory benefit growth has tapered off in the past eight years, but that private, company-sponsored benefit plans have begun to become important, effectively keeping the cost increase rate constant.

The major components of the statutory portion of the remuneration maze are two:

Social Security: social benefits and insurance programs administered by government agencies and funded jointly by employer and employee.

Labor Law Benefits: extra cash and indirect payments which the employer must provide, usually at full company expense.

Prevalence and costs to the employer of the eight most significant Social Security programs in seven countries are included in Figure 2. Cost data are given in U.S. dollars per year and as proportions of the basic pay for an average semi-skilled worker, or mechanic in the language of Latin American statisticians. The pay rates are universally low by most Western standards; the benefit programs are comprehensive and costly by any standards, though there are considerable differences between countries. The most elaborate program is Chile's, and it costs nearly ten times more than the Brazilian counterpart. This great difference in apparently similar programs is caused by

Figure 1 ESTIMATED HISTORICAL AVERAGE INCREASE IN STATUTORY BENEFITS IN LATIN AMERICA—PER CENT OF BASE SALARY

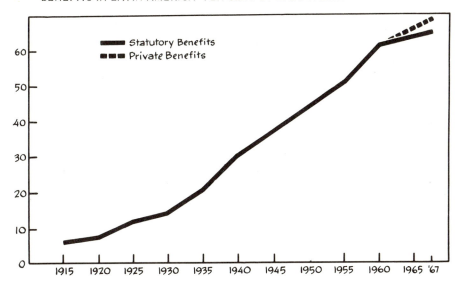

Figure 2   SOCIAL SECURITY IN LATIN AMERICA (1969)

	Family Allowance	Old Age Pension	Disability	Work Injury Compensation	Medical Care	Death Benefits	Unemployment	Maternity	Average Mechanic Annual Salary	Employer Cost	Employer Cost as % of Mechanic Salary
Argentina	X	X	X			X		X	$1,480	$256.56	17.3%
Brazil	X	X	X	X	X	X		X	1,430	60.44	4.3
Chile	X	X	X	X	X	X	X	X	1,600	550.00[a]	34.4
Colombia	X	X	X	X	X	X		X	1,050	140.00[b]	13.3
Mexico		X	X	X	X	X		X	1,780	196.00	11.0
Peru		X	X	X	X	X		X	1,450	166.75[c]	11.5
Venezuela		X	X	X	X	X	X	X	1,946	155.68	8.0

[a] Blue-collar workers only.
[b] Less than 20 years of service; includes contributions to National Training Institute.
[c] Blue-collar workers only; includes contributions to National Health & Welfare Fund.

differences in salary ceilings for tax purposes and amounts of benefits paid—both much greater in Chile.

The Social Security programs may appear overwhelming in variety and cost, but they pale beside the benefits required by the second part of the statutory maze, the Labor Laws. These payments are shown in Figure 3, and range from minor housing subsidies or mandatory union dues to severance pay provisions which in some countries are so high they effectively guarantee a worker a job for life. Unlike the Social Security programs, Labor Law benefits are not overbiased in favor of the very lowest paid workers. They add from 30% to more than 50% to the total pay of all employees from the janitor to the local manager.

In addition, the benefit costs are increased by staff time required for administration. Chile, with the most costly benefit program of the seven nations, also has a total of 41 separate government agencies which must be dealt with by most companies. (The record holder was pre-Castro Cuba which had 45 separate and independent Social Security agencies.)

These costs are high and cannot be avoided. What can multinational corporations do? First, they can be fully aware of employment costs and, second, they can plan for the future—plan for both the future growth of government programs, and continual change of company plans so they are responsive to employee needs and desires which are not met by the government.

As the Latin American economies expand and become more unified, there is little doubt that social benefit programs will follow suit. The precedent for amalgamation of Social Security plans in conjunction with economic integra-

Figure 3 MANDATORY LABOR LAW BENEFITS (1968)

	Argentina	Brazil	Chile	Colombia[a]	Mexico	Peru[b]	Venezuela
Severance Pay	X	X[c]	X	X	X	X	X
Vacations	X	X	X	X	X	X	X
Paid Holidays	X	X	X	X	X	X	X
Compulsory Life Insurance				X		(d)	
Accidents/Illness Benefits	X	X			X	X	
Compulsory Annual Bonus	X	X	X	X		X	
Compulsory Profit Sharing	(e)		X	X	X		X
Technical Education Tax	X	X	X	X			X
Union Tax		X					
Transportation Subsidy		X					
Provident Funds				X			
Social/Labor Services Tax			X	X			
Housing Subsidy/Tax			X		X		
Annual Cost % of Average Mechanic Salary	38.3	45	45.4	36	48.4	40.1	47.8
Annual Cost as % of Local Manager	37.3	43.5	30	38	51	49	56

[a] Workers engaged after 1966
[b] Workers engaged after 1962
[c] Workers opting for new scheme or hired after 1966
[d] White-collar employees only
[e] Unapplied constitutional provision

tion has already been set by the European Common Market. To project future developments, one can simply fill in the blanks in Figures 2 and 3. Political facts of life in Latin America, as anywhere else, dictate that a government benefit, once given, cannot be taken away; unity of social programs will be achieved by addition of benefits where they are presently lacking. It is safe to assume that by 1980 most of these nations will provide all of the more common benefit programs.

This process need not mean that mandatory benefit costs will continue to rise as a constant percentage of payroll. Social Security programs are heavily biased in favor of the lowest paid workers; there is no reason why this situation cannot be retained or strengthened in the Labor Law benefit programs. In this event, government program costs would drop as a percentage of payroll as better skilled and paid employees become a larger proportion of the work force. It is these personnel whom management will wish to retain and motivate through private benefit and other remuneration programs tailored to specific corporate needs. However, it is reasonable to assume that without a strong management voice in future government deliberations over benefit plan and Labor Law extension, the corporation will have a decreasing area of latitude in determining its own compensation and benefit structure in Latin America.

PRIVATE BENEFIT PLANS

Given the variety and extent of present government social benefit programs, it may appear surprising to find private pension and other benefit plans in existence, but they are, and research indicates they are on the increase in all countries but Peru. Private benefits are used to fill existing gaps in type and amount of coverage of government plans. They can be very useful in obtaining and keeping personnel with scarce skills. The comparative abundance of private benefit plans refutes the commonly held attitude (among U.S. and Europe-based "experts") that Latin American governments have forced private enterprise to pay for a full schedule of benefits for the population. This is not so; Social Security benefits are adequate only for the very lowest paid, and many programs are brand new or still financially immature. As shown in Figure 4, Venezuela promises to pay an old age pension of over 40% of final pay to persons earning $20,000 per year. This sounds good and may actually come to pass—but not until the year 2007, when the program is projected to be funded adequately to pay full pensions.

This situation—financially immature programs and benefits appropriate only to the lowest paid—holds true of most Latin American Social Security programs. In addition, benefits are available to only a very small proportion of the population. Generally, social benefits are easier to administer to inhabitants of urban areas. Coverage by Latin American government benefit programs roughly corresponds to the proportion of population concentrated in the rapidly growing cities. The highest coverage rate (28%) is in Chile, which also has the largest urban population (69%). The second highest coverage rate is in Argentina, which has over 60% of its population in cities. Not surprisingly, these two countries also rate 1 and 2 in employer cost of statutory benefits.

Figure 4 details the prevalence of private benefit plans. Despite government programs, familiar benefits such as group life insurance, disability and medical insurance plans are found in varying degrees in Latin America. Of most importance financially are private old age pension plans, found in all seven countries and quite common in four of the seven, among the largest companies. Not surprisingly, Chile and Argentina, with their high urban populations, have a relatively large number of private pension plans. They share this distinction with Mexico, which is something of an anomaly. It is unique among Latin American nations for its well-established insurance

Figure 4 COMPARISON OF RETIREMENT PENSIONS

	Argentina	Brazil	Chile	Colombia	Mexico	Peru	Venezuela
A. Projected Social Security Pensions (As a percentage of final pay) Final Pay (in U.S. dollars per year)							
$1,000	70%	100%	100%	70%	77%	75%	87%
$2,000	50	100	100	70	66	75	67
$5,000	27	50	80	57	40	75	54
$10,000	18	26	37	27	20	38	48
$20,000	14	13	19	14	10	18	42
B. Population Distribution—% in Urban Centers	60%	45%	69%	38%	52%	48%	65%
—% covered by Social Security	23	10	28	5	6	7	7
C. First Year When Full Social Security Pensions Paid	1984	1968	1970	2001	1953	1998	2007
D. Private Pension Plans (1) % of major local companies providing retirement benefits	40%*	20%	45%	30%	†	5%	30%
% of major foreign companies providing retirement benefits	10	5	20	10	56†	10	20
	50%	25%	65%	40%	56%	15%	50%

*Informal plans for higher paid employees
†Includes major local and major foreign companies

E. Prevalent Voluntary Benefits (1)

	Old Age Pensions	Group Life Insurance	Long-term Disability	Medical Plans	Thrift and Savings Plans	Profit Sharing
Argentina	1	1	2	1	(a)	(b)
Brazil	2	1	2	1	(a)	(b)
Chile	1	0	0	0	(a)	(b)
Colombia	1	1	2	1	2	(b)
Mexico	1	1	2	1	(a)	(b)
Peru	0	1	2	2	(a)	(b)
Venezuela	2	1	2	1	(a)	(b)

(a) Banking and financial institutions.
(b) Informal policy, mostly for executives.

Code: 1. Often provided.
       2. Few companies provide benefit.
       0. One or two companies provide benefit.
       (1) Benefits prevalent among 100 largest companies in each country, foreign and local companies included.

247

industry, a government which encourages private annuities, and relatively low inflation rates—all of which greatly simplify funding and payment of retirement pensions.

Past experience suggests that the more urbanized a country becomes, the more concentrated is its economic machine, the more comprehensive its statutory benefit programs will become and, at the same time, the more stimulus there will be for installation of "gap-filling" private benefits. Though in time government programs will become uniformly comprehensive, private benefits will continue to be a useful management tool where the coverage of statutory programs is inadequate. Peru has no family-size related allowance; there are no mandatory housing subsidies and medical benefits in Argentina; Colombian Social Security will provide a $20,000-a-year man an annual pension of only $2,800—and that not until the year 2001. These are just a few areas of possible, and as research shows, common private supplementation. The unanswered questions are: are such private plans desirable; will they perform a useful function or be simply a waste of money—or worse?

Analysis of Latin American wage and salary data shows a recognizable pattern:

Very low paid unskilled workers receive annual pay of under $400 in rural areas, up to $650 in the cities—the great mass of the population;

Skilled workers, white collar personnel and lower-level managers receive from $1,000 to $3,000 per year—the emerging middle class;

Top professional and executive personnel earn at the $10,000 level or higher—the local socio-economic elite or "oligarchy" in Latin American terminology.

The effect of these wide differences in salary levels is evident when the compensation structure of a company located in a developing country is compared to the compensation structure of a company in a developed economy. As shown in Figure 5, the distribution of compensation among employees in the first firm has a strikingly different shape from that of the firm in an advanced economy. A few employees can earn high salaries, and a large gap exists in salary levels at the middle section of the curve where a very small group of employees earn salaries exactly midway between the highest and the lowest salaries.

However, salary information in Latin America is difficult to obtain and is seldom definitive—the countries are just beginning to develop a working labor market, where the interplay of supply and demand is facilitated by the mobility of a work force which is knowledgeable about pay rates and job opportunities. At the present stage of development such a labor market exists only for the top group—the executives.

Salary survey data covering top managers in each of the seven countries is given in Figure 6. The figures are not surprising. The highest salaries for local nationals are found in the wealthiest nations, Venezuela and Mexico. Among the others, the larger countries appear to provide the higher pay.

Figure 5   COMPENSATION STRUCTURES IN UNDERDEVELOPED AND
          DEVELOPED COUNTRIES—PER CENT WORKERS EARNING BELOW

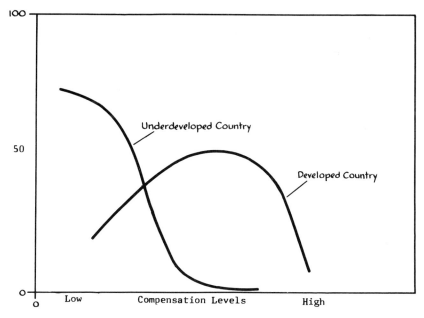

Figure 6   COMPARISON OF TYPICAL EXECUTIVES' SALARIES

(United States dollars per year)

Country	Local National Top Manager	Foreign National Top Manager
Argentina	$19,000	$38,400
Brazil	17,000	34,000
Chile	14,500	26,500
Colombia	15,500	29,300
Mexico	21,200	37,800
Peru	14,000	25,800
Venezuela	22,500	36,000

Data represents typical average salaries paid in each country for top operating executives in major enterprises having over 500 employees. Basic position responsibilities are similar, but averages include data from all important sectors. This information is valid *only* for country-to-country comparisons.

Comparison of pay for local national and foreign top managers also produces no surprise. In all countries, the foreign expatriate receives a salary approximately twice that of a local national, though both are performing substantially the same job. The most common apology for this apparent discrimination is that rates and expectations are greater in the expatriate's North American or European home economy.

A more persuasive reason is the total remuneration cost represented by the local base salary figures (Figure 7). The combination of Social Security costs, mandatory bonuses, etc., required by the Labor Laws plus costs of a conservatively competitive private benefit package increase the local executive's total pay by some 60% in each of the seven countries. The total pay of the typical local manager in Venezuela, for example, is $38,000 plus. This compares to a base salary of $36,000 for an expatriate. If we assume a typical added U.S. fringe benefit cost of about 25% of base, the expatriate will receive a total of $45,000, less than 20% more than the local counterpart. In most Latin American countries expatriates qualifying as resident aliens are entitled to full or almost full government-required benefits. Most multinational firms, however, consider all mandatory cash payments and employee-recoverable deferred benefits as deductions against home base salary when negotiating pay in the foreign location.

Another factor in the take-home value of a Latin American salary figure is the personal income tax situation. Each country's theoretically effective tax rates for a married man with two dependent children is charted in Figure 8. We say "theoretically effective" because the efficiency of tax collection in many Latin American nations has been notoriously poor until very recently. Collection procedures are now improving very rapidly, and new tax structures being adopted.

With changes in tax rates and in efficiency of collection, the take-home pay of a good many Latin American executives is going to change practically overnight. Peru has just adopted—and intends to enforce—the tax curve

Figure 7 LOCAL EXECUTIVES' TOTAL COMPENSATION (U.S. DOLLARS 1968)
TOTAL COMPENSATION IN U.S. DOLLARS PER YEAR

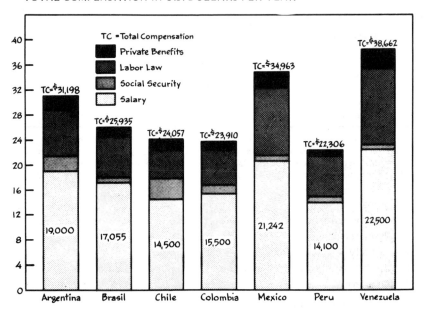

Figure 8   EFFECTIVE PERSONAL INCOME TAX CURVES FOR SELECTED
COUNTRIES (1968)—PER CENT TOTAL SALARY TAKEN AS TAX

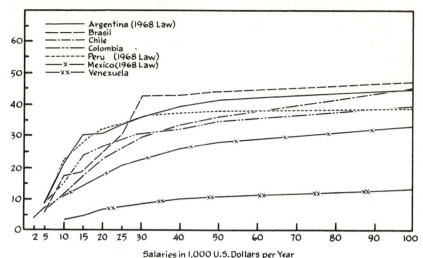

Salaries in 1,000 U.S. Dollars per Year

Source: OAS-Organization of American States, IDB-Inter-American Development Bank Joint Tax Program, Washington, D.C. 1967-Updated.

shown in Figure 8. The sudden reduction in net income may tempt an executive earning $20,000 per year in Lima to accept another position at the same pay just down the coast in Santiago, where the tax system would give him 20% more in take-home plus somewhat higher government benefits.

Changes and improvements in tax laws will also modify the present use of special executive remuneration devices in Latin America. Many multinational firms include top Latin American managers in the parent company's special bonus plan, deferred compensation and equity participation schemes; ideally those eligible would be all top personnel who are actually or potentially transferable regardless of nationality. However, for the Latin American national, many such programs will be a mixed blessing. The tightening tax regulations plus the chronic inflation being experienced by many countries can make deferred cash or many forms of funded future benefits less valuable than current income.

As a single example, the U.S. and Canadian tax laws making stock options desirable do not apply to a Latin American. Few Latin countries would permit a citizen to export funds necessary to exercise an option and buy foreign securities. Even if he did, a foreign tax advantage on increases in stock value would do him no good when the stock was sold; indeed it would be an unusual "blue chip" that would provide as much return as if the money were invested in the local real estate markets, where 20% interest isn't unusual, and specific tax provisions do apply.

If the present state of executive remuneration is a maze, the future will be even more complex. There exists strong evidence of a "leveling out" of executive pay through all of Latin America, due largely to the increasing mobility of the better informed and trained younger generation of managers. (This pattern is the same in continental Europe, where there is less and less difference between pay for local and U.S. nationals.) As indigenous Latin economies continue to strengthen, multinational firms will be under increasing pressure to replace the *"gringo"* top manager with a local man. The already strong competition for top Latin American executive talent will intensify, and the cost will keep going up.

Consequently, it is important that the multinational firm keep a close eye on what is happening to the total executive remuneration picture in all countries. With the extensive government benefits, an increase given to a good man who may be contemplating a job change will cost almost twice the base pay "face value." On the other hand, a recent tax change may have reduced his take-home pay by 25% or more.

To keep those scarce Latin American executives, top multinational management must keep fully current on:

Competitive pay; what salary and voluntary fringes are being paid by the competition—which may be located several thousand miles away.

Net value of salary; what are the current personal income tax laws and how well are they being enforced; what is the current real value to the employee of his salary and fringes.

Salary substitutes; what perquisites, such as gratis or subsidized housing, automobiles, etc., might provide a tax advantage or an added status symbol which an executive would find attractive.

WHITE AND BLUE COLLAR WORKERS

Mobility among lower levels of industrial workers in Latin America has just begun to be statistically significant, and then only in special circumstances. The only important instance of mobility below the executive level is the continuous migration of rural populace to the growing urban complexes. It is projected that by 1980 over 60% of the total population of Latin America will live in 10 urban-industrial centers. As a result, for the present and foreseeable future, the supply of unskilled and semi-skilled workers will far exceed demand; at the same time there will be more technical and skilled trade jobs than personnel to fill them.

These imbalances usually tend to reduce mobility. The unskilled urban worker must be paid the statutory minimum wage—low rates, but set by the government at much higher figures than if a completely free labor market existed. The unskilled worker values his job and seldom leaves voluntarily. The abilities of a highly skilled worker, on the other hand, are in short supply and both employer and employee know it. In this case, the employer will go to considerable lengths to retain personnel with valuable skills.

Mobility is further reduced by the extremely high termination pay required by the Labor Laws and the survival of a traditional attitude toward the employer-employee relationship. In much of Latin America, the "job-for-life" attitude is still strong. Statistics indicate extremely low turnover rates in most countries.

With little knowledge among workers or employers of competitive pay practice, there is no widespread concept of a "fair wage" or a "going rate" for a particular skill. Consequently, wage and salary surveys below the top executive level are nearly worthless. Large foreign companies starting up in Latin America will usually make a wage and salary survey for guidance in setting their own rates. Analysis of the best available salary data shows the the median pay rates for an electrician, to pick an example, are $1,390 in Peru and $1,400 in Brazil. This is what the figures say, but they are completely misleading. The actual pay for any semi-skilled or skilled worker varies ±50% to 150% of the median figure—in contrast to a normal differential of ±15% to 30% in an industrialized country with a functioning labor market. An employer can pretty well pay anything he wants and still get all the workers he needs. The lowest he can go is the statutory minimum, about $700 per year in most countries, and, of course, there is no upper ceiling.

It may appear that the traditional objectives of a remuneration program—to "attract, retain and motivate employees"—do not hold in Latin America. To a certain extent this is quite true. There are more people than jobs (except in top executive and some skilled categories), so the "attraction" goal is largely academic. "Retention" is taken care of by the labor laws and the severe job shortage. What remains, then, is "motivation," and that is perhaps the toughest part of the remuneration maze. How do you motivate an employee to work toward company objectives when he has almost 100% job security (guaranteed by the government), when his annual pay increase is set by the government and the national, politically affiliated unions? Employer-union negotiations are merely the first step before the government steps in and wrangles with unions over company- and industry-wide pay increases. The answer lies in the final part of the maze—worker attitudes.

To motivate Latin Americans, a foreign employer may as well forget money as measured by labor markets and to a lesser extent by workers—except for top executives, who have become more Americanized they they care to admit, and for whom acquisition of money and the things it buys is an acceptable life goal. For most of the rest of the working population, affluence is so unattainable a goal that it is neither expected nor sought. Money has little incentive value when internal wage differentials are so wide and differences in socio-economic status so marked as shown in Figure 6. What is important is that pay rates are in keeping with the social attitudes and expectations of the populace—in keeping with the company's "image" and objectives as seen first by the greater population and, secondly, by the company's own work force.

THREE APPROACHES

On establishing a facility in Latin America, a major international mining company opted to "maintain local consistency" in its remuneration policies. The work force consisted of rural peasants hired out of the hills. Pay and productivity were extremely low, the management extremely paternalistic. This was eminently successful for the decade it took the work force to become urbanized and develop more sophisticated attitudes and radical leaders. In the course of time, the people changed but the company did not; the eventual result was a plant burnt to the ground, riots and much bloodshed. At present, the work force is reduced by half, pay and productivity are up, and someday the shareholders may start getting dividends again.

A well-known extractive company had long been the subject of intense national debate over the familiar political question: should foreign financial interests profit by exploiting local national resources? This firm was the local "wage leader," with an elaborate compensation system, paying the highest salaries in the area, and creating a widely resented economic elite of their personnel. A premium was placed on employees' becoming "North Americanized" and the company was accused of buying loyalty and even of subverting the patriotism of its employees. Reportedly the work force was sincerely upset when the government nationalized the entire operation without paying a cent in damages.

A European-based appliance manufacturer has operated for years in Latin America. At first, its remuneration system was paternalistic. Workers received low pay but were provided company housing. However, that was many years ago. Today, wages are about average for their location—higher than in the old paternalistic days, below those of wage leaders. There are still company clinics and other benefits that some companies would consider paternalistic, but wages have gone up and most of the obvious reminders of the past are gone. This company has changed with the times—has adapted its policies to changes in its people's attitudes. Its labor history has been unusually tranquil, and it can boast of a distinction shared with only one other foreign-owned company in its area; instead of putting pressure on the government to obtain across-the-board increases, the union has agreed to negotiate selectively according to increases in company productivity.

These three examples point up the danger of ignoring societal attitudes—attitudes of the general population as well as the company work force—in setting remuneration policy. The firm which failed to grow with its workers and kept to traditional methods was literally destroyed. The "100% modern" remuneration policies of the company which was either unaware or unconcerned that its policies were worsening an already sensitive political situation produced an overpaid employee group which alienated the general population. The company which paid attention to its social environment, changing itself as its workers and the host population changed, exemplifies the success of an open-minded management. In fact, this company discovered that the external competitiveness of its compensation structure was far less important than gradual changes in the internal distribution and structure of compensation (leading to a curve somewhere between the two curves of Figure 5).

Sensitivity to local attitudes is the key to developing a successful remuneration policy. It would be helpful if we could prepare a chart pairing attitudes with remuneration devices—a quick and easy guide to remuneration planning in Latin America. Unfortunately, people are the most complex part of the maze, and such a chart can only be done in general terms. However, individual firms can and should undertake surveys which produce data on the worker's ratio of expectation to reward.

WORKER CATEGORIES

Three general categories of workers of major interest to industry can be identified as well as their basic attitudes. Suggestions can also be made on the remuneration which would be most appropriate for them. One of Latin American management's toughest problems is discovering where in the social/attitudinal continuum its work force fits.

Rural migrants are not only impoverished peasants seeking economic survival in the city, but also "country boys" who recently left the security of the family or small rural business in an attempt to climb another step up the social and economic ladder. The rural peasants tend to be passive and indifferent workers, easily led, difficult to motivate. Paternalism works with these people, at least until they get used to impersonal city living; a system of non-financial rewards (subsidized housing, medical care) can be effective. To hasten development of more modern achievement/financial attitudes, some firms successfully introduced simple piece-work bonus systems.

Many social benefits are not so much desired as taken for granted by these family-oriented people; the more the employer provides familiar services (housing, retail stores, etc.), the more he provides opportunity for expected social interaction (social clubs, subsidized fiesta celebrations), the more contented will the work force be. However, such contentment may do little to increase low levels of productivity (the elimination of chronic worker undernourishment would be far more effective), although it may postpone and cushion industrial conflict.

It is from the ranks of the rural migrants that a good portion of radical elements of Latin American society come. After a period of living at an urban subsistence level, the former "country boy" begins to resent the material wealth of the more fortunate—wealth which he has begun to covet but lacks the industrial skills to obtain. His resentment and "frustration of rising expectations" finds many outlets, including a variety of anti-employer activities. The basic problem is cash remuneration and its internal distribution within the firm. Another factor in this resentment is the strong barrier between manual and non-manual workers created by government labor law, unions and social attitudes. There is ample evidence that this barrier is not accepted by a number of blue-collar employees. It may be to a firm's advantage to establish training programs or performance appraisal systems that provide blue-collar workers an opportunity to rise into the higher status and better paid position of a white-collar worker.

The characteristic urban worker is the blue-collar worker. He is a recent migrant who has become assimilated by the city and probably has the training and the job to accumulate something more than basic necessities. He might be considered to have a "traditional" orientation. He has fairly low socio-economic expectations, is basically conservative and intent on keeping the little he has. The remuneration key is security. With this group added social benefits might be effective (medical care in Argentina, where there is no federal program, for example). The primary social ambition of this group is upward mobility for their children. Company-subsidized child education facilities or allowances would be one way to meet this desire. Incentive pay related to individual or group productivity can also be effective in further improving worker acceptance of a productivity/reward relation.

The modern urban or white-collar worker constitutes the group in which the most progressive and constructive forces in Latin America can be found. These are people, not of the hereditary oligarchy, but of the emerging middle class. They have managed some social and financial success and want more. Although money is important, their major interest is status, the power and growth potential obtainable through training and education, both for themselves and for their children. An effective motivator might be performance-related formal training courses or higher education "bonuses." Genuine opportunities for advancement and in-company training programs should be provided for this group.

In sum, the most complex part of the remuneration maze is the people. The desire for personal wealth—taken for granted as a prime motivator and an attitude on which remuneration policies are based in Western society—does not have a comparable intensity for many Latin Americans. The task of management is to define the goals and desires of its work force, and then design a remuneration program in response to all their varied needs, to discover the real ratio of expectation to reward.

A WAY OUT?

Remuneration is, and for many years will continue to be, a labyrinth in Latin America. Government social benefit programs and taxes will keep on growing and changing. Labor awareness and mobility will increase, and social attitudes toward work and the employer will change greatly as industrialization continues. Management of the multinational enterprise must be fully aware of all these changes if it is to keep its remuneration program responsive to the environment. This will certainly take a good deal of time and effort. However, firms operating in Latin America are not going to get out of the remuneration maze; all they can do is keep current on its ever-changing complexities—if they do not, they may find themselves at a dead end.

Public Relations

PROBLEMS IN INTERNATIONAL PUBLIC RELATIONS

EDMUNDO LASSALLE

For companies operating in foreign fields,[1] management's skill in relating itself to community and government may well make the difference between failure and survival. This need provides the opportunity for the public relations man.

So far his performance has fallen far short of meeting the need. For this, there are two main reasons. In most cases, the public relations man's activities are not grounded in any body of systematic knowledge. He acts on the basis of hunches and personality. His hunches are not always good, and personal charm is no substitute for knowledge. Furthermore, when he is right, his recommendations are often disregarded by operating management.

Through an examination of several cases, we are going to try to present the approach that should lead to the systematic knowledge that is needed. First let us consider the role of the public relations man. What can he be expected to do?

THE ROLE OF THE PUBLIC RELATIONS MAN

Many people think of the public relations man as a sort of glorified press agent, whose job is to place favorable publicity concerning his organization. To be sure, the task of preparing press releases and other publicity is assigned to his department, but this should be a function of minor importance for the public relations man. His main functions can be summed up under three headings:

1) *He interprets the culture and social organization of the country to other management people.* This means more than just knowing who the important people are. It means knowing how people come to be important and respected in this particular society. It also means knowing what types of behavior are appropriate (and appreciated) in a wide variety of social circles and situations.

Edmundo Lassalle, Problems in International Public Relations, reproduced by permission of the Society for Applied Anthropology from *Human Organization*, vol. 16, no. 3, 1957.

2) *He aids other management people in their contacts outside of the company*—which means that he maintains a wide circle of acquaintances in community and government. However, it emphatically does not mean that he can handle the company's external relations by himself. People in community and government will naturally assume that the top operating people are the really powerful figures in the company. On any matters of real importance, they will not be satisfied to deal with the company through a contact man. The public relations man then can guide the president or general manager and help him to develop effective external relations, but he cannot personally substitute for them.

3) *He helps management to interpret the company to the community*, in an effort to enhance its reputation. In this activity, he faces a two-fold problem. The company has to *earn* acceptance through developing a program that fits with community interests. No publicity program can be effective unless the actions fit the words. On the other hand, just doing good (and talking about it) hardly helps management's position. Virtue does not bring its own reward in this field any more than it does in rural development. Management's efforts to do good in the foreign field are resented almost as often as they are appreciated. Management needs knowledge as to how it may not only make a constructive contribution but also be sure that the contribution is well received. And much of this knowledge is already available from research in applied anthropology.

The public relations man should not be called upon only for what management should *say* and *write* about the company. In the field of management's relations with its external environment, he should be called upon also to advise management on *what to do* and *how to do it*.

The following cases of successes and failures in international public relations will show what these general statements mean in practice.

LAUNCHING A NEW ACTIVITY

A large steel company had been negotiating for some time to secure valuable ore deposits in southern Mexico. When arrangements for the concessions were finally completed, management made a public announcement in its main office in the United States. The Public Relations Department at the home office followed up this announcement by inviting a group of U.S. newsmen to visit the ore deposits. They were flown to the site in a company plane and were entertained in the best style by management. They responded with newspaper stories regarding the importance of this new development to the company's operation and the contribution the company was thereby making to the economic and social development of Mexico.

At this point, it occurred to someone in Public Relations that it would be a good idea to let the Mexicans know what was going on. The Director of Public Relations for the company thereupon invited a group of Mexican newsmen to be guests of the company at a similar visit to the mine site. He was shocked to receive curt refusals from all of the invited guests.

Since this beginning, management has had great difficulty in getting publicity for its Mexican mining operations and has lived in constant fear than an unfriendly press would build up any small unfortunate incident into an adverse news report of large proportions. Furthermore, management thought it had received a promise from the government to build a road from the nearest town to the mine site. When it finally became evident that no road was forthcoming, management had to undertake the project at great expense.

Quite a different approach was taken by another company[2] in another Latin-American country. The occasion was the dedication of a new plant which would contribute importantly to the conservation of the country's most important natural resource.

For this occasion, there was no advance publicity in the United States. Prominent guests (and newsmen) from the United States were flown down for the ceremony, *but* they were joined by high Latin-American government officials, dignitaries of the Catholic Church, newsmen, and others whose prominence was limited to the local area.

In the entertainment preceding the ceremony, there was no separation of Latin Americans from North Americans. The archbishop gave the church's blessing at the dedication ceremonies. The main speech was delivered by a cabinet minister, who took credit for the government for its conservation policies—but also lauded the company's contribution. The President of the company responded in a speech (in Spanish) in which he pointed out that the new plant was a very tangible evidence of the company's dedication to the government's conservation policies.

The ceremony brought the company a great deal of favorable publicity, especially within the country. A less tangible but more important result was the strengthening of management's ties with government and community.

In this case, a special inauguration committee had the primary responsibility in developing plans, from the list of invited guests to the sequence of dedication activities. The committee also advised the company president on the preparation of his speech. However, the ability of the president to deliver that speech in fluent Spanish was an asset quite independent of the most skillful public relations planning.

CONTRIBUTING TO ECONOMIC DEVELOPMENT

A U.S. public utility company was interested in the economic development of the areas in Mexico where it was operating or considering development of new facilities. Management decided to carry out a study of the possibilities for economic development in one state of Mexico. The company engaged a U.S. research group for this purpose. After making their program known to the provincial authorities, the research men went about their survey. When the preliminary results of the research were announced, management was astonished to learn that the federal authorities in Mexico City were alarmed by this effort designed to contribute to the advancement of Mexico as well as to that of the U.S. company.

Management had failed to recognize the much greater centralization of authority that exists in Mexico compared with the United States. A company planning a survey of economic development in Arkansas would need only to consult with the relevant people in the government of Arkansas. In Mexico, and indeed in any Latin-American country, the company must consult with federal government officials before embarking on any such local program. Furthermore, in Latin America, the promotion of economic development is assumed to be a primary function of government much more than is the case in the United States. It is therefore inevitable that the federal authorities will look with suspicion upon any economic development activity in which they are not consulted.

A quite different approach to economic development is being promoted by the Business Council for International Understanding. This Council was created by President Eisenhower "to inspire, encourage and assist American firms and their overseas representatives to aid in the task of creating in other nations understanding of U.S. objectives and building better relations with the other peoples of the world. To enlist their aid in counteracting and dissipating any unfriendly attitudes that may exist in other countries." Instead of carrying out an economic development survey for Mexicans, the Council is trying to help them to set up their own organization and carry through their own program of studies of economic development. A U.S.-Mexican meeting on economic development, held in Mexico City, was an important step in this direction. The Council's staff consulted extensively with officials of the federal government and leading Mexican businessmen in setting up this meeting in an effort to secure their participation and to assure itself that their ideas were being incorporated into the meeting. In planning U.S. participation in the meeting, the Council deliberately decided to minimize the role to be played by officials representing the U.S. government. The planners felt that if this seemed to be a program sponsored by the U.S. government, it could be looked upon by Mexicans as an instance of our big government coming and telling their little country what to do. Instead, the prominent roles were assigned to officials of various state planning agencies. These men were coached to avoid giving the impression that they were telling the Mexicans what to do. They were simply to report "This is what we have done in our state." The spirit of the meeting was expressed in this way by one of the U.S. participants: "We hope our experience will be of some help to you, but you are the only ones who can decide how best to develop your own program."

The Mexican participants seemed quite receptive to this approach. They commented that they were pleased that they had not been called upon to listen to experts from Washington, New York, Chicago or Detroit; that they were able to talk with people who were working on local level problems and even people who represented underdeveloped areas—Arkansas for example.

The meeting led to the formation of a Mexican council for economic development, which is now beginning to carry out its own studies. The Business Council for International Understanding is active in a consulting role, but the program has been accepted by Mexico as its own.

DELIVERING A PROMINENT DELEGATION

A U.S. company with a large and important plant in Mexico was about to open a large new plant in Canada. Top U.S. management decided that this should be the occasion of a ceremonial, which would dramatize international understanding and the contribution the company was making to Mexico and Canada as well as to the United States. The President of the company decided when it would be convenient for him to visit the Canadian plant and set the inaugural date for that time. The word was then passed down to the general manager of the Mexican operations that he should arrange to have a delegation of Mexican officials of top prestige at the inaugural as guests of the company.

The Public Relations Manager in Mexico of the company then called upon the Minister of Finance and the Minister of National Economy to invite them to attend. They both informed him (rather coolly) that they had important matters scheduled in Mexico on that date. The Public Relations Manager then advised the local general manager that the junket should be abandoned. The general manager would not hear of this. He had been ordered to send up a delegation of prominent Mexicans, and he felt that his standing in the company depended upon his ability to deliver such a delegation.

The Public Relations Director then returned to the field and began working his way down the ladder of prestige and power until he was able to round up a group that was interested in a trip to Canada (with a stopover in San Francisco) at company expense.

The Public Relations Director knew very well that his delegation was composed of men of no real importance in Mexico, and he so reported to his general manager. The general manager replied that nevertheless they were indisputably Mexicans and who up in Canada was going to know the difference? (At the last minute, the Public Relations Director found himself "sick" and unable to accompany his delegation.)

The company flew this delegation from Mexico City to San Francisco, entertained them in the finest hotel there, flew them on to the plant site in Canada for another round of elaborate entertainment, and then flew them back to Mexico. The trip was a good deal more expensive than management had anticipated. The Mexican guests, seeing money flowing so freely, even went on an extensive shopping tour in San Francisco and charged everything to the company!

So far as we know, the top management officials never did discover the real standing of the members of the delegation. They had ordered a prominent delegation, and neither the delegates themselves nor the general manager of the Mexican plant wished to disillusion them.

However, the junket from Mexico was worse than a mere waste of money. Any effects it had upon international understanding must have been of a negative character. U.S. management people who were involved with the junket or heard about the behavior of the Mexicans, were inclined to think that if this was the way important Mexicans behaved, then Mexico could hardly be much of a country. Nor were the Mexicans impressed by the attention lavished upon them. They knew very well that they were not worth all this fuss and money and that anyone who treated them in that way must be a fool. A fool with money is widely regarded all over the world as a legitimate target for exploitation. These delegates made the most out of a good thing.

For this type of situation, we do not have an actual case which illustrates what might have been done. However, the analysis of the case readily suggests a different approach.

If it had indeed been important to have a top-level Mexican delegation, then the date of the ceremonial inaugural of the plant should not have been set before consultation with the Mexican Cabinet Ministers. If that had been the case, the General Manager and the Public Relations Director, after explaining the significance of the inaugural to the Ministers, could have asked them to name the date within a period of several weeks or even months when it would be convenient for them to make the trip. This approach would have made it evident that the inaugural ceremony was being built around their presence and one or both of them would have been much more likely to have accepted the invitation and set the date. Once management had secured the acceptance of a Cabinet Minister, everything else would have been easy. Noting that a Cabinet Minister would be on the trip, many other high-level Mexican officials would have been eager to go along. Whatever their interest in the U.S. company and the opening of the new plant in Canada, they would not fail to recognize an important opportunity to cement their relations with such a top figure. Of course, it is quite possible that some governmental emergency might have arisen so as to force the Cabinet Minister to drop out of the trip, but even this would not then have been a great loss. By this time, a number of other almost-as-prominent people would have been committed to the trip, and they could hardly have found legitimate emergencies that would have enabled them to drop out at the last minute.

Had such a delegation been sent to the inaugural, they would have carried the dignity of Mexico—the responsiblity of representing their country at an important event—with them, and we can be sure that their behavior en route would have been quite different from that of the actual delegation.

This approach makes one key assumption: that the Mexican Cabinet Minister will set the date for the inaugural and the president of the U.S. company will arrange his own plans accordingly. Why should it be this way? For ceremonial functions, whose dates are not determined by the calendar, it is customary to work out a schedule in terms of the convenience of the most important person who is to be involved. No doubt, to the members of management, the company's president seems the most important person on earth. However, unless management is prepared to concede that a Mexican Cabinet Minister is more important than the president of the company, then management had better abandon altogether the business of importing prominent delegations from Mexico. No doubt, it might be inconvenient for the president of the company to meet the schedule proposed by the Cabinet Minister. It might involve the rescheduling of activities highly important to the company. If the president of the company felt that he could not afford to risk a date that would be inconvenient to him, then it would have been far better to cancel the junket than to squander money on an effort that was bound to do more harm than good.

CONCLUSIONS

What lessons can we draw from these cases? They may be summarized in this way:

1) *Other people are different from us.* In the case of the Mexican economic development survey sponsored by a utility company, management failed to recognize differences in governmental structure and activities. It should be the function of the public relations man to recognize these differences, whether in governmental structure or in culture and social organization, and to help other management people to see the implications of these differences for their action programs.

2) *Other people are like us.* In some respects, people everywhere are similar. Management sometimes makes serious errors overseas through failing to recognize considerations that would be obvious at home. This seems to have been the case with the opening of the mine in Mexico. Suppose a company with its main office in New York were planning to open an important new plant in Chicago. If newsmen from New York were invited, it would hardly require any conscious thought to see that newspapermen from Chicago should also be included in the party.

The problem seems to be that management people, when in the United States, often do the right thing, without any conscious thought, because of their *implicit* understanding of U.S. culture and social organization. In a foreign country, the U.S. executive cannot assume that his intuition will guide him correctly. He needs to give conscious thought to the matter.

3) *There are also important people outside the company.* Some of the blunders we find in this field seem to stem from an excessive preoccupation with the prestige or status system of the company itself. Unless top management within the company emphasizes the importance of these external relations, it can expect that subordinates will develop plans for company-community activities primarily in terms of the convenience of top management. This means that important Nationals will often find it inconvenient to fit in with management's plan.

4) *Doing good is not necessarily appreciated.* Whether in rural communities or in cities, people do not respond favorably to having good done *to* them. The best way to gain acceptance for an activity is to involve the people in question in the planning and carrying out of the activity. This point was overlooked in the utility company's economic development survey and in the ceremonial opening of the mine. It was the key to success in the Mexican economic development program and in the ceremonial opening of the resource conservation plant.

5) *The words sound better when someone else says them.* What a company says about itself (in press releases, speeches by management, etc.) is bound to be greeted with some suspicion. This is true even when the company enjoys a good community reputation, because, after all, management's statements are issued by an interested party. If respected figures outside of the company make the same kind of statement, it is likely to carry much more weight with the community.

Managers may fear that outsiders will not say all the nice things that could legitimately be said about the company—and would be said if the public relations department could write their speeches. Of course, this is true. Management can never enter into any activity with the guarantee that its contribution will receive full public recognition. However, if management gives proper attention to community relations and takes care to involve significant members of the community in the carrying out of company-community activities, then some of these people will speak and write in ways that will enhance the reputation of the company. They will not express the gratitude that management sometimes mistakenly seeks. They will express their own pride in their *joint* participation with management and in that way give a much healthier form of appreciation to management's contribution.

REFERENCES

1. This article is based on the paper presented by Dr. Lassalle at the Management Seminar on Human Problems of U.S. Enterprise in Latin America, New York State School of Industrial and Labor Relations, Cornell University, June, 1957.

2. We are indebted to the Creole Petroleum Corporation (Venezuela) for the information on this case.

Selected Annotated Bibliography

CONCEPTUAL MODELS AND
METHODOLOGICAL APPROACHES TO
CROSS-CULTURAL COMPARISONS

Adleman, Irma and Morris, Cynthia Taft. "A Factor Analysis of the Interrelationship Between Social and Political Variables and Per Capita Gross National Product," *Quarterly Journal of Economics*, 19 (November 1965), 555-578.

> This study was designed to determine the amount of variance in gross national product per capita predictable or common with twenty-two other variables used to scale seventy-four underdeveloped countries.

Banks, Arthur S. *Cross-Polity Time-Series Data*, Center for Comparative Political Research, State University of New York at Binghamton, New York (Cambridge, Mass.: The MIT Press, 1971).

> Contains longitudinal data from 1815-1966 for 102 variables and over 150 countries. Data include macro and micro economic variables, sociological, cultural, and political variables. An indispensable source for further reserach and study in cross-cultural methodology and applications. This data can be usefully combined with in-company data to conduct cross-cultural studies in long range planning, organizational behavior, marketing, and financial management.

Bertil, Liander; Terpestra, Vern; Yoshino, Michael; and Sherbin, A. A. *Comparative Analysis for International Marketing* (Boston: Allyn and Bacon, 1967).

> This study uses three empirical methods in comparing countries, of which a form of cluster analysis is considered the most complex and thorough. The clustering of countries was done on the basis of the number of shared attributes (8 out of 12 variables). Despite its imaginative approach, its research methodology is open to serious question and therefore its findings are of only limited reliability.

Farmer, Richard N., and Barry M. Richman. *Comparative Management and Economic Progress* (Homewood, Ill.: Irwin, 1965).

> The authors' central thesis is that effective management of private enterprise is essential to economic growth. They pose the ques-

265

tion: "Why is management activity and effectiveness so different from country to country?" and attempt to provide a methodological framework within which to answer this question. An effort is made to bring together all the disciplines that have relevance in comparative management studies; qualitative and quantitative inputs (legal, sociological, political, educational, economic, cultural) are combined toward achieving this end. The authors perceive their model as having applicability both at firm- and macro-level policy making.

Haire, M., Ghiselli, E. E., and Porter L. W. *Managerial Thinking: An International Study* (New York: Wiley, 1966).

A 14-country study making comparisons among various aspects of managerial attitudes. This study was the first of its kind and broke new ground in cross-cultural research.

Harbison, F. H.; Maruhnic, Joan; Resnick, Jane R. *Quantitative Analyses of Modernization and Development* (Princeton, N. J.: Princeton University, 1970).

The authors make use of quantitative indicators of development to explore and apply methods of ranking, clarification, and comparisons of countries or regions within countries. They list the indicators which they deem relevant, apply taxonomic analysis for inter- and intra-country comparison, perform single- and multi-period correlations and regression analyses, do a graphical profile analysis, discuss the Harbison-Myers composite index of human resource development, and examine relationships between expansion of education and rate of economic growth. Analysis includes both a time period study (112 countries, 40 variables), and four time period studies (40 countries, 29 variables). Also contains a "workbook" for use by analysts who are interested in the measurement of modernization and development. They conclude by expressing reservations about some of the techniques discussed and by suggesting the usefulness of others. The purpose of the volume is to provide a reference matrix for the comparisons of one nation with other nations on scales of economic, cultural, health, and educational development.

Irancerien, John M. and Baker, James C. "A Comparative Study of the Satisfaction of Domestic United States Managers and Overseas United States Managers," *Journal of the Academy of Management*, March 1970, 69-77.

The article is an account of a comparative study of job satisfaction of American business executives in Europe and in the United States. The conclusions are reached from the results of a Porter need-satisfaction questionnaire, based on the Maslow theory of motivation, from the top- and middle-level U.S. company managers in Europe and the United States. The results purport to shed light on how the satisfaction for each need, and how the perceived opportunity for need-satisfaction, differs according to the level of the managers, their job locations, and whether they are in Europe or in the United States. Another finding is that the rank order of cluster scores is different in Europe to what it is in the United States and that it diverges from that which Porter postulated.

Lindzey, G., *Projective Techniques and Cross-Cultural Research* (New York: Appleton-Century-Crofts, 1961).

> The concern of the book is to study "the problems and contributions generated by extensive use of projective techniques in cross-cultural research". The author begins by discussing the interest in, applications of, and unrest about projective techniques in anthropological research. He then describes projective techniques, their varieties, and their theoretical foundations. Treatment is given to the interpretative process, its hazards and general issues. The case against projective technique in cross-cultural investigation is stated and cross-cultural application of projective technique is discussed.

Negandhi, Anant R. and Estafen, Bernard D. "A Research Model to Determine the Applicability of American Management Know-How in Differing Cultures and/or Environment," *Academy of Management Journal* (December 1965), 309-318.

> This article constitutes an attempt to enhance the case for the transferability of American managerial know-how to other countries. While they recognize the importance of environmental factors in influencing the performance of managers, the authors take a more moderate stand than Farmer and Richman and seek to isolate particular environmental forces and theory to identify those elements of know-how that are transferable. A more revealing model, they find, is one that includes management philosophy as well as process and effectiveness among the key variables.

Roberts, Karlene H. *International Research Related to Organizational Behavior: An Annotated Bibliography* (Stanford, California: Graduate School of Business, Stanford University, 1971).

> An excellent source for reference material on organizational behavior research.

——. "On Looking at an Elephant: An Evaluation of Cross-Cultural Research Related to Organization." *Psychological Bulletin*, 74 (1970), 327-350.

> A good review article which analyzes the current cross-cultural research in the field of organizational behavior, classifies this research, evaluates its applicability to management problems, and points out avenues of future research. Has extensive bibliography.

Tryon, Robert C., and Bailey, Daniel E. *Cluster Analysis* (New York: Mc-Graw-Hill, 1970), 347 pp.

> Gives a description of the theory and application of a quantitative technique in the analysis of multivariate data., i.e. BC TRY System of Cluster Analysis. BC TRY System is a set of computer programs designed to analyze multi-variable data and is especially suited for cross-cultural research. Topics included in the book range from the basic concepts of observation of natural phenomena and the logical foundations for the cluster analysis of variables, to the mathematical formulation of cluster analysis, the logical and operational bases of cluster analysis of objects, and the technology of cluster analysis computer systems. An application of this technique has been demonstrated in an article entitled "Variable and Object Clustering of Cross-Cultural Data: Some Implications for Comparative Research and Policy Formulation," by S. Prakash Sethi and David Curry. This article appears in the book of readings to which this annotated bibliography is appended.

Udy, S. "Cross-Cultural Analysis: A Case Study," from P. E. Hammond (Ed.) *Sociologists at Work* (Garden City, New York: Doubleday, 1967), 187-212.

> The article is a detailed account of how the author went about performing a cross-cultural analysis to explain the influence of social setting and technological process on work organization in different societies. It describes the procedure that was used in conducting the preliminary survey, in sampling, exploring, and in processing and analyzing the data. The author brings to light the sort of problems that are associated with each phase of cross-cultural research and the decisions, assumptions and simplifications that must often be made to render the task feasible and yet have it yield a meaningful result. He shows how common sense, trial and error searching, ad hoc methodology and arbitrary judgement must sometimes be introduced in the process. By candidly discussing the procedure used in an actual case, the author gives insight into the problems associated with cross-cultural analysis and (unpretentiously) provides useful hints to the researcher.

Whiting, John W. "Methods and Problems in Cross-Cultural Research" in Lindzey, G. and Aronson, E. (Ed.), *The Handbook of Social Psychology* (Reading, Mass.: Addison-Wesley, 2nd Edition, 1968), 693-728.

> The cross-cultural method is described by the author as utilizing data collected by anthropologists on the customs and characteristics of various peoples to test hypotheses concerning human behavior. The article states the advantages of the method (it embraces many cultures and widens the range of variations in many variables) and discusses the many problems that are associated with it. Problems and approaches to cross-cultural research are also considered in terms of sampling, transcultural definition of variables and coding procedures.

LONG RANGE PLANNING

Balassa, Bela. "Planning in an Open Economy," *Kyklos*, Vol. XIX, No. 3 (1966), 385-410.

> This paper deals with some problems of long-term planning in developed countries. Marketers must look beyond national boundaries in the long run, because governments cannot offer indefinite stability to the market.

Christopher, William F. "Marketing Planning That Gets Things Done," *Harvard Business Review*, Vol. 48, No. 5 (Sept./Oct. 1970), 56-64.

> The author contends that many key performance areas that determine long-range profitability and success go unnoticed. In this article he describes how three concepts of "mission," "perspective," and "management style" are applied within various corporate operations so that a practical and successful approach to long-range marketing planning can be developed.

Gaddis, Paul O. "Analyzing Overseas Investments," *Harvard Business Review* (May-June 1966), 115-122.

> Managers can make better analyses and comparisons if they take into account all relevant forms of earnings or losses that are expected to flow from proposed investments.

Garrett, Robert. "Opportunity in Foreign Bonds," *Harvard Business Review*, (July-Aug. 1970), 73-80.

> An analysis of the investment problems presented by recent developments in the international capital markets, the solutions for coping with them, and their relevance to U.S. investors.

Hovell, P. J. "International Operation and Corporate Planning," *Journal of Management Studies*, Vol. 6, No. 3 (Oct. 1969), 302-317.

> This paper is excellent in describing the need for management to realize the link between corporate planning and the international business environment. The author suggests a conceptual corporate planning framework for international operations.

> Hovell's main point is that a firm should consider its international operations as an integral part of its overall strategy and that this should be cast in a corporate planning mold.

Leontiades, James, "Planning for the New Common Market," *Worldwide P & I Planning*, Vol. 4, No. 4 (July/Aug. 1970), 53-62.

> When (not if) Britain joins the Common Market, multinational strategies geared to the old boundaries must be restructured. For maximum benefits the firm's planning should start early—even before the EEC firms up its traditionally vague guidelines. The author discusses pertinent implications of the EEC's enlargement.

Mockler, Robert J. "Theory and Practice of Planning," *Harvard Business Review*, Vol. 48, No. 2 (March/April 1970), 148-159.

> The author reviews the published material on planning since 1958 and singles out those which he believes would be most useful to the executive. He also predicts the development of several trends in planning for the 1970's. The author additionally presents a bibliography which cites thirty volumes.

Pryor, Millard H., Jr. "Planning in a Worldwide Business," *Harvard Business Review*, (Jan.-Feb. 1965), 130-139.

> What are the most common mistakes made in planning business operations in foreign countries? What steps will improve marketing, production, and other functional programs?

Steiner, George A. "Rise of the Corporate Planner," *Harvard Business Review*, Vol. 48, No. 5 (Sept./Oct. 1970), 133-139.

> The author sees the role of the planner becoming intimately involved in the affairs of corporate management to such an extent that the planner will become the prime mover in guiding the firm toward new opportunities and away from environmental dangers.

——, and Cannon, W. M. *Multinational Corporate Planning.* (New York: Macmillan, 1966).

> The authors discuss the recent growth of the multinational firm and its reliance upon corporate planning for effectiveness. They point out the importance of long-range, strategic, and tactical planning to the firm's operation.

Stobaugh, Robert B., Jr. "How to Analyze Foreign Investment Climates," *Harvard Business Review* (Sept.-Oct. 1969), 100-108.

> The author discusses four techniques of investment-climate analysis: (1) the go-no go method, (2) the premium for risk, (3) range of estimates technique, and (4) risk analysis. The author compares and contrasts these methods of taking risk into account when investing abroad.

Vancil, Richard F. "The Accuracy of Long-Range PLanning," *Harvard Business Review,* Vol. 48, No. 5 (Sept./Oct. 1970), 98-101.

> This article presents a summary report of a large-scale project which is investigating corporate formal planning systems.

Williams, Simon. "Negotiating Investment in Emerging Countries," *Harvard Business Review* (Jan.-Feb. 1965), 89-99.

> The planning required is intensely introspective and personal. The businessman should decide before leaving the United States how much he is prepared to give in order to get.

——. "Private Investment in World Agriculture," *Harvard Business Review* (Nov.-Dec. 1965), 95-105.

> One of the most exciting challenges ever issued to U.S. management, this article defines the role of private enterprise in a situation that promises both profitable investment and needed contribution to worldwide social and economic stability.

"Your Company Can Gain From International Long Range Planning," *Business Abroad* (May 1, 1967), 21.

> Large multinational organizations are convinced that a formalized long-range plan is necessary to run their business efficiently. The author presents various elements of guidelines of long range

planning and shows how large international organizations put these principles into practice.

Zenoff, David. "Objectives for Multinational Management in the 1970's," *Worldwide P & I Planning*, Vol. 4, No. 2 (March/April 1970), 22-28.

> To meet the international challenge of the 1970's, the multinational firm must review its present position, forecast the future and establish explicit goals and how to reach them. The author lists the broad objectives into which specifics will fit.

ORGANIZATION AND MANAGEMENT

Bain, G. S. "The Growth of White Collar Unionism in Great Britain," *British Journal of Industrial Relations*, Vol. 7, No. 3 (Nov. 1966), 305-335.

> This paper examines the extent and nature of the growing white-collar labor force and reports the progress of the British trade union movement in their attempts at recruiting white-collar workers.

Barkin, Solomon. "The Manpower Policies of the OECD," *Business Topics* (Autumn 1963), 7-16.

> A discussion of the functions of the OECD, and its means for reaching an end goal.

Barnes, William S. "Guides to International Operations," *Harvard Business Review* (July-August 1970), 26-37.

> Regarding the new sources of knowledge that tend to reduce the confusion which surrounds foreign operations.

Barnet, S. "International Public Relations," *International Advertiser*, Vol. 9 (Oct. 1968), 13-15.

> The address traces the evolution of domestic and international public relations. In light of the present state of the art, the author discusses current international trends in the industry. In doing this he explores marketing, nonmarketing, financial and corporation problems in the area plus the role of the U.S. government.

———. "New Era Opens for Public Relations Abroad," *Public Relations Journal* (Dec. 1968), 10.

> Centralization of international public relations as the interrelationships of markets requires the necessity of the corporation speaking with one global voice.

Barovick, Richard L. "Labor Reacts to Multinationalism," *Columbia Journal of World Business*, Vol. 5, No. 4 (July/August 1970), 40-46.

> The emergence of the multinational corporation has been a disturbing development to labor unions around the world. The author discusses the ways and means that the unions are trying to come to terms with the situation.

Bowman, M. J., and Meyers, R. G. "Schooling, Experience, and Gains and Losses in Human Capital Through Migration," *American Statistical Association Journal*, Vol. 62, No. 319 (Sept. 1967), 875-898.

> This article suggests the need for new census tabulation which would allow more sophisticated application of human capital concepts to migration.

Bradley, Gene E. "Building a Bigger Atlantic Community," *Harvard Business Review* (May-June 1966), 79-90.

> The main requirement, this study shows, is that U.S. management cope successfully with Europeans' fears that they will be left too far behind in technological competition.

Bussey, Ellen M. "Organized Labor and the E.E.C.," *Industrial Relations*, Vol. 7, No. 2 (Feb. 1968), 160-170.

> Organized labor in the EEC is trying to establish a more powerful position for its workers. The article tells of the new problems that the workers are facing since the beginning of the common market and the unions' attempts at correcting them.

Butler, W. Jack, and Dearden, John. "Managing a Worldwide Business," *Harvard Business Review* (May-June 1965), 93-102.

> Despite much progress, a variety of control problems still get in the way of "operating" the ideal world enterprise. New management tools are needed and they can be developed.

Cantril, H. "A Study of Aspirations," *Scientific American*, Vol. 208, No. 2 (Feb. 1963), 41.

> This article tells of research that may lead to a systematic approach to many fundamental questions about people and their societies in the present period of rapid social change and political evolution. The development of a "self-anchoring scale" makes it possible to study the hopes and fears of people in different countries.

Chorafas, D. N. "Developing the International Executive," *American Management Association Research Study No. 83*, 1967.

> This study is taken on information collected from interviews with executives throughout the world. It is broken down into eight articles discussing the role, source, development, and appraisal of the international executive. In three of the articles executive development is discussed from worldwide points of view and from different national viewpoints.

Clark, D. C., and Mosson, T. M. "Industrial Managers in Belgium, France and the U.K.," *Management International Review*, Vol. 7 (1967), 95-100.

> The authors consolidate various studies examining education levels and social background for industrial managers of the three countries. They give percentage breakdowns and comparisons in these categories and try to project trends wherever possible.

Clee, H. G. "Organizing a Worldwide Business," *Harvard Business Review*, Vol. 42, No. 6 (Nov. 1964), 55-67.

> Three basic organizational structures have evolved in response to the growing pressure to the major U.S. companies who are committed to invest abroad: (1) variants of the traditional international division structure; (2) the geographic structure, replacing the international division with line managers; (3) the product structure replacing the international division with executives.

"Co-ordination of International Operation," *Fabian Research Series*, 279, 5s.

> The coordination of activities in different plants, which can be thousands of miles apart, requires a high degree of organization; the implications and the urgent needs are going more and more toward a centralized organization.

Crissy, W. J.; Marple, G. A.; and Conant, E. "Field Assignments for Individual Managerial Development," *Business Topics* (Winter 1963), 49-65.

> This article primarily deals with the development of sales managers. Criteria for management development programs are also discussed.

Crowther, F. D. "Organizing for Overseas Operations," *Management Review*, 48 (March 1959), 9-13.

> The same organizing principles that apply in domestic operations can be applied in international operations. Differences between

the two are not in principles but rather in degrees. The most important starting point is determining the objectives and purposes of the enterprise within the organization-components being considered.

Davis, Stanley M. "Management's Effects on Worker Organizations in a Developing Country," *Human Organization*, Vol. 27, No. 1 (Spring 1968), 21-29.

This paper examines the processes of social change in Mexico and investigates how and why independent worker organizations originate within business enterprises. Davis's point is that management plays a key role in influencing worker behavior.

——. "U.S. vs. Latin America: Business and Culture," *Harvard Business Review* (Nov. 1969), 88.

This article describes some fundamental differences in the meaning and emphasis that Latin America and America attach to the four spheres (the individual, the group, the organization, and the community) in the social environment. The basic difference described is that of the uniqueness of the individual in all relationships in Latin America as opposed to the integration of the individual in the American enviornment.

de Mente, Boye. "Can We Learn From Japan?," *Worldwide Projects and Installations Planning*, Vol. 4, No. 2 (March/April 1970), 51-58.

The author presents a good case for the adoption of traditional Japanese management techniques by U.S. industry, instead of forcing U.S. management theories on Japan.

Demeure, Joseph A. "Labor Legislation Considerations for American Companies Investing in Mexico and South America," *Business Lawyer*, XXIV (Nov. 1968), 267-279.

Presents a brief discussion on Latin American labor legislation with emphasis on those areas which differ significantly from U.S. labor legislation such as job security and profit sharing.

Fornasier, Raffaello. "Toward a European Company," *Columbia Journal of World Business*, Vol. IV, No. 3 (Sept.-Oct. 1969), 51-57.

Nationalistic attitudes and practices continue to obstruct full integration of the European Common Market. Remedies may be found in current proposals for a European company law.

Friedrich, Otto A. "German Co-Determination: Parity Is the Goal," *Columbia Journal of World Business*, Vol. 5, No. 1 (Jan./Feb. 1970), 49-55.

> The trade unions are claiming as a fundamental right equal participation with management in all phases of decision-making. German business views this as a radical restructuring of the economic power base and as an infringement of ownership. Currently an angry debate rages.

Gavian, R. W. "Adapting the Corporate Structure to Foreign Operation," *Management Review* (August 1967).

> When a company goes international it soon is faced with new problems of internal relationship and finds that new concepts of organization are needed. The company organizations vary in the changes according to the size, experience, and the line of business of a particular company.

Gerring, W. J. "How to Minimize Overseas Recruiting Risks," *Management Review* (March 1967).

> Gerring presents an illuminating appraisal of the key considerations involved in recruiting Americans, third country nationals, and local nationals for executive jobs abroad.

Hall, David. "The French Business Elite," *International Executive* (Spring 1969).

> The article reports the prevailing image of top executives in France as a self-perpetuating elite, also there is considerable mobility of managers among companies, and awareness of their deficiencies in marketing.

Havens, A. E., and Potter, H. R. "Organizational and Societal Variables in Conflict Resolution; an International Comparison," *Human Organization* (Fall 1967).

> A useful case study about a strike in Latin America.

Hayden, S. "Organizational Problems in Overseas Operations," *Personnel* (March 1968).

> The problems facing U.S. oversea's companies are numerous. The most demanding problems are: (1) to organize along regional lines or centralized corporation, (2) keeping abreast of local political and economic changes and maintaining correct relations with local officials, (3) costing technical know-how and management skills, (4) maintaining proper organization with home offices, and

(5) determining optimistic amounts of autonomy for local managers abroad.

Heller, Robert. "Motivation and the British Manager," *Worldwide Projects and Installations Planning* (July-August 1970), 32-42.

A wave of mergers and reorganizations has changed British business. A new breed of managers is taking over. He is better trained and better educated with a very healthy attitude towards money. "Job satisfaction" as a motivational factor has slipped down the list.

Hitchin, D. E. "Pressures on the Key Executives Overseas," *Business Horizons* (Spring 1967), 85-90.

Corporate survey focuses on success abroad of managers.

Hodgson, F. X. "The Selection of Overseas Management," *Business Topics*, Vol. 11 (Spring 1963), 49-54.

The article emphasizes the need to send trained, qualified managers to overseas positions. It points out reasons for the reluctance of capable U.S. executives to accept overseas assignments and a possible solution. Facts to consider in selection of overseas personnel and training requirements are considered.

"International Coordination," *International Advertiser* (August 1968), 3.

Multinational companies are finding an ever-increasing need for centralized coordination and control, *not* because of governmental or economic arrangements, *but* because they must manage technology and resources more effectively in the present climate of heightened competition. The "coordination" approach recognizes diversity, but seeks uniformity within it.

Kassalow, E. M. "Professional Unionism in Sweden," *Industrial Relations* (Feb. 1969), 119-134.

This article gives a critical analysis of professsional unionism in Sweden. Problems such as the limits of bargaining and the right to strike are discussed.

Khuri, Fuadi. "The Eitquette of Bargaining in the Middle-East," *American Anthropologist*, Vol. 70, No. 4 (Aug. 1968), 698-706.

This paper attempts to show that bargaining incorporates elements of cooperation. Techniques of bargaining in the Middle East are used by the author in his discussion.

Lauter, Geza Peter. "Sociological-Cultural and Legal Factors Impending Decentralization of Authority in Developing Countries," *Academy of Management Journal* (Sept. 1969), 367.

> The concept of decentralization of authority as understood and practiced by managers in the U.S. may be of limited applicability in developing countries because of environmental factors. This article contains a study conducted in Turkey of the delegation practices of both Turkish and American managers in Turkey. Observations are made of the cultural and legal environment and managements reaction to it.

Layard, P. R. G., and Saigal, F. C. "Educational and Occupational Character of Manpower: An International Comparison," *British Journal of Industrial Relations*, Vol. 4, No. 2 (July 1966), 222-266.

> This paper discusses the proposition that there is a unique pattern of skill requirements for a given output per worker. A simplified model is presented which analyzes the manpower needs and skill requirements of several countries.

Lee, J. A. "Cultural Analysis in Overseas Operations," *Harvard Business Review*, Vol. 44, No. 2 (March-April 1966), 106-114.

> This article suggests that the unconscious reference to one's own cultural values is the cause of most international business problems overseas. An analytical approach designed to reduce the influence of cultural values is presented.

Lee, James E. "Developing Managers in Developing Countries," *Harvard Business Review* (Nov.-Dec. 1968), 55-65.

> Training potential leaders in American-owned companies overseas calls for programs tailored to meet key environmental problems.

Mace, Myles L. "The President and International Operations," *Harvard Business Review*, Vol. 44, No. 6 (Nov.-Dec. 1966), 72-84.

> This article discusses the total strategy for international ventures. Such aspects as the importance of data, the form of entry into foreign markets, the staff organization, and the needs of the foreign subsidiaries and corporate headquarters, are examined.

McKenzie, C. "Incompetent Foreign Managers," *Business Horizons* (1966).

> A common complaint of U.S. management is the incompetence of foreign managers—the result is a high and costly turnover of foreign managers. The symptoms are: (1) over-extensive control system by parent company, (2) managers have no grasp of what is

going on, and (3) the irrational fashion in which the manager reacts to either verbal or written instructions.

McLagan, C. B. "Measuring Executives Performance Overseas," *Management Review* (Oct. 1962).

> The present obsolete standards are based on subjective impressions and inadequate information. What is needed are the non-accounting measures: (1) market share of a manager, (2) market product distribution, (3) new product development, (4) improvement in productivity, and (5) quality and delivery.

Miller, Richard U. "Labor Legislation and Mexican Industrial Relations," *Industrial Relations*, Vol. 7, No. 2 (Feb. 1968), 171-182.

> Contrasts Mexican, American, and Canadian labor relations. The article examines two questions: (1) to what extent can the differentiation be traced to Mexican labor law and legislation? and (2) what significance does such legislation have for the development of alternative labor-management institutions?

Moore, D. S. "Compensating the Overseas Work Force," *Conference Board Record 5: 44-48* (Oct. 1968).

> The work force is made up of four parts: (1) wage payroll: — compensated on an hourly or daily basis; (2) local national salaried personnel—paid according to the existing salary patterns in the country; (3) the dollar payroll—paid depending on the duration of assignment and objective to be achieved; (4) third country nationals—paid a base salary and a premium for expatriation.

"More Workers in the Boardroom?" *Economist*, 226 (March 30, 1968), 65.

> Very short article on German workers' participation in management decision making.

"Multinational Organization: Management's New Dimension," *Business Abroad* (Sept. 5, 1966).

> Discussion of NICB study, "The Changing Role of the International Executive." Three dimensions in international organization—product, function, geography. Examples of types of organizations used, advantages and disadvantages of each type. Role of international unit—to serve domestic products division or to take over markets outside U.S. Importance of liaison-formal, informal, cross-fertilization (using executives in both domestic and international operations). Control of international operations therefore a top management responsibility.

Musgrave, P. W. "The Educational Profiles of Management in Two British Iron and Steel Companies with Some Comparisons, National and International," *British Journal of Industrial Relations*, Vol. 4, No. 2 (July 1966), 201-211.

> In this paper the results of a survey concerning the educational profiles of the management in two companies are shown and compared with some relevant national and international investigations. It is suggested that these educational profiles on an industry-wide scale could indicate future needs for management and future requirements from the educational system.

Negandhi, Anant. "Advanced Management Know-How in Underdeveloped Countries," *California Management Review*, Vol. X, No. 3 (Spring 1968), 53-60.

> Possible actions which will overcome the obstacles to the transfer of management techniques from country to country. The author suggests waiving the traditional objective of profit maximization as a first step.

Newman, William H. "Is Management Exportable?" *Columbia Journal of World Business*, Vol. 5, No. 1 (Jan./Feb. 1970), 7-18.

> Certain underlying cultural traits help distinguish U.S. management. Identification of these characteristics may determine their applicability in international environments. The author concludes that transferability is dependent upon prevailing attitudes and values and their receptivity to change. He also states that the body of concepts that can be transferred should not be diminished by the few that cannot.

Parks, F. Newton. "Survival of the European Headquarters," *Harvard Business Review*, Vol. XLVII, No. 2 (March/April 1969), 79-84.

> Reasons for the failure of European headquarters are given. Guidelines for making these headquarters more effective in the future are enumerated.

"Please Don't Call Me a Salesman," *Business Abroad* (February 20, 1967), 19.

> This article discusses the importance of titles and the role of prestige.

Robinson, D. E. "U.S. Life Style Invades Europe," *Harvard Business Review*, Vol. 46, No. 5 (Sept.-Oct. 1968), 140-147.

> This article suggests that the United States has come to dominate and direct international style currents.

Schnapp, John B. "The Case of Crisis in Caribia," *Harvard Business Review* (Nov.-Dec. 1968), 178, 185-188, 762-784.

> An up-and-coming North American is given a promising assignment in Latin America—and the roof falls in.

Schoenfeld, H. "Some Special Accounting Problems of Multinational Enterprises," *Management International Review*, Vol. 4, No. 5 (1969), 3-20.

> This article stresses the fact that multinational enterprises are largely dependent on the legal, tax, economic, and educational systems of the countries in which they operate. The author suggests intermediate solutions for the problems presented.

Stieber, John, and Paukert, Liba. "Manpower and Technological Change in Czechoslovakia," *Industrial Relations* (Oct. 1968), 91-107.

> This article examines the technological development in Czechoslovakia and discusses the anticipated impact of "planned management," a new system on manpower and employment policies.

Stuart, Robert D. "Purchasing in Worldwide Operations," *American Management Association*, 1966, Management Bulletin 75, 1-16.

> Stuart's contention is that as a firm becomes multinational, its purchasing problems become increasingly complex. To meet these problems he suggests the multinational firm must reorganize its purchasing function through decentralization. This article gives many insights into the problems encountered in purchasing in a foreign setting and ways to minimize them.

Sumiya, Mikio. "The Development of Japanese Labour Relations," *Developing Economics*, Vol. IV, No. 4 (Dec. 1966), 499-515.

> This paper describes the historical context in which the Japanese labor relations developed.

Tachi, Minoru, and Yoichi, Okazaki. "Japan's Postwar Population and Labor Force," *Developing Economies*, Vol. VII, No. 2 (June 1969), 170-186.

> This article discusses some of the quantitative and qualitative changes in demographic structure that have taken place in Japan since the end of World War II.

Teague, Frederick A. "International Management Selection and Development," *California Management Review*, Vol. XII, No. 3 (Spring 1970), 1-6.

> The selection and development of international management personnel is the subject of this article. The author considers sources

of management talent and discusses selection and criteria. He speaks of training for the international manager within the framework of management manpower planning.

"The Changing Role of the International Executive." New York, National Industrial Conference Board, No. 119, 1966.

Experience of 156 U.S. firms in international organization.

Vogel, P. P. "Round 2 in International Business," *Business Horizons* (Aug. 1968), 57-62.

The author maintains that the success of the international company will no longer lie solely in the area of marketing intelligence of technological achievement, but to an important extent in the type of men selected for international marketing executive positions. He then outlines the required talents an executive should possess and types of training.

Webber, Ross A. *Culture and Management*. Homewood, Ill.: Richard D. Irwin, Inc., 1969.

Culture affects management through motivation. Appollonian society stresses: security, friendship, mutual efforts, equality, altruism; Dionysian: need for security and affiliation satisfied through escape of nature and the misery of existence. Emphasis on gaudy, sensual, and the forbidden; Faustian: glorify the individual, competition.

Williams, Charles R. "Regional Management Overseas," *Harvard Business Review*, XLV (Jan./Feb. 1967), 87-91.

What are the main advantages of regional management, and to what companies do they apply? What are the best sites in Europe for regional offices?